HISTORIES OF INTIMACY AND SITUATED ETHNOGRAPHY

Histories of Intimacy and Situated Ethnography

Edited by

KAREN ISAKSEN LEONARD
GAYATRI REDDY
ANN GRODZINS GOLD

MANOHAR
2010

First published 2010

ISBN 978-81-7304-873-9

Published by
Ajay Kumar Jain *for*
Manohar Publishers & Distributors
4753/23 Ansari Road, Daryaganj
New Delhi 110 002

Typeset by
Kohli Print
Delhi 110 051

Printed at
Lordson Publishers Pvt. Ltd.
New Delhi 110 035

Contents

1

Introduction

This volume celebrates the work of Sylvia Vatuk, who recently retired as the senior South Asia anthropologist from the University of Illinois at Chicago. Our theme is 'Histories of Intimacy and Situated Ethnography', chosen to highlight the leading characteristics and contributions of Vatuk's work over time. The essays gathered here treat subjects ranging from kinship and family history to gender, aging, and the life-cycle to politics and law. All, however, involve intimate histories and situated ethnographies, and all are by daughters of India, whether by ancestry or by choice.

In the fall of 2007, Ann Grodzins Gold and Gayatri Reddy organized two panels honoring Vatuk at the Annual Conference on South Asia held in Madison, Wisconsin. Many of the papers in this volume originated then. When Karen Isaksen Leonard joined the editorial team, a few more papers were solicited from scholars who had worked closely with Sylvia Vatuk over the years, sharing interests and insights with her.

Vatuk's corpus of writings includes a range of topics: gift-giving and its impact on women's duties and roles in the family; folklore and its gendered meanings; women's agency within apparently male-dominated systems; history, life history and family history as subjects and fields for ethnographic practice; the relationship between orally transmitted and archived histories; domesticity as a realm of history; mutually pliable constructions of law and gender; colonial manipulations of 'native' speech and prose; and far more. Vatuk's abbreviated *curriculum vita* appears at the end of this volume. It reveals Sylvia Vatuk's ongoing research trajectory, one which signals not closure but new explorations. The papers gathered here testify also to the way she has encouraged others to explore intimate histories through situated ethnographies.

Sylvia Jane Dutra Vatuk grew up in Rhode Island, attending high school in Newport. Her father's family was Portuguese, immigrants from the Azores, and her mother was of Irish descent. Vatuk co-authored a number of important articles with her first husband, folklorist Ved Vatuk. Although the marriage ended, she kept the name, and their two sons and two daughters accompanied Sylvia on all of her research trips through the 1970s. She has been married for many years now to the economist, George Rosen, with whom she also shares an intellectual focus on South Asia.

Vatuk's intellectual biography included undergraduate training at Cornell University, an MA from the School of Oriental and African Studies at the University of London, and a PhD in Anthropology from Harvard. She held teaching positions at the University of California, Santa Cruz, and California State College at Hayward, but eventually she moved to the University of Illinois at Chicago in 1970. She remained there for over thirty years as a vital figure in Anthropology and Women's Studies, retiring as a full Professor in 2002. Vatuk continues, however, to pursue her research vigorously, presenting papers at conferences, publishing, and mentoring younger scholars.

Vatuk's early work was with white-collar migrants and Gaur Brahmans in north India (Meerut, Delhi), and it focused on kinship, family and neighborhood, and marriage networks and gift-giving. Her book on urban kinship remains a classic, and her incisive articles on Hindi kinship terminology, fictive kinship, and matrilateral asymmetry set high standards in the field. Vatuk's 'Gifts and Affines' article showed an unbreakable bond between a woman and her natal kin that was reaffirmed at every ceremony and at every meeting. This emphasis was unusual at a time when male anthropologists were interpreting women as decisively integrated, even in substance, into their husbands' lineages.

Vatuk's interest in women was clear from the beginning. Among her earliest writings were essays focused on savings practices among north Indian village women and on the image of lustful step-mothers in north-western Indian folklore. This original work highlighted gendered aspects of rural society and culture. Vatuk was also among the first to publish on Indian women's sexuality, aging, and life-cycle changes. Situated ethnography featuring the testimony of her informants marked her research. While she always oriented her findings to contemporary theoretical issues in anthropology, she often differed from other anthropologists by emphasizing women's agency and women's own views of their intimate worlds.

In the 1980s, Vatuk began a far-reaching research project which focused on an important Muslim extended family with roots in Madras and Hyderabad. She learned Urdu and worked with women to trace the construction of this family's identity over time. Vatuk tapped archival materials as well as living memories. Thus in an era when anthropologists loudly proclaimed a theoretical turn to history, Vatuk had already quietly embarked on a long-term project that involved an historical investigation of Islam and Muslims in India. Her article on the '*Qanoon-e-Islam*' in early and later colonial India is a significant intervention, again a standard-setting piece of research—as Raheja notes in her contribution to this volume. Showing the changing construction of an ethnography of India's Muslims, Vatuk highlighted the dialogic nature of early colonial ethnography and the later erasure of Indian contributors and agency; hers is a sophisticated and complex treatment of a subject often simplified and misrepresented.

In recent decades, Vatuk has taken up issues of marriage and divorce among Muslim women and Islamic feminism in India. She is combining archival work with observations in the civil Family Courts, speaking with Muslim women, qazis, and mosque officials as she investigates the impact of Muslim Personal Law on women's lives. These intimate histories have led her to a broader arena, to the India-wide efforts by Muslim women activists to change Muslim Personal Law; she is also doing comparative work on Hindu and Muslim dowry, divorce, and maintenance issues.

Contributing to work at the intersections of multiple disciplines long before inter-disciplinarity was a buzzword in academia, Sylvia Vatuk's scholarship has been central to theorizations and methodological innovations in analyses of gender, kinship, the family, and 'culture' writ large. Her research has been at the forefront of at least three 'turns' in scholarship, as it were, in Anthropology, Gender Studies, and South Asian studies: the turn to history, the affective turn, and the attention to the everyday and the performative as lenses to better understand modes of self-crafting, agency, and relationality. Taking the production of 'culture' as her primary lens, Sylvia Vatuk has repeatedly shown, through meticulous historical and ethnographic research, how what we take to be normative structures—from the dynamics of kinship and the family, to gender and inter-generational relations, as well as the law, to name a few—are in fact contextually produced regulatory mechanisms that permeate and construct and *re*construct everyday life in colonial and post-colonial India.

The production of such cultural knowledge, Vatuk argues, is essentially a 'heteroglot' and 'dialogic' *process*; the significance and endurance of Sylvia Vatuk's research is in allowing us to *see* this process at work—whether she is deconstructing the life of a colonial text (*Qanoon-e-Islam*), the gendered norms governing folktales (Lustful Step-Mother and Ethnography of Sang), forms and regulations of kinship and the 'family' (Fictive Kinship, Forms of Address, Gifts and Affines, Household Form and Formation, Making New Homes in the City, Changing Patterns of Marriage and Family), the interpellation of kinship and gender with the law (Moving the Courts, Domestic Violence and Marital Breakdown in India, Muslim Women and Personal Law, Bharattee's Death), or processes of aging and the regulations of sexuality among middle-aged women (Aging Women in India, South Asian Cultural Conceptions of Sexuality, Sexuality and the Middle-Aged Woman in South Asia, To Be a Burden on Others), to invoke just a few of her many publications.

Drawing on both archival and ethnographic fieldwork, the articles published here build on these theoretical insights and methodological innovations, unearthing the discursive productions of cultural knowledge, 'structures of feeling', as well as forms of resistance to normative regulations in everyday life in India and its diaspora. The articles draw on multiple strands of Sylvia Vatuk's work, providing testimony to the immense breadth and scope of her work as well as its ongoing relevance to subjects as varied as the encoding of 'family' and conjugality through the law (S. Basu), tracing the shifting meanings of conjugality and intimacy over time in one village in Karnataka (Ullrich), tracing changing family strategies in the twentieth century in a U.P. village (Kolenda), transnational 'ethnoscapes' stressing narratives of family continuity (Leonard), performative genres from discourses of the Shiv Sena (Bedi), *mehndi* rituals in the U.K. (Werbner), healing rituals in Hyderabad (Flueckiger) and Gujarat (H. Basu), and colonial practices of entextualization (Raheja). When read through the fabric of Sylvia Vatuk's work, all of these varied articles allow us to rethink the relationship among 'culture,' 'history' and 'politics,' ostensible 'public' and 'domestic' spheres, between intimate histories and reconfigurations of gender and the family in colonial and post-colonial India.

Building on some of Vatuk's earliest insights into relational identities, Tarini Bedi's essay, titled 'The (Im?) Possibilities of a Situated Feminist Subject in Shiv Sena: Shiv Sainiks, Governance, and Adjustment in Maharashtra', offers a fine-grained and revealing ethnographic account of women's aspirations, actions and experiences in urban politics, addressing the need to rethink feminist subjectivity with attention to cultural specificities. The subjects of her research are key players in the Shiv Sena women's wing in Mumbai, Pune, and Nashik. Bedi finds that Vatuk's observations on women's strategic uses of kinship relations and kin terms help to illuminate the ways Shiv Sena women position themselves, for example using terms that connote natal and maternal connections to take advantage of the greater freedom these relations generally carry for women. Vatuk's work on aging, shifting domestic dynamics and visibility in public spaces also informs Bedi's understandings.

Based on fieldwork evidently characterized by intimacy and trust, Bedi's essay deftly attends to situated complexities expressed through individual voices and stories while proposing some larger claims. Interview excerpts imbue Bedi's theoretical insights with persuasive life, as she examines the intersection of public and private in the constitution of gendered selves. Bedi is able to show 'how women's aggressive, and frequent public participation in Shiv Sena's politics unsettles private gendered relationships'.

Bedi works squarely in the realm of the political without losing sight of the ways it is dynamically embedded in domestic and cultural contexts. She proposes nothing less than rethinking the category of the family, arguing that it should be seen neither as emancipatory nor as oppressive, insisting on women's active agency. Particularly fascinating is Bedi's elaboration of the concept of 'adjustment' (a word adapted from English) as it is used by the Shiv Sena women. Bedi unpacks this term as it applies to a 'complex of relational processes between and among genders and generations'. The semantics of 'adjustment' unfolds through Bedi's numerous examples of its usage, revealing subtle negotiations and less subtle jostlings: women's awareness of limits imposed on them and their tireless capacity to undermine these limits.

Similarly working to rethink the category of the family (and arguably, the discourse of adjustment) in another context is the essay by S. Basu, titled 'The Legal Structures of Kinship: Re-Working Affinity, Residence and Entitlement in the Kolkata Family Court'. In the best tradition of Sylvia Vatuk's work on the productions of kinship in contemporary India, Basu's essay traces the constitution and reconstitution of kinship and the family through one such domain: the law. The 'family', Basu argues, echoing Vatuk, is discursively produced and it is through the workings of the law—in this case, the Kolkata Family Courts—that one can see this process in action. Taking as a point of departure the vexed relationship between the ideologies of the 'joint family' and discourses of conjugality—as evidenced through their (disarticulated) instantiations in Hindu property law and marriage law—Basu allows us to glimpse how categories of kinship, norms of gendered responsibility, and notions of intimacy are both negotiated and rendered 'real' through the legal discourses and invocations in these Family Courts. In this regard, her work parallels Sylvia Vatuk's work on Family Courts in Hyderabad that similarly demonstrates the affirmation of gender and class norms within and through the medium of the law.

Drawing on fieldwork in the Kolkata Family Courts, S. Basu examines litigants and court officials grappling with the slippages in Family Law, the multiple, oftentimes contradictory ideologies of normative femininity and the centrality of the patrilocal 'joint' family with constructions of intimacy and registers of conjugality in the nuclear family unit. What is revealed through this process is the 'ironic terrain' of the law, wherein not only are forms of customary entitlement re-negotiated, but 'new notions of kinship are constituted through such legal maneuvers'. In fact, as we see through Basu's rich ethnographic work, often court officials actively insert themselves into kin categories, representing themselves as the 'better' kin. Using actual cases to illustrate her point, Basu shows us how both litigants and court officials discursively draw—sometimes simultaneously—on normative scripts of gendered responsibility and extended familial obligations (the 'good wife', the 'providing husband', the needs of the culturally 'valid' joint family), as well as nuclear conjugal expectations and individual desire to, ultimately, remake notions of 'family', duties and responsibilities of nuclear and extended kin. Thus they recast kinship norms (and subjectivities, much as Bedi argues), in present-day India.

Moving from the legal (and urban) domain to the 'rural', Helen Ullrich's essay, titled 'Marital Intimacy: A Four-Generation Study of Change among Havik Brahmans' also explores a similar process of re-negotiating intimacy and conjugality among Havik Brahmans in the village of Totagadde, Karnataka. Following in the tradition of Sylvia Vatuk's pioneering research on intergenerational relations, familial ruptures, and shifting ideologies of conjugality, Ullrich's essay exemplifies the value of ethnographic fieldwork and long-term life-history methodology in illustrating changing modes of self-crafting through the lens of one particular ideology (and practice)—that of marital intimacy or companionate marriage. Taking advantage of her intimate, forty-four year relationship with the Havik Brahman families in the village of Totagadde, Ullrich explores shifting discursive constructions of marital intimacy in four generations of Totagadde Brahman families. Her careful explication of changing gendered norms and values across these generations allows us to chart the intricate relationships between history and culture, ideology and practice, economy and morality over the course of the past half-century in this village, and to discover anew Vatuk's point about the complex, shifting, multiply-indexed nature of 'culture' and 'history' writ large.

Tracing twentieth-century family strategies in a north Indian village, Khalapur in U.P., Pauline Kolenda also draws on decades of fieldwork, from the 1950s through the 1990s. She suggests that having few daughters and keeping some sons unmarried were early strategies to keep property concentrated in the *khandan* or minimal patrilineage, while educating sons for non-agricultural jobs and later educating daughters helped enhance resources and minimize obstacles to family prosperity in later decades. Kolenda sets her case study of one *khandan*, that of a Brahman teacher, in the context of economic and social changes in Khalapur over the course of the twentieth century. She also shows the impact of obstacles to family success such as high infant and child mortality, diseases, addictions, and accidents, showing, as Ullrich does for south India, intersections between 'history' and 'cultural norms' evolving over time.

Echoing these themes of inter-generational relations, complex life and family histories, and continuities and tears in the warp and weave of culture, Karen Leonard's essay on 'Degrees of Diasporic Separation: Family Narratives of Continuity' delineates the affective and material 'field of relations' occasioned by the Hyderabadi diasporic dispersal. Drawing on eight family narratives evoked from the perspective of those 'left behind' in Hyderabad, Leonard poignantly illustrates the felt meaning of spatial and cultural dislocation, revealing a powerfully articulated stress on continuity in the face of apparent rupture. The 'degrees of separation', she argues, are variously experienced by those 'at home' and 'abroad,' revealing multiple and shifting registers of longing and belonging, alienation and intimacy. Invoking Sylvia Vatuk's exemplary analysis of the ruptures and reorientations of culture experienced by a Nawayati Muslim family over the course of the nineteenth and twentieth centuries, Karen Leonard similarly allows us to explore with her the 'structures of feeling' and re-orientations of self, family, history, and culture revealed through the lives, longings and relations between Hyderabadis and members of their families—the Hyderabadi diaspora dispersed around the globe.

Pnina Werbner's essay on 'The Place(s) of Transgressive Sexuality in South Asia: From Ritual to Popular Culture' allows us to glimpse yet another aspect of culture's intrinsically dialogic and heteroglot nature in a diasporic context. Through the lens of sexuality—and gendered spaces for non-normative sexual performances in particular—Werbner undertakes a ritual analysis of *mehndi* marriage ceremonies in Manchester to reveal the symbolic and cosmological context and logics to better understand the performances of transgressive sexuality enacted therein. Following the trajectory and goal of much of Vatuk's work (and using Raheja and Gold's *Listen to the Heron's Words* as a mirror and foil to do this)—that is, in recovering subaltern (gendered) voices and perspective, disarticulating 'normative' assumptions about the split representations of women in South Asia (between the married, nurturing mother and the single, dangerous, sexually devouring woman), and troubling the notion of a single, unproblematized category 'woman'—Werbner argues for *mehndi* rituals to be interpreted in this multivalent light, while also calling for their contextual understanding within a broader cosmological frame of interpretation. *Mehndi* rituals, Werbner argues, and the play/performance of sexuality in these rituals, not only reveal women's agency and control, but also need to be seen within 'broad and complex ideas about the cosmos, nature and regeneration, which are based on the notion of balance, the juxtaposition of opposites'.

Further extending her frame (and framing) of ritual analysis, Werbner juxtaposes the 'private' *mehndi* performances with the more 'public' fund-raising performances of the women's group, Al-Masoom. Both historical colonial/missionizing movements and more recent (Hindu *and* Muslim) right-wing movements have targeted public intimations of women's sexuality as one focus of their ongoing attack. This, too, is another context that situates the interpretation of contemporary performances of transgressive sexuality, Werbner argues, calling attention to the multiple, shifting 'frames' that locate cultural and ritual analysis.

Linked to Werbner through a concern with negotiating gender in ritual contexts, but shifting observations from household confines to more public spaces, are contributions by Joyce Flueckiger and Helene Basu. Both approach places of religious and ritual healing, and the domestic politics at play in such places, but each from a rather different angle. H. Basu's essay, 'Healing Madness through Ritual Trials', discusses healing practices in a space where the quest for relief from suffering trumps religious and other identities. The shrine she describes uses the language of law courts; and as do courts of law, it deals with many domestic problems—thus revealing unexpected continuities in the domain of religion with Vatuk's and S. Basu's writings on family courts. An alternative 'moral court' is held in this unusual healing shrine in Gujarat, as H. Basu explains. Here 'human and non-human offenders are tried through rituals for specific misdemeanours creating trouble in people's mind, body and behavior'.

Legal language is used to describe modes of affliction and exorcism. Moreover, just as is a law court, the shrine court is characterized by a commitment to determining ultimate truth. As is often the case with secular courts and judgments, H. Basu points out that—rather than reconciliation—shrine treatment and prescriptions may result in rupture and entail a separation of conflicting parties. We also see in one case study that H. Basu provides the possibility for a woman cured of 'madness' to emerge from the healing process in an improved domestic situation. Thus an afflicted wife, who clearly does not enjoy her job as a servant and whose illness directly resulted from the polluting work she was required to perform, returns to sanity and in the process declares that she will quit her job and her husband will 'stop gambling and work instead'. Here is revealed, as in a number of Vatuk's studies of gender and kinship, the ways women may—in spite of manifold social constraints—assert strong claims for autonomy and well-being.

Flueckiger, like H. Basu, is concerned with a space of healing. But her focus—in the essay titled 'Courage and Authority in the Next Generation: Shifts in Gender Expectations and Performance in a Hyderabadi Sufi Healing Tradition'—is on a family of healers rather than on the afflicted who come to them. Acknowledging the precedent set by Vatuk's extensive explorations of Muslim family history, Flueckiger herself investigates the transmission of power and authority across generations. Writing in a uniquely personal voice, characterized by lucidity and honesty, Flueckiger describes relationships within a family she has come to know very well. She discusses the ways these relationships have been altered in the aftermath of the death of Amma, the female healer who was the central figure in Fleuckiger's recent book, *In Amma's Healing Room* (2006).

Having encountered the courageous and charismatic figure of Amma, Flueckiger is looking for her successors. What happens after the death of such an extraordinary woman? Flueckiger finds a 'routinization of charisma': potential female successors, none of whom are quite what Amma was, yet who nonetheless make claims to ritual authority on the basis of Amma's legacy. Within this perhaps predictable pattern, Flueckiger observes many additional subtle transformations at work.

While less dramatically transgressing normative gender roles and boundaries than did Amma, the women in Amma's family nonetheless seem to find some slightly altered roles and positions as a direct result of the precedents set by Amma. Vatuk's insights into change through the life cycle as well as transmission through generations are significant to Flueckiger's findings. It is especially interesting that while Amma described herself as 'like a man', her daughter, daughter-in-law and grand-daughters 'have internalized the potential for expanded gender roles' and 'have experienced Amma as a woman like themselves'. Interesting also is a cross gender move observed by Flueckiger: the grandson Akbar, a young man, sees himself as an heir to his grandmother, unlike his father who lacks her patience and caring capacities. In other words, in following Amma's model as a healer, he follows a more female mode of practice. As does Bedi in a very different context among women of very different religious and social backgrounds, Flueckiger is able to portray distinctive individual personalities, even as she shows how their lives are conditioned and constrained by their social milieu.

Flueckiger emphasizes as influential Vatuk's tracking of a family through time and history, including the methodology entailed by such a focus on a single family: that is, the deliberate choice to observe in a limited context but think outward from it. As do several of the other essays gathered here, Flueckiger's contribution demonstrates the many ways long-term, attentive, intimate ethnography entails personal involvement. She describes how she has become so close to Amma's family that she herself has become literally incorporated into their collective past and ongoing story.

Gloria Raheja's essay '"A Splendid Thing for the Empire": Some Reflections on Ethnography and Entextualization in

Colonial India' is neither about gender nor kinship. Rather, Raheja reflects on another very significant line of Vatuk's scholarship—one that is not adequately represented in this volume. Raheja acknowledges a link with Vatuk's 1999 article on the '*Qanoon-e-Islam*' in which, as Raheja describes it, Vatuk addressed processes through which the speech, words and voices of colonized citizens were 'entextualized' in colonial administrative reports and ethnographic documents. In her own essay, Raheja pays particular attention to those British 'entextualizing practices' that concerned acts the British regarded as criminal or rebellious, and she demonstrates some of the links between ethnography and colonial disciplinary practices in nineteenth-century India.

Raheja provides some extraordinary and varied examples of the use of ethnography in colonial India. She is able to show, with Vatuk, that colonial ethnographic practice was marked by 'heterogeneity and contradiction' and shot through with considerations of power. Raheja explores this in a range of contexts, focusing on the uses of ethnographic description in the colonial archive and the ways that the recording of native speech came to play a role in the project of producing an illusion of consent to colonial rule and a justification for the colonial enterprise. She also shows that the texts inserted into colonial documents were shaped far more by the exigencies of colonial rule than by native speakers themselves. Among the diverse examples Raheja unfolds in detail here are an imaginary conversation between a 'sahib' and a woman about to commit sati—produced to exemplify both customs and grammar in the late eighteenth century; the diverse reactions of 'natives' to the mark-stones installed by the 'Great Trigonometrical Survey' in the nineteenth century and the reductive colonial diagnosis of these reactions; folk songs questioning the value and equity of colonial irrigation projects and the ethnography whereby the voices of the singers were marginalized and discounted; and ethnographic and fictional reports of the customs of the Thugs and the ways in which Thug narratives came to be inserted into these texts to serve contradictory colonial purposes. As are all the authors gathered here, Raheja is attentive to voice, and to divergent voices; remarkably she is able to uncover these within archival materials.

Together, all nine of these essays critically examine and extend Vatuk's contributions to the intersections of historical and ethnographic work, exploring anew the ways in which constructions of culture are inextricably and intimately tied to the specifics of historical and political context, as well as attending to the implications of such situated knowledge for contemporary understandings of history, culture, and politics in present-day India. Through these essays—and Sylvia Vatuk's immense corpus of work—culture is indeed revealed as necessarily 'dialogic' and 'heteroglot', requiring scholarship attentive to intimate histories and situated ethnographies in order to represent this complexity meaningfully. Although a single collection could not by any means contain a comprehensive representation of Sylvia Vatuk's influence, we offer this volume as a modest tribute to an exemplary scholar and a good friend.

KAREN ISAKSEN LEONARD, GAYATRI REDDY
& ANN GRODZINS GOLD

2

The (Im?) Possibilities of a Situated Feminist Subject in Shiv Sena: Shiv Sainiks, Governance, and Adjustment in Maharashtra

TARINI BEDI[1]

INTRODUCTION AND AIMS

I was always the one who was slightly different in my family. I was always interested in the outside world; I was never interested in sitting at home. If any of my neighbors ever wanted anything from the markets they would call out to me since they knew that I enjoyed being out of the house; I tell you, my personality has always been like that, and that's the way I am even now. As far as the house goes, I really hardly ever cook; and since my daughter has got married and left the house, there are only two of us, my husband and me so I don't need to do much cleaning. I much prefer to work outside the house. I am not very domestic. For the last 5–6 years I have stopped eating any dinner. And my husband comes home so late he often eats on his way home. Or else we have a *dabbawalla*[2] that we order our food from. It's so much easier to just adjust like that. You have seen what a state my house is in; I told you I really don't like housework; that's my *swabhav* (personality).

(Sarite Mohite, Shiv Sainik in Mumbai).

Like the speaker above, I am explicitly concerned with the examination of the relationships between public, performative (Butler 1990a, 1990b; Turner 1986) politics and gendered dynamics within the home and the political party. I particularly examine how women's aggressive, and frequent public participation in Shiv Sena's politics unsettles private gendered relationships. My fieldwork with Shiv Sena women was conducted between 2003 and 2007 across three field sites: in the northern suburbs of Mumbai city, Pune city and Pune district, a region about 160 km (approximately 100 miles) south-east of Mumbai, and in Nashik city and district, about 185 km (approximately 115 miles) north-east of Mumbai. During this time, I followed the lives of 29 Shiv Sainiks in Mumbai, 13 in Pune city and districts, and 3 in Nashik city and districts. I conducted multiple interviews with the same women over the years so that I came to know them during different phases of their political careers and their personal lives. Throughout this paper, I illustrate many of the responses of my informants in their own words. However, it is a deliberate decision on my part to omit exact dates and times of interviews, a decision I make through most of my writing on the subject, and one made in order to protect the identities of my informants. Given that many of my informants are local public figures, the clear identification of responses and interviews, opens up the possibility for my informants to be identified in ways that could affect both their political and social careers. Therefore, in order to maintain the anonymity of my informants, apart from simply using pseudonyms in my writing, almost all my informants are composites, who are expressions of common themes without being individually identifiable.

I have three related goals, and all three are deeply influenced by many of the pioneering themes examined by Sylvia Vatuk in her admirable body of work. There is no doubt that this paper has been influenced by Sylvia's writings and her approach to ethnography; I have additionally had the privilege of having her as a member of my dissertation committee at the University of Illinois at Chicago, and have therefore had the benefit of her wisdom and guidance on much of my work, and my thought on gender and the cultural dynamics of the South Asian household more broadly. I am extremely grateful to her for a close reading of a draft of this paper; and for her tremendously incisive insights into many of the themes that I tackle here.

My first goal is to examine and acknowledge the ways in which contemporary cultural negotiations between public and intimate life and the production of subjecthood through performance are deeply implicated in the broader social and historical relationships between capital, property, family, and legal subjecthood in western India (Deshpande 2007; Dobbin 1972; Glushkova and Feldhaus 1998; Glushkova and Vora 1999; Kosambi 2000b). It is through these very specific histories that contemporary discourses of empowerment emerge and unsettle each other in the lives of Shiv Sena women. I argue that subjecthood in this context is constituted not simply through individual action but through relational logics between men and women and between women themselves (Chatterjee 2004; Sturman 2005). In the course of my research, I found that everyday practices in Shiv Sena create numerous collective and relational conditions for women out of which both subjectivity and experience emerge (Rowe 2005). Throughout this paper, I unpack assumptions about the dynamics of home, family, and domesticity by placing them within broader cultural and historical processes. A great deal of my thinking on these topics has been influenced by Vatuk's approach to understanding the family through its historical and contextual textures (2004). In particular, I revisit Vatuk's earliest work on family dynamics and kinship within contexts of migration and urbanization in India (1969; 1972) as well as her later work on marriage and family change (1982).

Second, I look at how the imperatives of the very visible, public participation of Shiv Sena women in politics and governance affect the gendered relationships within both home and party. In unpacking the overlapping structures of power and the everyday use of kinship terms of address within the party, I am particularly influenced by Vatuk's earliest insights into the strategic use of fictive kinship terms and the ramifications this usage has for the expression of gendered autonomy within what are otherwise patriarchal structures (1969; 1971). Third and relatedly, I illuminate how gendered relations and possibilities for governance change over the life-cycle of women in public life. I find that for women in Shiv Sena, the dynamics of domesticity and public politics are deeply implicated in individual life-cycles as well as in the interactions between generations and genders within Shiv Sena households. As I unpack the interaction between life-cycle and women's governance in Shiv Sena, I am particularly influenced by Vatuk's writings on the relationship between age and changing normative constraints and the performative dimensions of aging in India (1987; 1992).

Much like Vatuk's work on the subject of ageing and sexuality suggests (Vatuk 1992), it is essential to problematize both age and gender as distinct (albeit related) feminist categories. This is particularly important when examining gendered access to governance, because the public gaze changes a great deal through women's life-cycles (Lamb 2000). Even more important, women in Shiv Sena seem to perceive this gaze very differently through different stages of their lives. These changing perceptions have pragmatic effects on women's styles of governance and on the degree to which they engage with public space and public audience. Many female Shiv Sainiks locate discourses of gender autonomy, as well as control over their political careers as rooted first in adjustment,[3] and as they get older, in the freedom of *umar* (age).

The first section briefly introduces the situated discourse of adjustment. I discuss some existing feminist approaches to women and politics and then go on to examine how ideas of family, domesticity, and intimate relationships are constituted within very particular historical and cultural dynamics. I also provide the background to the intersections between private kinship and party dynamics within Shiv Sena. The next section illuminates how the discourses of adjustment and *umar* are manifested in Shiv Sena and how they interact. The last section will focus on the performative dynamics of age and public life through the narrative of a key female Shiv Sainik in Mumbai.

ADJUSTMENT AS SITUATED FEMINIST DISCOURSE: SOME BACKGROUND

The three key goals of this paper stem from the need to examine the situated discourses and performances of autonomy of Shiv Sena women. I address these goals by engaging deeply with what actually happens to women's lives when they join political parties that reward high local visibility at the same time that they present immensely contradictory discursive associations of women with home and child-rearing using a variety of religious and cultural discourses.

The party's women's wing, the Mahila Aghadi (literally translated as 'women's front', though interpreted for me by my informants as 'women first'), is comprised largely of middle and lower-middle class women who often live in and on the edges of Maharashtra's cities and towns and their semi-urban peripheries (Sen 2007). There is only very vague official documentation on the establishment of the Mahila Aghadi (often referred to in this paper as the Aghadi).[4] Hence, much of the reconstruction of its birth comes through the narratives of women who see themselves as its 'original' founders (Sen 2006). The absence of a master-narrative for the founding of the women's wing is telling, especially given the almost mythic nature of the founding narrative of the larger Shiv Sena party. Instead, the Aghadi's narratives of its establishment take on the forms desired by the tellers. If there is a common thread, it is that all the narratives of women who see themselves as original members suggest very specific forms of public performative action as absolutely key to the founding of the Aghadi (Bedi 2007). The multiple founding narratives I collected despite their diversity, all focus on visible events where women's bodies were inserted into urban public space as the defining moment of the Aghadi's inception. In all the narratives, this entrance into an urban public space through a commitment to justice and service to the community seemed to be integral for the constitution of political selves for Sena women. It is out of the imperatives of work and direct action in local communities that the discourse of adjustment emerges as the enabler of a very specific kind of public life.

When it comes to public life and governance, structures of patriarchy and domesticity within the family and within the party often overlap. The party's official rhetoric casts party-cadre relationships in kinship terms that aim to discursively replicate familial relationships and therefore arguably also replicates the gendered hierarchies within the family. However, in the case of Shiv Sena women, what seemed at times undoubtedly a form of structural subordination both within the party and the home, was far more complicated when examined from a perspective of political practice. While a great deal of subordination is constituted rhetorically, it was often rejected performatively in collective and relational practice by the imperatives of everyday life paired with the personal and collective political ambition of Shiv Sena women. Thus I move away from a critique of gendered structural subordination within party politics.

Many feminist scholars have already contributed to this critique of structural subordination within parties on the political right (Bacchetta and Power 2002b; Dworkin 1982; Moghadam 1994a). Further, scholarship on women of right-wing political parties in India in particular has engaged very eloquently with the apparent disjunctions between these organizations' ideology of domesticity and the fact that they provide scope for women to venture into the public sphere (Bacchetta 2002; Sarkar and Butalia 1995). However, most of these studies make some assumptions about ideological consistency, both at the broader party-level as well as at the cadre-level. Shiv Sena is in fact, quite ideologically inconsistent with few consistent positions on either domesticity or politics. Most of its positions are performatively produced and are performatively subverted. The party therefore is a useful site at which to examine dynamic, situated practices of structural subversion. It is a somewhat fruitless attempt to 'locate' the feminist subject in Shiv Sena because it may never appear in its pristine, 'emancipated' form; I examine, instead, the subject in the relational imaginaries such as adjustment, through which Shiv Sena women attempt (by and large successfully) to locate themselves.

Broadly, Shiv Sena women located themselves in their everyday lives, within what they considered to be a subversive site of adjustment. This allowed them to constitute identities and selves in performative and narrative ways that often unsettled intimate relationships. Within this discourse of adjustment, audiences and bodies interacted largely to unsettle the conventional gendered relationships both within the home and the political party. This unsettled condition may better envision a feminism based not on the feminist discourse of emancipation or even on what has been referred to in the South Asian context as 'empowerment', but rather on what female Shiv Sainiks refer to as a relational politics of adjustment. At the risk perhaps of some naiveté, I move away from a structural critique of patriarchal power to an examination of contextualized expressions of gendered autonomy through Sena women's discourses on adjustment. Finally, I do find, and acknowledge, that these modes of power and autonomy are always in motion, appearing at times to reinforce and at others to unsettle gendered relations of power. Moreover, I also found that while adjustment is a useful lens through which to look at expressions of autonomy, adjustment is rarely fully complete, nor is it entirely devoid of personal or familial conflict.

SHIV SENA WOMEN AND ADJUSTMENT

Early in my research, many of my Shiv Sainik neighbors in Mumbai, invited me to have dinner at *Ruchi* the local vegetarian restaurant that serves everything from *udipi*[5] *dosas* to *udipi Chinese*. Udipi restaurants in middle-class areas in Mumbai are popular places for women to visit in all female groups because they are generally crowded and very well lit (and hence considered safe). Their extremely quick food-service is not conducive to lingering and the assumption therefore is that they do not attract men with bad intentions; further, they do not serve alcohol which makes them appropriate, familial places for the Indian middle and lower-middle-classes at which to eat or drink tea and coffee.

For many of the women who were with me that night, the simple act of eating at a restaurant without male escorts such as a husband, a brother or a grown-up son, was itself an act of defiance and a transgression of a class-constituted notion of female propriety. Middle-class Maharashtrian women, even women who live in large metropolitan areas such as Mumbai and Pune, rarely eat at restaurants alone and when they do, the vegetarian udipi-style is the most popular choice. During the course of my fieldwork, I found this transgression practiced more and more freely, particularly when Sena women were out on party business in large groups. While we were at dinner, Sate madam[6] a Shiv Sena corporator[7] in the BMC, got a phone call on her mobile phone—it is from her husband. It was 9:30 p.m. and past his dinner time and he wanted to know when she would be home. She told us to stop our chatter and said to him very irritably, 'I am in a meeting, why do you disturb me? I will be back by 10:30 or so. Heat up your food and eat without me.' All the other women teased her 'yeah what meeting', and she just good-humoredly shook her head, 'what does it matter? I am building the *Sanghatana* (the organization). *Arre baba*, it is adjustment' (come now, it is adjustment).

That evening I began to think about how the political party and its access to public life and the imperatives of public audience for Shiv Sena women unsettle or adjust domesticity. Further, throughout the course of my fieldwork with women of Shiv Sena, I realized that the discourse of adjustment had taken on meaning in the lives of Shiv Sena women as a very particular narrative of domestic and public negotiation through which they cast themselves as politically powerful and personally autonomous subjects.

The notion of subversion cannot be discussed without unpacking the situated meanings of adjustment. The very particular linguistic use of the English word adjustment even when otherwise speaking in the native language of Marathi certainly draws from the larger processes of the profoundly eclectic linguistic usages in urban India (Pandharipande 2003). This is particularly true in cities such as Mumbai and Pune where several English words have become an integral part of the vernacular itself. However, since adjustment does not have an easy corollary in Marathi, I found that the English term acted as a mobile resource in constituting a new sense of self that cannot be accommodated entirely within a traditional Marathi discourse on family and domestic life.

This situated discourse of adjustment was always brought up in the context of describing the balance between the imperatives of governance in Shiv Sena and intimate life. Adjustment is therefore a profoundly relational conception that is cognizant of the reality that women in urban and semi-urban Maharashtra, whose subjectivity is constituted through their performance of what they see as a public good is also deeply tied to familial relations. Adjustment occurs on a variety of levels: Sena women themselves adjust to a balancing act of personal and public life, as do their families. They see adjustment in a myriad of ways. For example, two active Shiv Sainiks in Pune district, which includes agricultural communities between Pune and Lonavala[8] told me that their early political careers were rooted in this adjustment between public life and domestic duties.

Since my son was about 2–3 years old, I have been working in Shiv Sena. He is now 22 years old. I have worked for the party for 20 years. I have been working after his birth. But there used to be an adjustment. When I did all this, what I used to do was get up early, make vegetables and *chapattis*, not rice and *dal*.[9] Then who is tortured? The house is tortured. But they all have to make the adjustment; this is politics see, this is my social work.

After I finished my party work, I would get down at the bus stand. Over there, whatever I will need in the house all day, some vegetables, some flowers, but what I will do is when I get down at the stand, I used to have my plastic bag with me. How much ever I may be tired, but for my house, if I needed things in the house, some grains, and vegetables, I used to bring all this within my adjustments. I don't tell anyone else to do it. It is important that I do my own work. Only there is an adjustment. Now I like to do it, which is why I work in the Shiv Sena. And my family is also doing that adjustment for me, since I am doing work for our nation of Maharashtra.

I also found that this theme of adjustment as Shiv Sena women's situated discourse of autonomy was located in a local context of urban and regional history and was critical to a particular kind of 'modern' public agent. Moreover, the emergence of what may be looked at as a form of feminist subjectivity in Shiv Sena did not present itself simply within a male–female, masculine–feminine dyad of power. Instead, the sort of mobilization that Shiv Sainiks engaged in, and the access this mobilization provided, was both the product and the source of a complex of relational processes between and among genders and generations which is what Shiv Sena women referred to as adjustment. Pratibha Sawant, a Shiv Sena leader in Mumbai, discussed the dynamics of her household as we sat in her small sitting room while her twenty-one year old daughter served us tea and snacks. She told me:

See we have adjusted now. Now my daughter Megha has grown up. She has adjusted so I can now go and do party work and everything else. When she gets married, then my son will have to do some adjustment, until we bring my daughter-in-law in the house. But see my daughter-in-law will probably be *hi-fi* (colloquial term often used to refer to someone from a higher class or with a high level or education), she will be educated and will want to do service and not stay in the house. That is okay, then everybody will again have to adjust and do a little here and a little bit there because I also have to do my party work. See now if anyone knows me, they know me only with the four letters of Shiv Sena.[10] Otherwise, who is Pratibha Sawant? Nobody. Who am I if I am just sitting at home? I am nobody, and recognized by nobody; that is why there has to be adjustment.

As Pratibha points to above, adjustment is broadly conceived as a logistical shuffle between political and domestic space where generations and genders interact in dynamic ways. Female Shiv Sainiks recognize, and increasingly their families do too, that the adjustment demanded by the imperatives of party work (as perceived by most Shiv Sainiks) requires a de-centering of domestic relationships. However, this de-centering is not a formally debated form of domestic sharing in response to the demands of external party commitments. It occurs instead through an informal, unstated, and gradual process of adjustment led largely by women. Arguably, it is this informality along with the somewhat un-debated, even un-debatable cause that allows women degrees of autonomy.

Shiv Sena women routinely negotiate this important relationship between the demands of party and intimate life. This negotiation and what it means to feminist theories on politics and action, is not always adequately accommodated as a theory of autonomous action within existing feminist theory. Most Shiv Sena women, define themselves through very interesting and often contradictory discourses on home, family, and public life that are not easily categorized in existing feminist terms even feminist terms that have been termed 'third world' feminist perspectives (Jayawardena, 1986; Mohanty et al. 1991). As Balatai[11] Shinde, my key informant in Pune, reiterated to me:

My recognition outside the house is because of Shiv Sena. All the greetings I get, all the respect I get, all that has been given to me by the four letters of Shiv Sena. Had I been inside the house, I would have been known amongst relatives as the son's mother, the husband's wife, and the mother's daughter, I would have been known by these few relations. But if you see my name today, it is very big. And the most important thing with the fame is that I am recognized. Whoever has a problem should go to Shinde.

Mohanty, who has most explicitly argued for a more situated understanding of feminist action, argues that much of feminist scholarship in the western world assumes certain cross-cultural universalities in the understanding of concepts such as family, marriage, patriarchy, etc. (Mohanty et al. 1991). The case of religion and ethnicity has been particularly problematic for Western feminist thought. Mohanty argues that a feminist theorization of the post-colonial world must take into account the diverse ways in which the religious and the secular have interacted with discourses of colonialism to produce culturally and historically specific problems (and solutions) for post-colonial women (Mohanty 1991a, 1991b).

Thus, to analyze religious ideological structures as primarily and always responsible for patriarchy and oppression is somewhat misplaced. In India, the collective celebration of religious ritual has been a key strategy of mobilization, even within the liberal women's movement. In fact, Neelatai, a very prominent female Shiv Sainik in Pune who, during the course of my fieldwork was one of two women to hold a leadership role in the general party (not simply in its women's wing) and also to become one of the key party spokespeople, was recruited into the party after many years working in the women's movement in rural Maharashtra. As we sat in the bedroom of the government guest house she was staying at on an official visit to Mumbai, she described the strategies that she had used to mobilize high and low caste women collectively using religious ritual and told me that was the strategy she was now using in Shiv Sena.

I realized that women along with having the independent decision-making we have to strengthen ourselves on many different levels. One is in our own lives; secondly in the family. So we always talked about strengthening the family unit. The Indian women's movement is always accused of being anti-religion, anti-family. My movement, has always talked, dreamed, defined, publicized and decided to change the norms of the dignity of women within family, so that they will have a better life; so that women can set up their own agenda, so that we can strengthen the *parampara of prabodhan* (further the knowledge and ways of knowing). So we talked of not denouncing every festival, but we talked of festivals like *naga-panchmi*[12] where *dalit* and non-*dalit* women can come together and they can play *jhula* (swing) together, and they can sing songs, so the barriers due to caste and religion can be broken and women can come.

Mohanty's suggestion that religious discourses and women's attraction to movements that reify these discourses must be examined within social and political relations and practices is important (Mohanty 1991b). This approach allows feminist scholarship to dislodge religion, and in fact all other forms of assumed oppression such as conjugality and family from universal ideas of patriarchal oppression. Vatuk's most recent work, has examined these issues closely with regard to Muslim women in India (Vatuk 2008). These context driven explorations allow for the examination of women's oppression as the cultural and historical product of religious discourse as it interacts with a variety of other social and cultural practices. It is therefore a paradigm for the examination of both agency and oppression.

SHIV SENA AND FICTIVE KINSHIP NETWORKS: STRUCTURES AND PROCESSES OF POWER IN THE PARTY AND FAMILY

In Shiv Sena, female Shiv Sainiks arguably encounter dual structures of power. That is, the party's key strength lies in ensuring party loyalty by conjoining ideas of kinship and party membership. The complex politics of class and caste domesticity in the home and in a class and caste-flexible but hierarchical political party is based at least at the higher levels of the party on masculine paternalism. Shiv Sena propaganda and most of its discursive processes go to great lengths to recast the party in familial terms. Shiv Sainiks, both men and women, generally address each other with commonly used Marathi kinship terms. Not insignificantly perhaps, the kinship terms used consistently connote natal kinship and relations traced through maternal rather than paternal kin: *tai*, *bhau*, *dada*, *maushi*, *mama*, *mami*, *vahini* (older sister, brother, older brother, mother's sister, mother's brother, mother's brother's wife, older brother's wife). These relations of fictive kinship engendered by regular use of such kinship terms are according to most Shiv Sena women, important in setting the boundaries of sexual relations among party members. 'We are all brothers and sisters, that is why no one will ever do anything wrong. There is never anything *bura* (bad) between *ladies* and *gents*. That is why *ladies* get so much respect in Shiv Sena.'

As Vatuk has illustrated in the case of women in Uttar Pradesh, (1969, 1971), for many Maharashtrian women displaced by marriage from Maharashtra's rural areas and urban centers to urban peripheries, this construction of natal kinship networks, allows them to recreate communities of affiliation that they have left behind (Sen 2006). For many older Shiv Sena women it also recreates a political climate that they recall from their youth when familial participation in the urban politics of Maharashtra was quite commonplace. However, it has been suggested, with respect to other right-wing movements in India, that constituting an organization along the lines of kinship, fictive or otherwise, may in many cases replicate those gendered relations of power that are extant within the household (Bacchetta 2005; Mazumdar 1995; Sarkar 2001).

As far as the structural inclusion of women in the party goes, Shiv Sena's Mahila Aghadi gained more public prominence and was officially integrated into the structure of the larger party through the influence of Thackeray's late wife Meena Thackeray in the 1980s. Meena Thackeray died in somewhat mysterious and tragic circumstances in 1996, when she allegedly took ill rather suddenly and was unable to get to the hospital quickly due to inadequate ambulance facilities. Meena Thackeray is now widely referred to by both male and female Shiv Sainiks as either Meenatai or *Maasaheb* (lord mother or mother of the lord).[13] Interestingly this colloquial term in Maharashtra also refers to Jijabai, the mother of Shivaji, the warrior king after whom the party is named.

Several examinations of gender and politics have pointed to the predominance of 'mother' figures in both the liberal and conservative discourses of nationalism (Klatch 1994; Smith 1994; Yuval-Davis 1997). The Meena Thackeray figure is a critical mother icon, though not so much in the obvious sense as a cultural role-model of femininity. Rather, she is looked at as an almost paranormal, embodied source of a particular kind of devotion to the party that Shiv Sena women refer to as *nasha* (heady addiction). I have heard from more than one Shiv Sena woman that the day she felt changed was the day she ate refreshments prepared by Maasaheb: 'It was after that day, when I imbibed the food cooked by Maasaheb, that something got into my blood and I got this *nasha* (heady feeling); this is a *nasha* I cannot leave. It is in my blood, and right here in my heart.' Others mention similarly corporeal experiences with Meenatai:

> She touched and caressed my back like this, softly, powerfully. She was very nice. I have never met such a nice woman. She had come and taken us out of the house to do the work, I had gone with her and only a few days later she died. She had so much love and that is why I still feel like crying when I think about her.
>
> She would never let us leave *Matoshree* (home of the Thackerays) without giving us tea. And the tea was made by her hands. What was in that tea, I don't know, but it was something great, something that had given me strength.

These narratives of *nasha* and love are very personal ones. Many Sena women who narrated them wept with an intense emotion evoked by the memory of Meena Thackeray. Many in Mumbai's media circles decry Meena Thackeray as nothing more than an obedient, submissive trophy-wife, testimony to Bal Thackeray's ego-maniacal and paranoid desire for public recognition. From the ways in which her presence is reconstructed by Sena women, it is clear that she fulfilled many of the expectations of middle-class Maharashtrian femininity and domesticity; however, the deeper meaning that her involvement has for many of today's Sena women cannot be ignored as a very political reading of her conventionally feminine presence.

Also under Maasaheb's influence, the party's internal relationships were increasingly recast in terms of fictive kin networks, a unique organizational structure of Shiv Sena. Party workers are deeply embedded in both local neighborhood as well as more extended networks that are cast linguistically in kin terms, across neighborhoods in parts of urban Maharashtra. This is arguably the party's single most critical strength in local mobilization and party loyalty. It is also what has prompted many critics of Shiv Sena to refer to the party disparagingly as Bal Thackeray's clan particularly because any dissension is severely punished through a politics of shame akin to what might occur among kin.

This could be seen as a rather ingenious strategy. The networks that emerge when politics is constituted around neighborhoods have been very helpful to the party's influence. Party-workers and their constituents have become implicated in a complex of relations that revolve around residence, kin and the larger landscape of social and cultural life. Arguably, the locality of political action and the recognition that it brings to women, and by extension their families has also made it easier for women in this party to lead very public lives and to make adjustment less stigmatized. This is because of a woman's location within the safety of a kinship group, and her perceived contribution to a cause that will bring honor and fame to her relatives. As the grown-up son of one of female Shiv Sena leader in Pune district told me: '[My mother] does not get any money from this work, only what she gets is recognition. So the only profit is the name you get out of it. Otherwise there is no profit from this work. So papa and I take care of the business and mummy brings us the name.'

Therefore, for some, party work outside the house is not only important to a sense of self, but increasingly to the ways in which they constitute themselves for their children. Party work has an effect on the ways in which their children perceive their mother's autonomy. Moti and Pratibha, both active Shiv Sainiks in Mumbai echoed these patterns.

> One day my son came to drop me at night in that ward where we were working to get them some electricity. There was no electricity, it was raining. We had to cross that bridge; at that time there was just a small bridge. And my son told me '*ma* you come so far on your own late at night? Santosh Nagar is very far away from our home.' So I told my son, 'yes, now if I have taken this post, I have to go otherwise what is the use?' So now he knows that I am brave enough.
>
> I told my children when I became a Sena leader that I would be away from the house a lot and they supported me and said '*aai* (mother) you have this opportunity, you must do it. We will be okay and help in the house.'

While certainly Shiv Sena women share a perception that their families are dynamic entities that adjust and, in fact, often derive both symbolic prestige and pragmatic gain from their involvement in public life, this participation is often wrought with contradictions. Neelatai the Pune leader who I got to know very closely through my fieldwork talked at great length about her own negotiation of these personal contradictions. Neela is fluent in English and many of our conversations went back and forth between English, Hindi and Marathi. The following was told to me in English and I have therefore chosen to reproduce her conversation verbatim to reflect the local nuances in Neela's usage of English:

> I feel for women it is not only a question of family or about the family's adjustment. Because families also go on changing their notions, they go on adjusting this way and that way. So the way my family used to look at me 10–15 years ago was different. Now that family also feels that their prestige is elevated if I get better sanction by society. That is changing within the Indian system and it is not like it was 10–15 years ago. But it is a very hard struggle, I have faced it myself. After every success, I have seen that many times actually you have to work double to get success because you are a woman; and if you are woman and you are giving a lot of time [to your work] then people call you ambitious; then if you are not well then you are told, you are not taking proper care, you are getting sick; and basically as a woman I will say that all the time there is a guilt within your mind which gives you a haunting feeling that something, somewhere, you are doing a mistake, that I am doing a mistake. So it took for me at least ten years to grow out of that feeling of guilt. So society and people who are around you, they go on giving you a feeling of doing something wrong though you may be correct in your own way. It is a mindset; it is up to you to look at your mind and see whether I am happy with whatever I am doing. That is the positive feeling. But to understand and realize that positive feeling that takes a very long time, and it only comes as you get older and get some more experience with politics and life.

It would be erroneous to conclude simplistically that Shiv Sena women themselves are motivated by a sense of 'honor' that they bring to their families, though this recognition is an important by-product of women's participation in party politics. The demands of electoral politics and the sort of dedication that party-work requires is far more complicated than that. Most Shiv Sena women display very individual, very personal desires for power. Most also want to leave lasting civic legacies that go far beyond a simple understanding of women in public life as little else but repositories of cultural and social honor. In fact, the increasing presence of women in the party has actually succeeded in extending the party's local spheres of influence to include schools, bazaars, temples, and, of most relevance to this paper, households.

An examination of the ways in which familial structures and processes operate for Shiv Sena women shows that there are clearly contradictory processes in play. Arguably, for Sena women, the pattern of fictive kinship within the party constitutes a space of freedom akin to that experienced within the natal home. The usage of the kinship term of *bhau* (brother) for men in the party with whom they have to work closely, often late at night, on election campaigns and at party events, does away with the necessity of avoidance between men and women. As Vatuk has shown so clearly in her work, in most parts of India, women follow very different normative behavior in their natal and their conjugal homes; they are generally far more constrained by oppressive norms, in their conjugal than in their natal homes (1969). In addition, in Maharashtra (as in some other parts of India), when women enter their conjugal homes, they are given new first names by their husbands' families. All of my married informants were given different names in their conjugal homes, and while they are known politically by those names, they admit that visiting their natal homes means also going back to the comfort of their original names and less inhibited behavior. This effort at recreating an urban natal, extended family of sorts, in some cases rooted in actual kin relations, but in most, simply in fictive kinship, arguably helps to reconstitute the *ilaka* (neighborhood). To a large extent, this assuages the painful effects of rural and conjugal migration (Sen 2007; Vatuk 1972).

Arguably, for women, the wide use of kinship terms associated with natal homes is not simply a random choice as Sylvia Vatuk has shown in some of her earlier work (1969). Unlike the women's wings of other Hindu allied organizations such as the RSS where the most prominent women are unmarried and celibate (Ghosh 2002; Mazumdar 1995), most female Shiv Sena leaders are married and living in their conjugal homes. By constructing the possibility of extended natal kinship the party creates a space for women where they can behave as they do in their natal ones. The potential for the expression of individual personality, not simply in all female groups, but also in mixed male and female groups when out on party work, seems to be very appealing to Sena women. This lowering of inhibition, while certainly most obvious in all female groups, is also noticeable in mixed male and female groups of Shiv Sainiks. This is particularly evident among older members who have worked together in the party for a long time, and among whom the gendered negotiation of fictive kinship between *bhau* and *tai* (brother and sister) has an established history.

A feminist analysis of power in an organization like Shiv Sena must then problematize family, home and party as performative sites of control and subversion as they are imaginatively, discursively, and practically tied to each other in complex ways. The recognition that politics is constituted in everyday places is closely aligned with feminist analysis. However, the notion of domesticity, particularly, a domesticity that is rooted in religious structures is a problem for a Western-centric feminist approach. A large part of this unease comes from the fact that most sectarian and right-wing movements are rhetorically demand the strict separation of domesticity from public life (Bacchetta and Power 2002a, 2002b; Thapar-Bjorkert 1997).

Importantly there are strong structural differences between Shiv Sena women's everyday practice and organization and those of women of other right allied organizations in India such as the Rashtriya Sevika Samiti or the Durga Vahini (Bacchetta 2005; Bedi 2004; Sarkar and Butalia 1995; Sarkar 1998; Setalvad 1995). For one, most (if not all those who participated in my study between 2003 and 2007) female Shiv Sainiks, at some point or another admitted to wanting some form of real political power. By real political power, I mean that they desire some hand in governance across the levels of India's electoral and governmental system. Scholarly literature that examines women's wings of other organizations such as the Rashtriya Sevika Samiti talks very little about individual women's desires for legislative, electoral, or political power. This is what makes Shiv Sena women quite distinct from women in the other organizations (Bacchetta 2005; Katju 2005). However, because of the rhetorical denigration of overt 'ambition' in Shiv Sena for both men and women, though more so for women, political power is almost always viewed as an unintentional by-product of social work. Both Moti in Mumbai and Sauraksha in Pune reiterated this many times:

> See I got this post from god's grace. It must have been in my fate to get into *rajkaran* (politics). You know how they say you could never have dreamed something like this? I never could have dreamed of this. I never thought that I would be here sitting right in front with this post that I have. Now they say to get a post you have to run around, go, here, go there running behind the post. But for me, the post just came to me from the front. I am telling you the truth. I really do not know much about how to go about getting something like this, so they just gave me the post. And really I have never been in *rajkaran* in my life. I just did the social work and this is how I got the post.
>
> I kept saying no, no when they would say you should put your name for *Shakha Pramukh* (party office chief). In my mind it was just that everyone knew me. They also knew that I do all the work here. They also knew that I am always working with all the ladies here. They all recognized who I was. Now see, what the *netas* (ministers) give us, is that they decide and when they decide we have to do that only right? If it is in their mind to give it, then they will. They knew that I work for the party and that I come out and unite people . . . and if they wanted to give it to me they could. I was not going to go out and ask for it.

Despite continued efforts to dissociate themselves from the active pursuit of political office, most Sena women worked very hard to construct themselves 'politically' even if they did not talk about it. Power and autonomy was seen by them as constituted locally through the nominated posts that Sena gives its members or through elected office to the *panchayati* (village level) body, the district body or the zilla parishad or the civic bodies of the cities in which they lived and worked. Conversely others simply desired power as local patrons or protectors in their neighborhoods.

SHIV SENA WOMEN, AND INTIMATE POLITICS

While Shiv Sena has recently been examined within the rubric of Hindu nationalist organizations, it is erroneous to assume that its electoral alliances and the discursive agendas of its male leadership preclude a lack of individually or collectively constituted agency, particularly for its women at the local levels. If one looks at the organization entirely through the lens of its undeniable involvement in the brutal, anti-minority violence through several decades, the predominance of ideological 'religious' elements entirely precludes any possibility of really examining the tremendously flexible processes and networks that operate during periods of communal peace. These processes and networks provide women with many ways to negotiate both their intimate and public lives through cooption and rejection of traditional forms of femininity.

Further, the Sena's Mahila Aghadi is flexible without the formal initiation, or formal moral indoctrination and training camps noted in other right-wing organizations. Also Sena members in their everyday lives perform very flexible everyday practices of Hinduism (Mazumdar 1995; Sahgal 2007). While a Hindu discursive agenda frames the party's symbolic and performative agenda and has emerged in violent ways at volatile political moments in Maharashtra, party membership and indeed party work itself is first and foremost rooted in acceptance of Bal Thackeray's leadership, then in action, *kaam* (work) *samaj-seva* (community service), and of course *mara-mari* (violence). Moreover, the party's wide caste base means that even at its discursive level, it has to create Hindu imaginaries that appeal to those outside the fold of the strict, scriptural, Brahminical Hinduism that is associated with other Hindu allied organizations such as the RSS (Bacchetta 2005).

Feminist theorists who examine women's participation in nonliberal movements recognize that one of the most striking features of right-wing women is that their subjectivities are often constructed from a well negotiated system of 'double standards' (Bacchetta and Power 2002b; Scheck 2002; Vervenioti 2002). These authors suggest that there is a significant gap between the ways in which female leaders of right-wing movements live their own lives as individuals and the subjectivities that they propose for other women. While acknowledging that the often unconventional behavior of female leadership might actually be protected by class privilege, it seems obvious that 'in many cases right-wing women, leaders and activists alike, fight for societies that would totally eliminate women who behave as they do' (Bacchetta and Power 2002a: 6).

Shiv Sena women, interestingly advocate few, if any consistent normative or moral positions on Hindu women in general. They certainly see their own behavior in public space, particularly with regard to violence and aggression as 'exceptional' for other women, both Hindu and Muslim. The 'visibility' of their own power depends on the numbers of other women they can mobilize and make visible, so they do seem to advocate that other women at least symbolically venture out of their homes to protest and to fight for 'justice' that is not necessarily confined to a notion of gender justice *per se*. The focus on locality and local visibility in Shiv Sena's politics is particularly important to the unsettling of notions of home and public space. The imperative of grass-roots party work for ambitious Sainiks turns a great deal of the rhetorical separation between public and private, between home and party, and between the intimate and the public on its head for the most part.

A discussion of domestic adjustment and the boundaries between intimate and party lives, must examine the assumption that 'home' has the same meanings, one rooted in 'private' space, everywhere and throughout time. In Marathi the word *ghar* is used for what in English is 'home' as well as the physical building or 'house' (Glushkova and Feldhaus 1998; Glushkova and Vora 1999). Moreover, many Shiv Sena women when talking about their homes and families routinely used the word *sansar*, which literally translated into English means 'world' but for most women encompasses notions of both home and family, as well as more metaphysical meanings of domestic peace, and tranquility.

Most Sena women actually saw their homes as important sites of their public service. It is not unusual in India for politically powerful men to use an outer room in their homes to receive official visitors. However, in Shiv Sena's locally embedded political style where streams of constituents require resolutions to everyday problems throughout the day, I observed that Sena women's homes were used far more as sites of party business than were the homes of male Sena leaders (the men were perceived as being out during the day). Given the Sena's key strength of local and direct action (Eckert 2003), the private space of the home was itself intertwined with the public space of the party. Most women holding posts in the party, for example, had boards outside their homes with their names and party titles and Shiv Sena's logo of the tiger or the party symbol of saffron bow and arrow. These spaces were 'home-offices' in the true sense of the word, where domestic duty generally took a back-seat to party business, where a steady stream of neighborhood residents came in to ask for advice about their problems long before the official Shiv Sena *shakhas* (party branch offices) opened for business, and long after they closed at night.

A great deal of Western feminist debate has placed at its very core the distinction between the public and private. This distinction between a public masculine sphere and the private feminine sphere is assumed to be at the core of unequal gendered power relations. Indeed, in the case of India, masculine and feminized spheres have been critically intertwined in constructions of a nationalist discourse, particularly in the colonial context (Mani 1998; Sinha 1994, 1997). Partha Chatterjee's now famous discussion of the development of Indian nationalist discourse in the late nineteenth century within the context of imagining an 'authentic' but 'modern' national culture albeit one keenly differentiated from Western modernity has also reified this public/private and masculine/feminine divide

Chatterjee suggests that the central problem posed to the Bengali middle-class nationalist was the problem of 'modernizing' the Indian nation while at the same time retaining an essential national identity that underpinned the political claim to nationhood. Nationalist thought attempted to resolve this contradiction by distinguishing between a 'spiritual' and a 'material' realm: the nationalist could imitate the West in the outer material realm while at the same time retaining the inner 'spiritual' sphere as the un-colonized space of 'authentic' Indian-ness. Women as the guardians of the inner, spiritual sphere became regarded as the embodiments of an essentialized 'Indian-ness'

(Chatterjee 1986, 1993). Chatterjee's separation of an outer political sphere and an inner cultural one allowed him to relocate women's nationalist resistance from the political to the domestic sphere, but in the process he reified this divide without attempting to problematize it. My situated analysis of the ways in which women in public life move between what are deemed private and public spaces helps to problematize and unsettle this reification.

Needless to say, Shiv Sena women who are ambitious need to be very 'visible'. Their regular insertion into the public sphere is critical because public audience is perceived as being translated into electoral power and indeed it often works that way. Shiv Sena, and its reliance on local patronage systems operating at the level of each neighborhood (for example, through a remarkably vital shakha network in Mumbai), requires key personalities at every local level (Eckert 2003). Generally, I have found that all Sena leaders (both male and female) spend much of their efforts in office making sure that they are known (and to some extent feared) in their localities (Bedi 2007). The imperative of visibility has key electoral ramifications but also unsettles the everyday domestic lives of Sena women. For one, it requires long hours outside the house traveling through municipal wards and attending neighborhood events (condolence meetings, weddings, funerals, or housing redevelopment meetings). So the political strength of Shiv Sena really lies in the erasure of the abstract or distant aspect of politics. Almost all female Shiv Sena party workers and holders of both nominated and elected posts, publicly share their home phone numbers, cell phone numbers, and home addresses with their constituents. Anyone in the locality can gain direct access to them at any time of the day or night, and this is what makes adjustment on all fronts almost an imperative.

I came to see that, in Shiv Sena, appropriate public dedication was far more politically and often personally remunerative than conventional domesticity, and this was so despite Bal Thackeray's rhetorical efforts to place women within the confines of *ghar-grahasthi* (home and household). Most feminist examinations of right-wing women in South Asia relevantly point out that the most important difference between the women's movement and right-wing mobilization of women in India is that the women's movement challenges notions of women's subordination within the family and society, while Hindutva ideology places women squarely within the home and propagates a patriarchal model (Sarkar and Butalia 1995). While this discursive agenda is certainly useful to acknowledge, it is equally necessary to examine how top-down rhetoric is consumed by party-workers at the local levels. For example, the fact that Shiv Sena, does not pragmatically separate male and female wings for purposes of party events and rallies means that party rhetoric is directed and consumed collectively rather than separately by either men or women. Madhumati Dandekar, my key informant in Nashik district for example expressed this contradiction well:

> See what we teach our women is that first you look after your house. Even our Balaseheb says this. He says that 'the one who manages their *grahasthi* well that person will also look after the party well, isn't it?' See he will tell us these things at the party meetings. So it is not that he is separating women and men, he just says it to everyone. He says that the person who looks after their *grahasthi* well, will also look after the party well. This applies to everyone.

In this context, the more conventional debate over home (private) and party (public) is not particularly useful. Admittedly, it is impossible to ignore that the public and the intimate have routinely been conjoined in both colonial and post-colonial discourses of politics and sociality (Chatterjee 2004; Srinivas 2004; Sturman 2005). Therefore, any situated examination of feminist subjecthood can only assume the analytical categories of public and private as temporally contingent, rather than historically or culturally fixed. In practice, at least in Shiv Sena, the message is profoundly contradictory. Even Thackeray sometimes seemed to simply be playing lip-service to the ideological stance, since what ultimately got rewarded in the party is visibility in the *ilaka* (locality) at Sena public events—everywhere else but inside the house. Most female Shiv Sainiks also reiterate this ghar-grahasthi command rhetorically, though it seemed more of a political strategy than a moral one; this rhetorical reiteration in fact had a strangely subversive effect: By giving women this rhetorical tool and numerous performative outlets through domestic and feminized rituals that got performed in public space and sponsored by Shiv Sena, the party actually provided women with remarkable opportunities to access the female electorate as audience to these events outside the male gaze. I have always found the Shiv Sena's official ghar-grahasthi command, which is related through Hindu religious iconography, '*ghar ka diya pehle jalao, phir mandir ka diya jalao*', (first light the candle at home then light the candle at the temple) rather amusing. To be honest, during my fieldwork most of my informants were never home! Most gained far more satisfaction from their social work. Ragini Tawde, a Sainik in Mumbai who suffered from diabetes and asthma kept telling me again and again, whenever I inquired about her health:

I am really telling you that even if I am unwell at home . . . when I go outside, my illness just runs away. I become *ekdum fresh* (completely fresh). If I sit at home I go mad. I cannot sit at home and be happy. It was like this from before. Right after I got married. If someone needed me to go with them to the doctor's office or go to get their ration card, I would always go with them. I would not tell my husband that I was going out. I would run back before he came home. He did not know that I had been gone.

HOUSE, HOME, FAMILY AND DOMESTICITY: HISTORICIZING CONTEMPORARY DYNAMICS OF ADJUSTMENT

The discourse of adjustment for Shiv Sena women therefore means many things. On one level, it is certainly a discourse that refers to the changing logistical relations with the 'home'. However, it is also refers to a certain transgression of the physical space of the 'house', and to the changing dynamics of the family over time. Further, it also refers to the different and transgressive notion of domesticity and femininity. It could be questioned whether one could conceive of a South Asian feminism that navigates and unsettles domesticity through a politics of adjustment? Arguably, adjustment may be actually be a safer way to talk about increasing freedom by suggesting that other women in the family take over domestic responsibilities while the Shiv Sena women is out of the house. Adjustment is therefore a profoundly relational conception that depends on various negotiations within the home and the party and therefore adjustment becomes the enabler of public life. And while this may not fully de-center the gendered division of labor or the place of a female figure in the home it does quietly (and in many cases not so quietly) unsettle the individual practices of feminine conventionality.

It is essential at this point to unpack the various meanings of adjustment within the local contexts of house, home, domesticity, and family. Any discussion of the ways in which contemporary dynamics get narrated and performed must also be sensitive to how ideas of family, domesticity, and intimate relationships are constituted within very particular historical and cultural contexts. It is particularly important to recognize that the discourse of adjustment is rooted in a very specific sphere of performative action both within the party and within the home.

As many scholars now acknowledge, the boundaries of the home and domesticity are set by the larger culture (Sangari 1993). Therefore, critical analyses of the home trying to avoid both essentialization and romanticization of the allegorical power of the 'home' must be attentive to the specific languages, metaphors, and tropes through which it is narrated by historical subjects embedded in specific times and places (Burton 1997). In the case of Shiv Sena women, conceptions of home are locally and culturally embedded in the experiences of urban migration, both class marginalization and class mobility, and the complex relationships of political affiliation and ethnic and linguistic expression. The narrative of adjustment that emerges out of Shiv Sena women's everyday lives as a narrative of unsettled domesticity is locally embedded quite outside a Western narrative of the home and family. It is also, perceived by Shiv Sena women as uniquely located outside more conventional South Asian conceptions of domesticity and it is in this way, I argue that it becomes a unique and subversive discourse of feminist action.

For Shiv Sena women, the spatial and physical dynamics of the home are closely entwined with the dynamics of the party. For example, many civic wards in and on the edges of slum neighborhoods in Mumbai and Pune city or in more rural sections of Pune and Nashik districts often either do not have the space to set up shakha offices or have little non-residential space available for party business. In these neighborhoods, Shiv Sena leaders, both men and women host party meetings in their homes and provide counsel and advice to local constituents while sitting on plastic chairs outside the house or in front rooms of the home that in the evenings double as TV and family eating areas. I observed that even in the evenings when the family is home watching television or eating dinner, many Sena women would not stop conducting business, leaving their children and others at home to adjust. When the home and shakha are thus conjoined here, it was Sena women who were approached more often and in fact all day by local constituents since they were perceived more likely to be home than their male counterparts. While this assumption on the part of the public certainly drew from the assumption of a family with a single male earner and a female housewife, all Sena women to whom I talked, seemed to exhibit a certain kind of agency as they disbursed justice and advice to their neighborhoods while sitting by their stoves. Being within the physical space of the home but not normatively confined while working for the public within it, was a critical way in which Sena women distanced themselves from a wide variety of 'others'. These others were the north-Indian, and the Muslim woman in particular, people who are viewed by Sena women as bound to a drudgery of domesticity and child-rearing. As one female Sena corporator summed up very well:

> So for me, my *prabandha* (composition of area of governance) is made up of three areas and there are three people (in charge), but I ended up working in all three wards. The other two Corporators who are gents are never available, so people all come only to me. See ladies can be found at home in the mornings and in the evenings, so people come mostly to me. They go to the others very little. So I have done work in all three wards. I am known best. These other UP/ Bihari women, they just sit at home.

In actual practice, the private space of the home is an increasingly fluid category. Moreover, the stark realities of displacement and the aspirations of class mobility that are so much a part of urbanizing India and especially true of those attracted to the Sena's lumpen form of political action, play no small part in unsettling the spatial notions of the home. The economic and social upheavals of post-colonial Maharashtra and their accompanying pressures of migration from rural areas into the cities has provided an important historical background to this unsettling. The displacement of urban populations from urban hubs into the urban peripheries has further unsettled the physicality as well as the abstraction of the 'house' as much as it has the dynamics of the 'household' and the family.

One should also note, that in practice historically, the Marathi home in several parts of Maharashtra, while spatially designed to preserve public and private spheres, did not actually clearly demarcate the distinctions between gendered public and private lives. For example, many lower-middle-class Maharashtrian women, and a majority of the Shiv Sena women I have talked to who are now in their late forties and fifties have at some point lived in and continue to live in homes that are designed around the regional *wada* (also sometimes colloquially called *wadi*) style of architecture. The wada is a form of building that derives its norms from Hindu treatise on architecture, the *Vastushastra* and seems to have its roots in the Vedic period (Dengle 1998).

The wada is a multi-family dwelling and consists of rooms and verandahs built around courtyards (in the Desh region of Maharashtra), or around a *majghar* or inner room (in the Konkan region). Conventionally, those families who occupied wadas were generally all part of the same extended family, and in many cases this practice continues. In other cases, because most wadas, at least in urban Maharashtra are in centrally located areas, families rent out their portion of the wada for high rents, and live in less central, and cheaper areas. While the traditional wada architecture does make room for spaces that are strictly for domestic work such as cooking, they are not designed for either gender seclusion or female invisibility. While wadas occupied by the wealthy allowed for more privacy for women, with outsiders only invited into the front courtyard, the wadas that most middle-class Maharashtrians lived and live in are single courtyard wadas where women are far more visible.

The really significant feature of the wada lifestyle was that there were always rooms within the wada used as meeting rooms, discussion rooms, and consultation rooms for meetings with outsiders. While these meetings rooms were traditionally reserved for men, in the course of my research with Sena women who lived in wadas, I found that these meetings rooms were now exclusively used by the women to conduct party business, while the privacy of the inner rooms was where their husbands or children watched television, or did their homework undisturbed by women's visitors. Many Shiv Sena women associated the centrality of wada living with political activity dating back to their childhoods. Many also admitted that their formative exposure to political, cultural, and literary movements in early postcolonial western India was in the wadas of friends and family; wadas at the time were centers of political and literary debates. For many of these women home and political life was deeply intertwined in memory and interestingly, many, who now live in more contemporary buildings with private spaces demarcated more clearly along the lines one might find in the urban west, or even many who live in slum communities, when talking about their homes would sometimes inadvertently refer to their home as a wada.

Therefore, the modern-day overlap between home and party office, where public and private life coincide spatially with public business taking place within the wada, has historical roots in the Maharashtrian wada home. Saurakshatai, the Shiv Sena corporator in the Nashik Municipal Corporation sums it up well:

> Some people come here to the wada at 10 at night. They could not find me all day, so they come at night. I have made an office downstairs. And there is no timing written on the board there. When I have guests in the house they are always telling me 'what is this, your work is always going on'. Even when my guests come to the house I have no time to sit down and talk to them. My guests tell me 'put up some timing on the board. In the mornings from 9–11 and in the evenings 6–8 and give us the time in the middle.' I said 'no, I cannot do that.' I have no fixed time. Anyone can come at any time. I am the one who has to suffer, and my family will suffer but we can bear it. We all adjust.

Sauraksha has a keen recognition for the kinds of constituents she serves and of her adjustment to their needs at the same time that she adjusts domesticity. This goes a long way towards creating the kinds of political and social networks that she desires for the reproduction of her own symbolic and electoral appeal.

> See people have to come when it is convenient for them. This area has a lot of traders so they close up their shops at night and then come to me. They cannot leave their shops during the day. So they just come to me at home in the night. I have those kinds of relations with everyone around, it is like they are from the family. The *Marwari* community here, the Gujarati community here, they are so close to me that in their homes I can even go into their kitchens. They also just think of me as someone from the family. They come anytime. And even they tell me and laugh 'it is 10 at night, how come you still look so fresh and not tired?' That is what no one can understand. But see that tiredness is on me only. It does not matter how tired I am inside. I do feel it inside, but I cannot show it to the outside world. If someone comes to me late in the evening and I behave as though I am tired and I don't help them and just go into my house without saying anything, then that person will be angry. He will say 'what kind of *nagarsevak* (corporator) is this?' So that I cannot show anyone, so even that I have to adjust.

Durvatai is another key female Shiv Sainik who lives in Pune city. She is a large, very articulate woman with short cropped hair, always dressed in crisp saris. Durva is well educated and trained as a doctor. She began her life in public service by working for tribal women in an area close to Talegaon in Maharashtra. She now runs a clinic in the Kothrud area of Pune and has started her own NGO to work for the health and rights of the sex workers within whose midst she currently lives. The fact that she lives in the middle of Pune's red-light district is key to her sense of marginalization from larger middle-class mores as well as to the sense of power that she derives as an advocate for the downtrodden. Her only daughter Priya is now in her twenties, and Durva first entered a public career when Priya was four months old. She has always had several responsibilities to her home, her clinical practice, her work in Shiv Sena, and more recently, the running of her NGO. However, like many female Shiv Sainiks, the nexus between her membership in the party and other parts of her life were not clearly delineated between public and private spheres. They are also always conceived of within relational processes of the constitution of the self and this relational process is talked about within the discourse of adjustment.

Both Sauraksha and Durva live in wadas, one in Nashik city and the other in Pune city. Both live in multi-family arrangements within the wada, where rooms on each floor are occupied by the families of their husbands' brothers. Each also has a significant amount of space dedicated to 'office' space where they conduct their party business. At odd hours, they will also often meet their female constituents inside their living rooms, kitchens, and, in some cases, even in their sleeping quarters when excessive privacy is required. Durva in particular, because of the counsel and health advice that she provides to the sex-workers who ply their trade through the night right outside her home, is awakened at odd hours of the night to resolve issues of violence against women, or to deal with a client who refuses to pay a woman the price she wants. Her wada is, she says, 'always open' and her family 'always adjusting'.

Both Durva and Sauraksha's politics of adjustment are closely related to the forms of family arrangements in which they live. The role both families have played in these situated discourses of adjustment is important to understand. In both cases, multi-family and multigenerational living arrangements coupled with some degree of independence for each family were conducive to the possibilities of adjustment and indeed to varying degrees of freedom for the women. This is an important retort to Western-centric analyses of the family that problematize only a limited notion of the nuclear family as the site for the emergence of female subjecthood. In the case of Durva, I found that her living arrangements, which encompass the complexities of family arrangements in India to include both nuclear and extended arrangements, significantly enabled her very militant and public life. Discussing her everyday household routines she says:

> I do all my housework myself. If I have to go somewhere in the morning, then it is my responsibility that I cook the meal for my husband and my daughter and keep it aside. Or that I pack their *tiffin* (lunchbox) and leave it for them. But, the work that I do, the hand of my husband is quite influential in this. If he does not agree, then I cannot do what I do for 24 hours a day. So he will also sometimes adjust. So if today there is no chapatti, then he will just eat

bread. So of course, this does not happen everyday; if he had to eat bread everyday, then I would be made to sit at home everyday also (laughs); so in the house I do try to do all the work. I have a *bai* (household help) who washes the dishes and the clothes, but otherwise, I do all the housework myself. I also have a very good relationship with my in-laws. My sisters-in-law come to my house and ask to eat food cooked by my hand. So I have kept up my relations very well. I keep one day of the week, Sunday for the family. That is the day I just spend with my family. Of course, if something comes up unexpectedly from the party, then I do go.

When I was first inaugurated, Priya was four months old. So I would come home every two hours to feed her and then go back to attend the event. And after she was seven months old, I would just put her in a bag and take her everywhere. And I had my mother-in-law here also, she also helped and gave me a lot of support. So really, if you have the support and adjustment from your family that makes a big difference. Because, I have taken beatings with *lathis* (sticks) from the police, I have taken part in so many *andolans* (riots and protests), I have had to spend time in jail all day. So when that happened, the family has made sure that the house is okay.

Familial arrangements in India are far more complex than the generally assumed dichotomy between the nuclear and the joint family. These complex dynamics have been the most important enablers of gendered autonomy for many Shiv Sena women. The assumed dichotomy in the scholarly literature on the Indian family is greatly bedeviled by the reality that there is no shared definition of what makes up these ideal types of 'joint' or 'nuclear' (Kolenda 1968). Most family arrangements in India do not fall into these ideal categories, and even if they display some of the characteristics generally assigned to these ideal types, they rarely display all of them. Many Shiv Sena women's family arrangements have changed many times over the course of their political lives, ranging from extended family households to nuclear family households with some unmarried relatives of their extended families pursuing higher education either in Mumbai or Pune, to extended family households which include their married sons and grandchildren. All of these changes have had significant effects on the relationships of adjustment and on the possibilities for political access for Shiv Sena women.

The 'joint family' in India, or rather a debate over the joint family and its ambiguous relationship to the modern has received a great deal of attention among sociologists of the family in India. Post-war modernization theory whose influence continues to be prominent in Western approaches to the family posits the idea that the nuclear family comprising of parents and unmarried children of the 'modern' Western variety is the form of family best suited to a modern, industrial society (Parsons and Bales 1955). This approach assumed that modernizing societies would replace the joint family with a nuclear one, with the path to what is modern following an upward developmental trajectory modeled on the developmental path of the West. However, the everyday formations of the family in the non-Western world particularly in South Asia, have problematized this Western-centric approach and its singular conception of the modern family. Early examinations of the family in India focused either on the family in its institutional form or as structure of kinship and social organization (Kapadia 1958 [1955]; Karve 1953; Khatri 2005). Others clearly pointed to the need to be cognizant of the referent when using the term 'family' in the Indian context. The family was theorized as having genealogical (joint or extended family), and functional (in the sense of household or joint family) referents with clear differences between the family and the household dimensions (Shah 1974, 1998).

Interestingly, Indian examinations of the family as a social organization have also mostly centered around the joint-nuclear family dichotomy, even if they have not framed the debate around a theory of modernization as Western sociologists have (Patel 2005). One of the most relevant critiques of the use of this dichotomy between individualism and collectivism in social science writing came from A.M. Shah (Shah 1998). Shah suggested that the association of individualism and modernization with the nuclear family is deeply problematic. Shah argued that these dichotomies were in fact, embedded in complex factors of class, caste, urbanization, region and religion rather than simply within notions of tradition and modernity. Shiv Sena women's discourse of adjustment is rooted in these polysemic dynamics of the family and the household, forcing a move away from the preponderance of organizational and structural tropes in the examination of family and from assumptions that one or the other (joint or nuclear) is a static site for either gendered repression or enablement.

An examination of Shiv Sena women's own discourses on domestic and public empowerment, and the critical place that dynamic processes of adjustment played in the constitution of public identities and very public personas is rooted very much in a processual understanding of the family, both in its contemporary and historical forms. These processual negotiations centered, in this examination around the discourse of adjustment, not only unsettled the practices of domesticity for Shiv Sena women, but they also countered many of the publicly held notions of women, family and gender in Shiv Sena more generally. For instance, during my very first stint of fieldwork in 2003, I was warned by a journalist who wrote for a popular English newspaper in Mumbai that most Shiv Sena women who are in positions of power, were simply the wives of male Shiv Sainiks forced into running for local elections to take advantage of the 33 per cent electoral reservation for women. He indicated that real power was located not with the woman who held the political position but rather in the domestic relations of patriarchy; while the woman was politically expedient, she was not really politically relevant. This commonly held view was repeated by various people in various contexts, often said to pertain to the irrelevant and at best, symbolic, position of women in most political parties, and not simply in the Shiv Sena.

This latter assumption no doubt stems from a degree of disdain for the 33 per cent reservation as well as a cynicism about the 'always corrupt' practices of India's democratic system. However a close examination of the complexities of political participation in Indian politics and an ethnographic examination of what actually happens to women's lives when they join parties like Shiv Sena reveals that the imperatives of public participation deeply muddy the assumed relationships of power and propriety most popularly projected onto them. These projections emerge from an understanding of the Hindu-Maharashtrian family as static repository of patriarchy and religion, largely because the Shiv Sena itself has been associated with non-liberal stances such as regional and linguistic chauvinism, religious communalism, and anti-labor positions. Most likely, they also stem from the observation that being a Shiv Sainik is a family affair and that, in many cases, entire families are Shiv Sainiks. The assumption here is that families affiliate with and vote for Shiv Sena, guided largely by primary male involvement. While I cannot generalize enough to entirely refute this assumption, in fact only a few of the women whom I worked with between 2003 and 2007 had entered the party through domestic relationships with male Shiv Sainiks. Interestingly, primary female involvement independent of male Shiv Sena membership was more the pattern in the more rural and semi-urban communities in Pune and Nashik district than it was in urban Mumbai or Pune.

Admittedly, for many of my informants, family involvement in party activities was considerable. But, generally, family members were brought into the Sena through the involvement of the female Shiv Sainik, thereby countering the commonly held assumption that political involvement is always and everywhere led by male political membership; and in all cases the enabler of public life was some form of the discourse of adjustment. Among those who did enter and gain power in the party through a male relative (sometimes a husband, but often a brother or brother-in-law), the imperatives of public political participation and the considerable local flexibility to organize and host local political, educational and social events for the female electorate had usually propelled Shiv Sena women into political arenas almost entirely outside of the male gaze through a politics of adjustment, a renegotiation of domestic life.

The category of family, its history within the context of India and within Maharashtra more specifically and the ways in which it has been adjusted through Shiv Sena, is obviously a dynamic category, one that neither promises 'emancipation' in the Western understanding of the term nor always and everywhere acts as a site of oppression. Instead, it has the potential to function as an open social system where active agents constitute selves out of relational processes that are deeply connected to the social, cultural, economic and religious repertoires provided by a changing society and rapidly changing democratic politics.

These multiple forms of household, home, and family were critical in framing the ways in which public life gets carried out particularly for Shiv Sena women. In some cases, the negotiations were among women and their children, both sons and daughters; in other cases they were with husbands. In still others, they were with mother's in-law, or unmarried sisters and brothers of husbands who also live in the household, or with daughters-in-law, or with college-aged nieces and nephews who live with the family as they get their education. In still others it involved the adopted children of siblings who because of the loss of one parent spend half the year within the household of a paternal uncle or a maternal aunt. The discourse of adjustment has to be looked at within the context of these multiple uses as well as the multiple conceptions of how Shiv Sena women see their public service.

Adjustment thus emerges out of a very complex negotiation between the Maharashtrian imaginary of home and family as they get imagined and transformed through the complex politics of urban migration, industrialization and deindustrialization, and a particularly flexible caste politics of what it means to be a 'Maratha' and a Maharashtrian. It is somewhat alternative to a bourgeois middle-class narrative of the Indian middle-class discourse of home and family. It is also located within the larger cultural politics of women's entrance into the labor force in urban India. Women in the paid labor force do often also talk about adjustment between their work and their families, but for Shiv Sena women this goes beyond simply a pragmatic adjustment of schedules or routines. The unpredictability of the party's demands particularly around the routine family activities such as meal times certainly requires a pragmatic adjustment of domestic roles. In addition, the party's demands and the fact that aggression and violence are adopted as feminine virtues require an ideational adjustment within the home which in turn unsettles conventional domesticity.

Domesticity in the Indian context cannot be discussed without acknowledging that historically, India has had a variety of different forms of family, and that family forms were transformed in the context of colonial reforms around a variety of 'private' questions such as age of consent, and *sati* (Anagol-McGinn 1992; Mani 1998; Sinha 1997; Uberoi 1993, 1996). Nor can domesticity be discussed without acknowledging the variety of crosscutting relationships of power and resistance within the context of the family in modern India and particularly in modern Maharashtra. In western India (and modern Maharashtra) the particular histories of religious and women's reform and changes in family and household have been deeply intertwined with the political histories of caste, language and territory (Cashman 1975; Glushkova and Vora 1999; Kosambi 2000a; Phadke 1979).

In the case of Shiv Sena women, the imperatives of work and direct action in local communities produce the discourse of adjustment as the enabler of a very specific kind of public life. However, the logics of adjustment do not operate uniformly for all Shiv Sena women and much variation depends on the positions women hold within the party. Sena women, much like the men in the party hold either nominated or elected posts. Some of my informants held elected positions within their civic bodies or municipal corporations. For these women, the imperatives of elected office and the need to be consistently available to constituents also meant the greatest demands for adjustment, and not surprisingly, most of these positions were held by women who were at stages in their lives where adjustment had become less necessary. The vast majority of my informants held nominated positions: therefore there were *shakha sanghataks* (shakha organizers), *vibhag sanghataks* (ward organizers), *upavibhag sanghataks* (deputy ward organizers), and *gata sanghataks* (neighborhood organizers) in Mumbai. In addition, in Pune and Nashik there were, *shehar sanghataks* (city organizers), *zilla sanghataks* (district organizers), and *gram panchayat sanghataks* (village council organizers). Many informants in all of my fieldsites held no post at all and were simply the most active of the *karyakartas* (party workers). While women in all these positions, shared the narrative of adjustment, for those whose work entailed the most 'local' levels of action, such as at the village council level in more rural settings or at the *gata* (neighborhood) level in dense urban areas, a different form of adjustment was apparent than that narrated by those in less local positions of power. It is significant that most of these local organizers are women who are younger than those who hold more powerful positions and in most cases have young children who are still in school.

For Sena women who work in and around small residential

clusters in particular neighborhoods, adjustment was talked about more as a personal adjustment to being placed in the public sphere and as a way of juggling of the schedules of their children's school and homework. Those who are educated (and many have completed at least the equivalent of the 10th grade) run what are locally referred to as tuitions. This involves group classes for children from the neighborhood who come to their homes for a low monthly fee to get help with homework and exam preparation. Many Sena women design their tuition classes around the grade level of their own children so that they can help their children with their homework at the same time that they can earn some money from others. Many then use the money that they earn for party work such as for the organization of local party events (which in turn builds their visibility opening up the possibility to rise in the party) or simply for their own travel to party events (also to increase their visibility) so that they do not have to depend on their husbands. While many of these more locally focused Shiv Sainiks also narrate adjustment as located in party life, adjustment here is not always a decentering of domestic relationships as it is a discourse of autonomy, both of time as well as of financial resources.

Shalini Naik was recently appointed shakha sanghatak in suburban Mumbai's Goregaon area, after running tuition classes in her neighborhood for over eight years. Because of the tuitions, local families who sent their children to her know her well and trust her deeply. Both Shalini's children now attend a local college. She lives in on the first floor of a two-storey *chawl*.[14] She has two large, colorful signboards posted on the front and side of her building, both of which have the Shiv Sena logo of bow and arrow and that read 'Shalini Naik, *Shiv Sena Shakha Sanghatak*; Tuitions. Maths, English, Science, Marathi. Nursery to 8th Standard'. She admits that it is through her classes that she has made her presence felt in the area, and it is also this knowledge of her influence that has led senior Sena leaders to promote her in the party.

> One day this Shiv Sainik brought [senior Shiv Sena leader] to my house. He introduced me and said 'this is the ladies *gata pramukh*; she is a very good social worker'. So, *saheb* just said 'you do not

need to tell me anything more. I can tell just from her board how much social work she does. This is a woman who teaches young children, that is the proof of her social work.' He immediately recognized that I am doing a lot.

If the logics of adjustment function differently at different levels of the party, there is also a great deal of variability in the kinds of support that Sena women perceive as coming from their families. Many talked about feeling entirely supported, while others did not feel as supported, but through adjustment they had managed to get around oppressive demands made on them and had therefore carved out what they saw as a sphere of autonomy for themselves. Radhikatai, one of my informants in Pune, admitted that she chose her husband largely because she felt that he would support her interests outside the house (at the time her interest in dance and music). She tells me that she married a man who was not very good-looking and who had educational qualifications that were inferior to hers largely because of his supportive and adjusting nature.

I am myself a double graduate. My husband has only passed his SSC.[15] And after that he had only done his diploma. But he and I had mingled during childhood. And the two of us had special interests . . . dance, drama, our interests were the same. And secondly his nature never stopped me anywhere. A woman faces obstructions; I was not obstructed in any way. I always had his support. And we always think—we see—educated women have one perspective: to have a nice big house—high earning husband . . . a handsome husband, but my own perspective—I myself felt that instead of seeing the man's appearance, it is more important to see a man's actions and nature. If those two match, only then the woman can go and find her way well. Then she can ensure progress for herself and for her family. If you want a handsome husband, just so that you may look at him, but then he eats dung outside then what is the point. Then does this woman's life have any use? There is no use. The husband is very rich, but if he has just kept his wife locked at home, then does that woman's life have any use? No. In all these respects, my husband whatever I am, behind that I give my husband more credit. Fine—my husband may not be that educated he may not be so good to look at, but he is proud of me—he doesn't think that my wife is so educated, why should I send her outside? In fact he tells me—do this—do that—he encourages me so much—so I feel good to do anything. . . . I do it with enthusiasm.

Motitai, one of my key informants in Mumbai, talked less kindly of her husband. While she said that her family has adjusted in many ways to her public life, she lamented that her husband, and increasingly her grown-up, married son have bad tempers and put a great deal of pressure on her to stop her party work. I visited Motitai several times during the day when none of the men of the house were home. During these times I got a chance to talk to both Moti and her daughter-in-law Kanti, on maternity leave from her job as a bank teller with a large Indian bank after the birth of her first son. Moti and Kanti had a close and supportive relationship framed largely through both women's resistance to the bad tempers of their husbands and a shared love of reading and classical music. I often saw them at the market together admiring new saris and once ran into them eating lunch at a local tea-shop with Moti's younger sister and the sleeping baby, where they laughed and talked animatedly about a film they had just been to see.

Motitai says that her husband and son have been forced to adjust to her public life by agreeing to pay for some household help because she does not expect her daughter-in-law to give up her job and stay at home.

Moti: I don't really raise my voice and fight at home. And I know that he wants me to be at home when he gets back. So what I do is I go out and just don't tell him. But I make sure that I am back when he gets here.

Kanti: We both go out and we have to run back before our husbands come back. They are both the same only. We do not tell them that we have gone out.

Moti: So now I have a woman who just does the clothes washing and mops the floor. I do everything else. I have kept this woman on purpose just to show the men how much I have to do. And she can even help me with the child a little bit. That is why I have kept her. That is why I said that if there is a girl here with me that would be helpful. Let them [son and husband] also see how things work out. If they come home a 9 p.m. then let them come, I will go to get the *atta* (wheat for chapattis) ground at 9 p.m., and they can eat their dinner at midnight, I don't care. Let them know what it takes to run a house and do the work for the party.

THE INTERACTION BETWEEN GENDER, PUBLIC POLITICS, AND AGE

Generational negotiations between mother-in-law and daughter-in-law in the case of Moti and Kanti, lead to me to my next argument in this paper. This next argument revolves around the suggestion that de-centering of domestic relationships through adjustment is closely tied to the age and life-cycles of women who are most active in Shiv Sena.

Sauraksha, a Shiv Sainik elected to the Nashik Municipal Corporation for two terms, presented a good example of the often contradictory dynamics of age and gender. She also illustrated the ways in which women's autonomy in public life is deeply connected to her generational place and autonomy within the household and vice versa. Sauraksha, like most women of her generation and class, is vague about her exact age. She, like many others, estimated her age through the relational logics of having recently become a grandmother for the first time: 'I must be somewhere like forty or forty-five, because my grandson was just born.' Throughout the duration of my fieldwork in Nashik, Sauraksha's married daughter, Manjari, who had returned to her natal home to give birth to her son, played a significantly supportive role in running the household while her mother attended to party business. Sauraksha told me that the others in her husband's extended family in the multi-family ancestral home in the middle of Nashik's old city have adjusted as she took over the party position, but she said that her daughter's presence, (which she has sorely missed since she left for another city after marriage) was of great help to her. As Vatuk (1972) pointed out, membership in the household is continually changing to accommodate different stages of the life-cycle for several generations within the same household, and Sauraksha's story clearly illustrates that.

Sauraksha's example clearly shows the ways in which extended family dynamics both constrain and enable women's public success through various stages of the life-cycle. She was one of the few Sena women in my study recruited into the party through a male relation. She had spent all of her married life as a housewife and had raised two children, her daughter Manjari, and a son Kailash. She has lived in the Nashik wada that she is in now, throughout her married life where each floor of the building is occupied by the families of her husband's brothers. Her oldest brother-in-law was the political figure in the family, and had held a post in the Nashik Municipal Corporation on a Shiv Sena ticket in the 1990s. However, when his municipal ward was declared a 'ladies ward'[16] the family convened a meeting to discuss the possibility of putting up one of the women in their household to contest as a Shiv Sainik from their ward. They chose Sauraksha, got the entire family to campaign for her locally, and she won the election.

It was probably no accident that Sauraksha though not the oldest in age, was the oldest physically able woman with grown children at the time. Her older sister-in-law who had older children, is mildly physically disabled and did not therefore have the physical mobility required for the job. However, the latter's grown-up sons had participated significantly in campaigning for each of Sauraksha's two election campaigns, and one of them often sat in the small office she has on the ground floor of her wada building taking messages for her when she attended to party business elsewhere. In the context of politics and political campaigning in India, it is quite acceptable, in fact expected, that extended family ties will be utilized to garner support for the political figure and in Sauraksha's case, she sees this as an immense source of support. She is both grateful and amused at how her young nieces and nephews rally around her.

The elections are going to be next year. So for one month before the election my whole family will start working for my campaign. I don't even have to tell people what to do, they just do it all. I even tell my husband to take a holiday from his bank [laughs]. All the children get to work also. We have ten grown up children in the household. So even if each one of them brings ten of their friends, then there is a lot of political *hungama* (activity). That is what is so good about family involvement because just like that, automatic we have 100 people working for me.

At the time of her nomination for the election, Sauraksha was assuming a certain degree of autonomy within her own household where her daughter, at the time unmarried, was able to take over a lot of the household duties. She admits that until she won the election, she was terribly shy, rarely ever spoke in public, and rarely ever left the house. However, ever since she won the corporation seat she says that her entire personality has changed and that she is now unafraid. Sauraksha's early inexperience in public life meant that early on, she worked closely with her more experienced brother-in-law in governing her ward. However, I found that Sauraksha, now elected to her second term in office has become the primary political figure in the family, and most of her constituents, called on her rather than on her brother-in-law when they needed representation. She, like most Sena women who are very active in the party, did not desire outright confrontation with her family and recognized that the less confrontational she was, the more autonomy she would receive. An informally negotiated adjustment was far more beneficial for her. Sauraksha admitted that her husband and son supported her political career, but did not really do much housework. She told me that instead that it is the extended family context that she lives in that has been the greatest source of support:

I have been adjusted by my joint family. My husband and son, they don't do much in the house. And you know how they got into the habit is that they all lived in a joint family. See, we were in a joint family so if one was out then the other could make the tea. But actually even now, we help each other. I am older, my children are older. I had gone out of town for two days for some election work, and my sister in law would cook the food. After all, we are from the same house. So everyone looks after things. I have the support of everyone. See what has happened is that now my children are grown up. And my *umar* is also such that I can now work outside the house. I have less responsibility now. Women who have young children, and have a lot of household responsibility, they have to fulfill those responsibilities first before they can do any other work. Now I say that to women when I have programs and have to give a speech. I say to them, that they must certainly work outside and do social work, (*samaj seva*), but do not make anyone at home angry as you step out. Do not disturb your family life for this. What is the use of doing that right? What is the use of working outside if your children give you *gaalis* (curses) at home?

In Sauraksha's case, there was a significant interaction between gender norms, adjustment and age. In a party like Shiv Sena which depends so much on local personalities who are continually in the public eye as well as on a form of governance framed around a very specific gendered conception of 'social-work' where wisdom, experience, and deep involvement in the lives of local constituents is imperative, age must necessarily be problematized as a distinct feminist category. It is particularly important because so far scholarly examination of Shiv Sena and its maverick, sometimes criminalized persona has looked at the party largely as a youthful, masculine organization (Banerjee 2000; Hansen 2001). Sen, in her rich and sensitive work on Shiv Sena women in the Mumbai slums, does present us with narratives of older Sena women, though Sen's subjects narrate age largely as a source of marginalization from the youthful discourse of the party (Sen 2006, 2007). My analysis departs from Sen's in this respect. I find that for women in the party, age operates in complex and often enabling ways for women, particularly if one examines age through the discourse of adjustment.

No doubt, the party's founder and chief ideologue Bal Thackeray has a deep desire to preserve a rough, youthful, masculine, party image. The now almost eighty-five-year old Thackeray probably dyes his hair a jet black and uses make-up (Heuze 1995). Despite his fast-diminishing physical and cognitive acumen, Thackeray continues to show up on party posters and in wall mounted photographs in every Shiv Sena shakha, and on a variety of party memorabilia, such as calendars and postcards with a full head of youthful, dark, black hair, and smooth, pink skin. Therefore, it is hard to argue that this youthful, masculinized, persona is irrelevant. What I do here is to read against the grain of youth and masculinity. Throughout my fieldwork I found that despite Bal Thackeray's efforts to present a highly dictatorial, and centralized model of charismatic, masculine leadership, in fact Shiv Sena's pragmatic action and local power is dispersed and localized in various informal networks across urban and peri-urban Maharashtra (Hansen 2001). This dispersal allows for a great deal of collective and individual flexibility at the local levels, where Shiv Sainiks actually exercise considerable autonomy, which escapes the critical gaze of senior leadership as long as it presents the potential for high local mobilization and community dependence on particular, locally powerful Shiv Sainiks. Therefore, a situated analysis of female party workers at the local levels of Shiv Sena's highly dispersed and localized spheres of 'direct action' (Eckert 2003) must necessarily engage with the deeply complex relationship between the self-presentation that gets constituted by party leadership and the accompanying, more flexible processes of rejection, and transgression that take place at the level of the party-worker.

The politics of personality around which Shiv Sena's political strategy revolves is quite intricately tied to age and generation, particularly for Shiv Sena women. Indeed most of the men who are very active party workers tend to be younger Maharashtrian men still in the workforce, who feel marginalized by higher skilled non-Maharashtrian workers from the white-collar service sector. They find in Shiv Sena an appropriate forum from which to protest their marginalization and are therefore active participants in all the party events and are for the most part, the public and media face of the party. In all the time that I spent at Shiv Sena shakhas, while older men do take on advisory roles, they tend not to participate as actively in either the party's work or its militancy. For male Shiv Sainiks, therefore, age functions very differently within party politics than it does for women. Their contributions to the internal morale of the party seem to increase as they grow older, while their actual service to constituents tends to be less involved. However, for women, involvement with constituents, creativity in planning party events, and in fact political militancy, seems to increase as they grow older and as household responsibilities diminish or get passed on to younger women in the family. Therefore an engagement with adjustment as a discourse of women's autonomy in public politics and governance must also engage as Vatuk does in her work with the constitutive logics of the changing realities of women's autonomy and power within their domestic spheres as they age and their increasing visibility in public space (Vatuk 1987). As Kalpana Sate, the Mumbai corporator said to me on several occasions:

If I had stayed home and made *rotis* (Indian flatbread) in the kitchen who would have known my name? They would say who is Kalpana Sate? Now you ask anyone and everyone knows Kalpana Sate. My name has become very well-known. Everyone, every *neta* (minister) in our party knows my name well. If I ever have any problem they will come to my help. And through the party my children have also made names for themselves. They also get some *izzat* (honor). People give them *respect* because their *mummy* is doing all this good work. If I did bad work that would not have been good for my children. No one really has the *himmat* (courage) to say anything in front of my children either. So that way my image is good, it is very good. But now I am old, so my image does not matter, I can do what I want.

In the months that I followed Sate around during my field-work, I witnessed the many ways in which she cultivated what she referred to as image. Moreover, on the one occasion that her extremely quiet husband accompanied us to a party event at a local Hindu temple, many Sena women teased him about Sate's outspoken image. He smiled shyly and said 'see she is what she is, her children are big, she is doing very good work; I adjust'.

ADJUSTMENT, *UMAR* (AGE) AND GOVERNANCE: THE SITUATED FEMINIST HISTORY OF KALPANA SATE

I now turn to examine the intersections between age and politics in greater depth through a situated discussion of Kalpana Sate. While her full name is Kalpana Sate, she was referred to as Sate *bai,*[17] Sate madam or simply madam within her municipal constituency. Sate was born and raised in a family that supported India's Congress party in a remote part of the Konkan. She is in her early fifties with three grown-up children. She was a corporator in BMC when I first met her. Before that she had spent many years working in a variety of nominated posts in Shiv Sena, all of which brought her the visibility she needed to get the coveted ticket to run for an election first in 1993 when she won the election, then in 1997 when she lost by 50 votes and again in 2001when she was elected once again. She was remarkably well known in Mumbai's western suburb of Goregaon which is where she lived and worked. While she was always impeccably dressed in often very ornate synthetic saris, complete with all the accoutrements of a middle-class Maharashtrian *suhaagan* (married woman), she had a loud booming voice, was always arguing with someone about something on her mobile phone, was quick to smack shopkeepers or auto-rickshaw drivers who charged her too much and was always among the first ones at any Shiv Sena riot or demonstration. The imperatives of self-promotion in the immensely transient halls of power that she was in, had become so much a part of her, that almost no conversation she had with anyone was complete without reminding them of her 'good works' in the neighborhood. I came to realize that this self-promotion was really a thinly veiled form of self-affirmation and stemmed from a very real desire to leave behind a civic legacy in the wards under her jurisdiction.

One evening at the local party office she simply turned to one of the many men there and asked him whether he had seen the terrific *nalla* (drain and sewage system) that she had built in ward number 32. He said, 'yes madam, it is a *mast* (wonderful) *nalla'*. She got a far off, almost misty look in her eyes and responded in childlike wonderment—'really?' A Muslim man called Bashir also sat down to talk to her about a drain and water in his locality. She said to him—'Bashir, I do all this work for you, but you better get your people (Muslims) to come over to our side. I want to see Shiv Sena *jhandas* (flags) in all your homes.' Bashir, who seemed quite strategic in his support for her, responded by saying, 'I have come so many times madam to get flags from the shakha or at least a board with the party name.' Bashir then assured her that for the next election he would get 45 or 50 Muslims from his area to vote for Shiv Sena. Then he slipped in a request to mend a broken toilet in the public bathroom in his ward. Madam immediately got on her cell phone with her contractor and yelled:

> I am standing right her in ward 30. I have just seen that the toilet in this ward number 30 is broken. I want you to fix it by tomorrow. And while you are about it, go ahead and put in two benches outside with my name engraved on them so that they know who did the work . . . immediately . . . *Jai* (hail) Maharashtra . . . bye-bye.

During her reign as corporator, all you had to do was go to the local market and ask any vegetable vendor where madam lives and he could point you to her home. Though of course, if you decided to pay her a visit before 11 p.m. you would almost never find her at home. 'You can reach madam on her mobile,' was always the response from her husband who was always at home to answer the door or phone. I had known her for at least eight months traveling with her all over her municipal ward in her bumpy Maruti van to every Shiv Sena event she was invited to, and to her family home in the Konkan during an election campaign, before I actually got to see her at home in the Mumbai suburb of Goregaon east. Her home was a modest one bedroom apartment or what in Mumbai real estate language is called 1 BHK (one-bedroom-hall-kitchen) which is an important distinction in an urban environment with one of the highest pressures on space in the world. She lived here with her three grown-up children, two sons and a daughter, her elderly mother-in-law, and her husband. The first time I entered her flat I saw a pile of copies of the *Harvard Business Review* sitting on a sofa at the entrance. Her oldest son is completing a diploma in business at a nearby college. Her twenty-three year old daughter dressed in shorts came out and greeted me. Sate introduced me to her daughter who I had heard a lot about already and then immediately started talking like most Indian mothers do and quite contrary to the persona I had seen her in so far, about her daughter's marriage prospects. She said, 'I only want someone from our caste. If we get anyone from another caste, it will only be a Brahmin.' However, so far her daughter has not seen anyone she likes—they are all too fat.

During the most recent elections for the BMC in February 2007, she was denied a ticket to run, though as appeasement the party had given her the nominated post of *upavibhag sanghatak* (associate ward organizer). This post requires far less running around, and when I met her last in June of 2007, I could tell that madam was very bored and was looking for other ways to get out of the house. She told me over and over again, that she is not in the *aadat* (habit) of sitting at home. She always talked about adjustment at varying stages of her life as responsible for propelling her to where she is now, allowing her to fulfill what I learned over the four years that I came to know her, to be a seething personal ambition while strategically escaping the microscope when it came to family and household duties. This is particularly remarkable considering she started her early married life living in a small one room tenement with twenty-three people from her husband's extended family in central Bombay in the late 1970s. It could easily be assumed that this home for this woman was a profound site for the reproduction of gendered forms of power; however, as she narrated her early married life, this large extended family was actually seen by madam as a source of freedom rather than as a source of containment. Her narrative pointed to how, in conceiving of a South Asian feminism, it is critical to unpack the varying understandings of family and move past assumptions of the family as always and everywhere nothing but a site of oppression.

KS: In a joint family you know how it is. I never had time to really even look after my own children. There are so many people around . . . you know my brother-in-law, this one, that one they would take the children. That is the nice thing about living in a joint family all the work gets distributed. Now my mother-in-law would wash all the clothes. Then my sister-in-law would cut all the onions and everything. Then my other sister-in-law would go to the bazaar if we needed anything. So in this way the work was distributed. But all the *andar ka kam*, *rasoi ka kam* (inside work, the work of the kitchen) was done by me. I did a lot of good adjustment with everyone. And then they did adjustment with me so I took another chance while I was living in the joint family. I would cook the food quickly and then I would go for training—for training of a *Balwadi*[18] teacher. So I did a 3-year diploma course in teaching for the Balwadi.

See right from my childhood in the fields, I used to cook for everyone. Now in my own house, all the workers, laborers, we used to have to cook for all of them. My mother had taught me all this. That is why in my husband's house, cooking for so many people was no problem at all. How much meat to put, how much chutney to put, how much *kopra* (coconut) to put, no one needed to tell me. My nature is such that everyone should live together in harmony and laugh rather than fight. I really liked the joint family. Our family was really very nice. My mother-in-law, father-in-law were all very nice. And my nature was very free-friendly. And I never thought 'how will I adjust to life here'. In fact I did not even go to my mother's place at all. I was so close to this family here. My father in law's mother you know, she was very old, she also lived there with us and

> she was very fond of my husband. And after I came here I looked after her a lot. She gave me a lot of *aashirwad* (blessings). She said to me that 'whatever you touch will become gold'. We were in a lot of financial difficulty it's not that we weren't. But I never asked my father for any money. Once I got married I forgot all about that. Now all my development is because of my mother in law. I have developed so much, developed so much, more than anything I have developed because she did this adjustment for me. . . . But one day [when we were living with everybody] I just went for a walk and I said to my husband that if we want our children to study, then this joint family is not going to be good for us. So we have to set up our own family . . . then we sat down and decided and they said that is good thought, a good idea to separate. See my name is Kalpana (Good Idea) that is why they kept my name Kalpana. I have good ideas. Then after we got out of the wada, our life became much better.

As Sate's description of the dynamics of her conjugal home illustrates and as Vatuk (1972) points to so clearly in her work on the Indian family in urban settings, the categories of both the joint and the nuclear family are far from homogenous. Neither of these categories are adequate in capturing the variety of household types or in fact the wide variety of perceptions that householders have of themselves and their families (Shah 1974).

The form of family structure does not automatically illuminate the modes of power and autonomy that prevail in everyday practice. It is only situated analyses of these varieties that consider the generational, gendered, and political factors that allow for a theorization of power and autonomy, particularly for women living within these units. These factors have complex ramifications for the gendered relations within the household and to women's access to the public sphere, as well as to the very unique discourses on empowerment that emerge out of these formations. In the case of madam, the unique formations within which she was born, then married into, and now lives in, are profoundly intertwined with her own experiences: first within her natal home in an extended agricultural family (where those who labored on the family land were also encompassed into the conception of 'family' unit), then with her experience as a rural migrant into her conjugal home in urban Mumbai, and later her experience of transition as an older woman from Mumbai's central city during the city's deindustrialization to the urban peripheries of the metropolis. The latter became for her a significant way of renegotiating a certain kind of mobility, as well as the form and the practice of both family and political life. These negotiations and renegotiations, expressed through the unique discourse of adjustment are as critical to madam's constitution of a political self as they are to the actual practices of local governance through Shiv Sena that madam has engaged in for over two decades. For Sate, adjustment may have left the gendered division of labor unaltered; however, the pressures of domesticity were distributed allowing her some flexibility to raise three young children at the same time that she pursued a course in education which later allowed her to start an adult literacy program which then gave her the local visibility she needed to be invited to join Shiv Sena and win the BMC elections twice. Her position as a Balwadi teacher, is what allowed her deep access to the communities that would later vote her to power as their BMC corporator. Many Shiv Sena women in Mumbai and in Pune city have risen to prominence locally through their involvement in the Balwadi program in varying capacities. Some have been teachers, others have been in charge of food and nutrition and still others in charge of health and immunization of the children who attend the Balwadi. This association of women with childcare and childrearing programs, certainly reinforces feminine positions as caregivers but at the same time allowed many of these women to gain personal access to people's lives and problems. This unique and consistent involvement in people's lives fits in very well with Sena women's conception of themselves as 'social workers' at the same time that it strengthens their positions as local patrons. As Sate expressed:

> I did not do the work for money. Of course everyone has a need for money. But from my end, I did not want to sit at home, I did not have an *aadat* (habit) of sitting at home. Sitting at home is a waste of time. Now if one can contribute to the public by doing some service then one should do that. That is why wherever I go in the area I always get to know people. Everyone had heard that this bai gives very good tuition, classes and Balwadi classes. So many children from the area used to come to me right? So there was an officer at this adult literacy organization. He phoned me and asked me to come and

work there. You know at that time they did not have too many women who could come and work. And they had this project of adult literacy. So they needed someone. They needed ladies to teach. Once I went there, they all knew about me. That is how it was. So after doing all this work, my name became very well known. So that is how I learned community development. I learned also how when you go into the communities, how to talk to people, how to give *bhashan* (public speeches). That is something that I picked up.

While Sate's early life as a public figure was a complex of adjustment she now talks about her *umar* as a source of freedom and critical to the political imperatives of Shiv Sena. Her children are grown-up and contribute to the household income through their jobs. Class mobility has allowed her to hire some household help, so madam's relationship to domesticity has become far more flexible. In fact, it many ways it seemed as though even expectations of domesticity had been lifted; and this deeply affected her own conception of self:

Now see I am older no one can say anything to me now. When I go somewhere on a riot everyone just runs behind me. No one can even stop me now. They all know me now because I have been around so long. They all know that madam will not come back before giving two slaps. People run away from me now. Now I am a *buddi* (old woman) so no one dares to say anything to me. In the beginning I used to feel quite afraid to give speeches and things because a lot of our ministers would come. But now after so much time, I have an *aadat* (habit). That *aadat* comes with age, with my experience. So it is not that is has been that difficult for me, since I had already learnt a lot of this before.

CONCLUSION

I have examined the possibilities of a situated feminist subject through the lens of women in Shiv Sena in Maharashtra. The paper has examined the ways in which very particular feminist discourses may be constituted in the global south, South Asia, in particular, through local, and everyday female action. A situated, and ethnographic exploration of the diverse discourses of power that emerge for women as they negotiate governance and domesticity problematizes a feminist subjectivity that is constituted in relational rather than in individual terms. I argue that to look at a 'South-Asian' feminism within the cultural realities of religion and communalism, it is important to look beyond the structures framing these realities towards the everyday practice of personal and public life. I therefore explore the ways in which structural subordination within Shiv Sena is constituted rhetorically but often rejected performatively in collective practice by the imperatives of everyday life paired with the personal and collective political ambition of Shiv Sena women. I suggest that subversive subjectivities get constituted in performative and narrative ways, where audiences and bodies interact to unsettle conventional gendered relationships both within the home and the political party.

This unsettled condition may perhaps serve to envision a situated discourse of feminism based not on a Western, feminist discourse of emancipation or even on what has been referred to in the South Asian context as 'empowerment,' but rather on what female Shiv Sainiks refer to as a relational politics of adjustment. Rather than fall back on assumptions about what movements with often non-liberal discourses don't do to further a feminist perspective, I focus on what they in fact often do, particularly at the level of everyday practice of governance and politics. The very particular discourse of empowerment that emerges out of the discourse of adjustment and umar is deeply rooted in the broader historical and social processes of family, conjugality, household and politics in urban India, and urban Maharashtra more particularly. While these processes are both conformist and subversive, they are in fact always constitutive of a wide variety of personal and collective notions of power and indeed of a unique form of female subject that is in the words of madam '*bindaas*. Do anything, but do it like you are *bindaas*.'[19]

NOTES

1. I am grateful for many comments and suggestions on a draft version of this paper from the participants in the South Asian Feminisms Pre-Conference convened as part the 36th Annual Conference on South Asia, in Madison, Wisconsin on 11 October 2007.

I would particularly like to thank Indrani Chatterjee for encouraging me to think about historicizing the South Asian family. I am also grateful to the American Institute of Indian Studies for their generous support of the fieldwork.

2. Packed meals cooked elsewhere and delivered to the home in a steel lunch box (*dabba*).
3. The discourse of adjustment is one of the most dominant among Shiv Sena women when talking about the negotiation between public and private relationships. All Sena women who talk about the critical place that adjustment has played in their lives use the English term adjustment to describe the process even when they speak in their native language of Marathi.
4. This paper uses the terms Aghadi and Shiv Sena women interchangeably; both terms refer to the same group of women.
5. Udipi refers to a particular style of south Indian vegetarian cooking. In metropolitan Mumbai, the popularity of the flavors used in Udipi cooking has resulted in the use of the base spices in other sorts of cuisine such as Chinese and even Italian to cater to the local palette.
6. The English language term madam is widely by used by both men and women across Maharashtra as a term of respect for women in positions of power; this applies to power derived from a variety of sources, class privilege, and political power being two of the most prominent.
7. Local term used for an official elected to office in the civic bodies in Indian cities.
8. Lonavala is a hill-station in the Western Ghats between Pune and Mumbai. It is about 45 miles from Pune and about 70 miles from Mumbai.
9. Vegetable and chapattis (Indian flatbread) are considered here more complicated to make while rice and dal (lentils) can be cooked later by someone else in the house.
10. In Marathi, the word Shiv Sena is spelled with four letters.
11. *Tai* is the Marathi term for older sister. Many Shiv Sena women are referred to by this kinship term by other party members, both male and female.
12. Hindu festival for the worship of snakes (*naga*).
13. Saheb is a term of respect given to people believed to be powerful masters. Saheb is generally the male gendered term while Saheba is the term generally used for women. The use of the male-gendered term in the case of Meena Thackeray is telling as

it allows Shiv Sainiks to refer to her flexibly as both 'lord and master' in her own right, as well as 'mother of the lord' as the mother figure whose greatness is dependent on the master that she gave birth to.

14. Building with several one-room tenements found all over Mumbai's working class neighborhoods.
15. Refers to the Secondary School Certificate examination which in the state of Maharashtra is taken as the culmination of grade 10.
16. This refers to a ward in which only female candidates may compete against each other as part of the constitutional amendment that mandates reservation of 33 per cent of all electoral seats for women at all levels of India's electoral system.
17. Bai is a Marathi term of respect given to an older woman.
18. Balwadis (Children's centers) are community based education programs for young pre-school children. Because they are early childhood programs targeted at helping children in working-class neighborhoods who often hail from families of low education and literacy get early preparation for school, they are often funded by both local and international NGOs. In many communities where I conducted my research, Balwadis are informally run out of the home of a woman in a particular neighborhood who has received some kind of a license and training in Balwadi teaching, and who brings in other women from her neighborhood to help out. Many Shiv Sena women have been, and continue to be involved with Balwadis in their neighborhoods and many see this involvement as being part of their social work. For many, this has allowed them to gain a great deal of trust among neighborhood families, something they call on during elections.
19. The word *Bindaas* is a colloquialism that means without fear and carefree. It is used a lot in Shiv Sena discourse also to mean brave and has a certain complimentary cache when applied to people in the party.

REFERENCES

Anagol-McGinn, Padma (1992), 'The Age of Consent Act (1891) Reconsidered: Women's Perspectives and Participation in the Child-Marriage Controversy in India', *South Asia Research*, 12 (2), 100–18.

Bacchetta, Paola (2002), 'Hindu Nationalist Women Imagine Spatialities/Imagine Themselves: Reflections on Gender-Supplemental Agency', in Paola Bacchetta and Margaret Power (eds.), *Right-Wing Women: From Conservatives to Extremists Around the World* (London; New York: Routledge), 43–56.

—— (2005), 'Hindu Nationalist Women as Ideologues: The "Sangh", the "Samiti" and their Differential Concepts of the Hindu Nation', in Christophe Jaffrelot (ed.), *The Sangh Parivar: A Reader* (New Delhi: Oxford University Press), 108–47.

Bacchetta, Paola and Margaret Power (2002a), 'Introduction', in Paola Bacchetta and Margaret Power (eds.), *Right-Wing Women: From Conservatives to Extremists Around the World* (London; New York: Routledge), 1–15.

—— (eds.) (2002b), *Right-Wing Women: From Conservatives to Extremists Around the World* (London: Routledge).

Banerjee, Sikata (2000), *Warriors in Politics: Hindu Nationalism, Violence, and the Shiv Sena in India* (Boulder, CO: Westview Press).

Bedi, Tarini (2004), 'Make Way for the "Mumbaikar": Shiv Sena Women and the Politics of Urban Identity', *33rd Annual Conference on South Asia* (Madison, Wisconsin).

—— (2007), 'The Dashing Ladies of the Shiv Sena', *Economic & Political Weekly,* 42 (17).

Burton, Antoinette (1997), 'House/Daughter/Nation: Interiority, Architecture, and Historical Imagination in Janaki Mazumdar's "Family History"', *Journal of Asian Studies,* 56 (4), 921–46.

Butler, Judith (1990a), *Gender Trouble and the Subversion of Identity* (London; New York: Routledge).

—— (1990b), 'Performative Acts and Gender Constitution: An Essay in Phenomenology and feminist Theory', in SueEllen Case (ed.), *Performing Feminisms: Feminist Critical Theory and Theatre* (Baltimore, MD: Johns Hopkins University Press), 270–82.

Butler, Judith and Scott, Joan (eds.) (1992), *Feminists Theorize the Political* (London: Routledge).

Cashman, C.J. (1975), *The Myth of the Lokmanya: Tilak and Mass Politics in Maharashtra* (Berkeley: University of California Press).

Chatterjee, Indrani (ed.), (2004), *Unfamiliar Relations: Family and History in South Asia* (New Brunswick, NJ: Rutgers University Press).

Chatterjee, Partha (1986), *Nationalist Thought and the Colonial World: A Derivative Discourse?* (London: Zed Books).

—— (1993), *The Nation and its Fragments: Colonial and Post Colonial Histories* (Princeton, NJ: Princeton University Press).

D'Monte, Daryl (2005 [2002]), *Ripping the Fabric: The Decline of Mumbai and its Mills* (2nd edn.; New Delhi: Oxford University Press).

Dengle, Narendra (1998), 'The Introvert and Extrovert Aspects of the Marathi House', in Irinia Glushkova and Anne Feldhaus (eds.), *House and Home in Maharashtra* (New Delhi: Oxford University Press).

Deshpande, Prachi (2007), *Creative Pasts: Historical Memory and Identity in Western India, 1700–1960* (New York: Columbia University Press).

Dobbin, Christine (1972), *Urban Leadership in Western India: Politics and Communities in Bombay City 1840–85* (Oxford: Oxford University Press).

Dworkin, Andrea (1982), *Right-Wing Women* (New York: Perigree Books).

Eckert, Julia (2003), *The Charisma of Direct Action: Power, Politics and the Shiv Sena* (New Delhi: Oxford University Press).

Ghosh, Bishnupriya (2002), 'Queering Hindutva: Unruly Bodies and Pleasures in Sadhvi Rithambara's Performances', in Paola Bacchetta and Margaret Power (eds.), *Right-Wing Women: From Conservatives to Extremists Around the World* (New York; London: Routledge), 259–72.

Glushkova, Irina and Anne Feldhaus (eds.) (1998), *House and Home in Maharashtra* (New Delhi: Oxford University Press).

Glushkova, Irina and Vora, Rajendra (eds.) (1999), *Home, Family and Kinship in Maharashtra* (New Delhi: Oxford University Press).

Gupta, Akhil and James Ferguson (2002), 'Beyond "Culture": Space, Identity, and the Politics of Difference', in Jonathan Xavier Inda and Renato Rosaldo (eds.), *The Anthropology of Globalization* (Malden, MA; Oxford, UK: Blackwell), 65–80.

Gupta, Dipankar (1982), *Nativism in a Metropolis: The Shiv Sena in Bombay* (New Delhi: Manohar).

Hansen, Thomas Blom (1996), 'The Vernacularisation of Hindutva: The BJP and Shiv Sena in Rural Maharashtra', *Contributions to Indian Sociology,* 30 (2), 177–214.

—— (1999), *Saffron Wave: Democracy and Hindu Nationalism in Modern India* (Princeton, NJ: Princeton University Press.).

—— (2001), *Wages of Violence: Naming and Identity in Postcolonial Bombay* (Princeton, NJ: Princeton University Press).

Heuze-Brigant, Gerard (1999), 'Populism and the Workers Movement: Shiv Sena and Labour in Mumbai', *South Asia,* 22 (2), 119–48.

Heuze, Gerard (1995), 'Cultural Populism: The Appeal of the Shiv Sena', in Sujata Patel and Alice Thorner (eds.), *Bombay: Metaphor for Modern India* (Bombay: Oxford University Press), 213–47.

Jaggar, Alison M. (1983), *Feminist Politics and Human Nature* (Totowa, NJ: Rowman & Alanheld).

Jayawardena, Kumari (1986), *Feminism and Nationalism in the Third World* (London: Zed Books).

Kapadia, K.M. (1958 [1955]), *Marriage and Family in India* (Bombay: Oxford University Press).

Karam, Azza (2002), 'Islamisms and Feminisms in Egypt: Three Generations of Women's Perspectives', in Paola Bacchetta and Margaret Power (eds.), *Right-Wing Women: From Conservatives to Extremists Around the World* (New York: Routledge), 225–41.

Karve, Irawati (1953), *Kinship Organization in India* (Deccan College Monograph Series, No. 11; Poona: Deccan College).

Katju, Manjari (2005), 'The Bajrang Dal and Durga Vahini', in Christophe Jaffrelot (ed.), *The Sangh Parivar: A Reader* (New Delhi: Oxford University Press), 335–41.

Katzenstein, Mary Fainsod (1977), 'Mobilization of Indian Youth in Shiv Sena', *Pacific Affairs,* 50 (2), 231–48.

—— (1973), 'Origins of Nativism: The Emergence of the Shiv Sena in Bombay', *Asian Survey* (13 April 1973).

—— (1979), *Ethnicity and Equality: The Shiv Sena Party and Preferential Policies in Bombay* (Ithaca; London: Cornell University Press).

Khatri, A.A. (2005), 'Some Neglected Approaches and Problems in the Study of Family in India', in Tulsi Patel (ed.), *The Family in India: Structure and Practice* (New Delhi; Thousand Oaks; London: Sage).

Klatch, Rebecca (1994), 'Women of the New Right in the United States: Family, Feminism, and Politics', in Valetine M. Moghadam (ed.), *Identity Politics and Women: Cultural Reassertions and Feminisms in Cross-Cultural Perspective* (Boulder, CO: Westview Press).

Kolenda, Pauline M. (1968), 'Region, Caste and Family Structure: A Comparative Study of the Indian "Joint Family"', in M. Singer and B.S. Cohn (eds.), *Structure and Change in Indian Society* (New York), 339-96.

Kosambi, Meera (2000a), 'Life After Widowhood: Two Radical

Reformist Options in Maharashtra', in Meera Kosambi (ed.), *Intersections: Socio-Cultural Trends in Maharashtra* (New Delhi: Orient Longman), 92–117.

—— (ed.), (2000b), *Intersections: Socio-Cultural Trends in Maharashtra* (New Delhi: Orient Longman).

Lamb, Sarah (2000), *White Saris and Sweet Mangoes: Aging, Gender, and Body in North India* (Berkeley: University of California Press).

Lele, Jayant (1995), 'Saffronization of the Shiv Sena: The Political Economy of City, State and Nation', in Sujata Patel and Alice Thorner (eds.), *Bombay: Metaphor for Modern India* (Bombay: Oxford University Press), 185–212.

Mahmood, Saba (2001), 'Feminist Theory, Embodiment, and the Docile Agent: Some Reflections on the Egyptian Islamic Revival.' *Cultural Anthropology*, 16 (2), 202–36.

—— (2005), *Politics of Piety: The Islamic Revival and the Feminist Subject* (Princeton, NJ: Princeton University Press).

Mani, Lata (1998), *Contentious Traditions: The Debate on Sati in Colonial India* (Berkeley: University of California Press).

Mazumdar, Sucheta (1995), 'Women on the March: Right-Wing Mobilization in Contemporary India', *Feminist Review*, 49, 1–28.

Menon, Meena and Neera Adarkar (2004), *One Hundred Years, One Hundred Voices: The Millworkers of Girangaon* (Calcutta: Seagull).

Moghadam, Valentine M. (1994b), 'Introduction: Women and Identity Politics in Theoretical and Comparative Perspective', in Valentine M. Moghadam (ed.), *Identity Politics and Women: Cultural Reassertions and Feminisms in International Perspective* (Boulder, CO: Westview Press).

—— (ed.), (1994a), *Identity Politics and Women: Cultural Reassertions and Feminisms in International Perspective* (Boulder, CO: Wesview Press).

Mohanty, Chandra Talpade (1991a), 'Introduction. Cartographies of Struggle: Third World Women and the Politics of Feminism', in Chandra Talpade Mohanty, Ann Russo and Lourdes Torres (eds.), *Third World Women and the Politics of Feminism* (Bloomington, IN: Indiana University Press).

—— (1991b), 'Under Western Eyes: Feminist Scholarship and Colonial Discourses', in Chandra Talpade Mohanty, Ann Russo and Lourdes Torres (eds.), *Third World Women and the Politics of Feminism* (Bloomington, IN: Indiana University Press).

Mohanty, Chandra Talpade, Ann Russo and Lourdes Russo (eds.) (1991), *Third World Women and the Politics of Feminism* (Bloomington, IN: Indiana University Press).

Pandharipande, Rajeshwari V. (2003), *Sociolinguisitic Dimensions of Marathi: Multilingualism in Central India* (Munich: Lincom Europa).

Parsons, Talcott and Roberta E. Bales (1955), *Family, Socialization, and Interaction Process* (Glencoe, Il: The Free Press).

Patel, Sujata (2003), 'Bombay and Mumbai: Identities, Politics, and Populism', in Sujata Patel and Jim Masselos (eds.), *Bombay and Mumbai: The City in Transition* (New Delhi: Oxford University Press), 3–30.

Patel, Sujata and Alice Thorner (eds.) (1995), *Bombay: Metaphor for Modern India* (Bombay: Oxford University Press).

Patel, Tulsi (ed.), (2005), *The Family in India: Structure and Practice* (New Delhi: Sage; London: Thousand Oaks).

Phadke, Y.D. (1979), *Politics and Language* (Bombay: Himalaya).

Purandare, Vaibhav (1999), *The Sena Story* (Bombay: Business Publications).

Rowe, Aimee Carillo (2005), 'Be Longing: Toward a Feminist Politics of Relation', *NWSA Journal,* 17 (2), 15–46.

Sahgal, Meera (2007), 'Manufacturing a Feminized Siege Mentality: Hindu Nationalist Paramilitary Camps for Women in India', *Journal of Contemporary Ethnography,* 36 (2).

Sangari, Kumkum (1993), 'Relating Histories: Definitions of Literacy, Literature, Gender in Early Nineteenth Century Calcutta and England', in Svati Joshi (ed.), *Rethinking English: Essays in Literature, Language, History* (New Delhi: Trianka).

Sarkar, Tanika (1998), 'Woman, Community, and Nation: A Historical Trajectory for Hindu Identity Politics', in Patricia Jeffrey and Amrita Basu (eds.), *Appropriating Gender: Women's Activism and Politicized Religion in South Asia* (London; New York: Routledge), 89–104.

—— (2001), *Hindu Wife, Hindu Nation: Community, Religion and Cultural Nationalism* (Bloomington, IN: Indiana University Press).

Sarkar, Tanika and Urvashi Butalia (eds.) (1995), *Women and Right-Wing Movements: Indian Experience* (London: Zed Books).

Scheck, Raffel (2002), 'Women in the Non-Nazi Right During the Weimar Republic: The German Nationalist People's Party (DNVP)', in Paola Bacchetta and Margaret Power (eds.), *Right-*

Wing Women: From Conservatives to Extremists Across the World (New York: Routledge), 141–54.

Sen, Atreyee (2006), 'Hindu Women 'Soldiers' Remember the Birth of Female Militancy', *Indian Journal of Gender Studies,* 13 (1), 1-35.

—— (2007), *Shiv Sena Women: Violence and Communalism in a Bombay Slum* (London: Hurst).

Setalvad, Teesta (1995), 'The Woman Shiv Sainik and her Sister Swayamsevika', in Tanika Sarkar and Urvashi Butalia (eds.), *Women and Right-Wing Movements: Indian Experiences* (London: Zed Books).

Shah, A.M. (1974), *The Household Dimension of the Family in India; A Field Study in a Gujarat village and a Review of Other Studies* (Berkeley: University of California Press).

—— (1998), *Family in India: Critical Essays* (New Delhi: Orient Longman).

Sinha, Mrinalini (1994), 'Gender in the Critiques of Colonialism and Nationalism: Locating the Indian Woman', in Ann Louse Shapiro (ed.), *Feminists Revision History* (New Brunswick, NJ: Rutgers University Press), 246–75.

—— (1997), *Colonial Masculinity: The 'Manly' Englishman, and the 'Effeminate' Bengali in the Late Nineteenth Century* (New Delhi: Kali for Women).

Smith, Joan (1994), 'The Creation of the World we Know: The World-Economy and the Re-creation of Gendered Identities', in Valentine M. Moghadam (ed.), *Identity Politics and Women: Cultural Reassertions and Feminisms in International Perspective* (Boulder, CO: Westview Press).

Srinivas, Mytheli (2004), 'Conjugality and Capital: Gender, Families, and Property under Colonial Law in India', *Journal of Asian Studies,* 63 (4), 937–60.

Sturman, Rachel (2005), 'Property and Attachments: Defining Autonomy and the Claims of Family in Nineteenth Century Western India', *Comparative Studies in Society and History,* 47 (3), 611–37.

Thapar-Bjorkert, Suruchi (1997), 'The Domestic Sphere as a Political Site: A Study of Women in the Indian Nationalist Movement', *Women's Studies International Forum,* 20 (4), 493–504.

Turner, Victor (1986), *The Anthropology of Performance* (New York: Performing Arts Journal Publications).

Uberoi, Patricia (ed.), (1993), *Family, Kinship and Marriage in*

India, ed. T.N. Madan (Oxford in India Readings in Sociology and Social Anthropology, New Delhi: Oxford University Press).

—— (ed.), (1996), *Social Reform, Sexuality and the State* (New Delhi: Sage).

Vatuk, Sylvia (1969), 'Reference, Address and Fictive Kinship in Urban North India', *Ethnology*, 8, 255–72.

—— (1971), 'Trends in North Indian Urban Kinship: The "Matrilineal Asymmetry" Hypothesis', *Southwestern Journal of Anthropology*, 27, 287–307.

—— (1972), *Kinship and Urbanization: White Collar Migrants in North India* (Berkeley; Los Angeles; London: University of California Press).

—— (1982), 'Changing Patterns of Marriage and the Family in an Urbanized Village in Delhi, India', in H. Safa (ed.), *Towards a Political Economy of Urbanization in Third World Countries* (New Delhi Oxford University Press), 119–50.

—— (1987), 'Authority, Power, and Autonomy in the Life Cycle of the North Indian Woman', in Paul Hockings (ed.), *Dimensions of Social Life: Essays in Honor of David G. Mandelbaum* (Berlin: Mouton de Gruyter), 23–44.

—— (1992), 'Sexuality and the Middle-Aged Woman in South Asia', in V. Kerns and J.K. Brown (eds.), *In Her Prime: New Views of Middle-Aged Women* (Urbana & Chicago: University of Illinois Press), 155–70.

—— (2004), 'The Family:' A Contested Concept in Early Nineteenth Century Madra', in Indrani Chatterjee (ed.), *Unfamiliar Relations: Family and History in South Asia* (161-191; New Brunswick, NJ; New Delhi: Rutgers University Press; Permanant Black).

—— (2008), 'Islamic Feminism in India: Indian Muslim Women Activists and the Reform of Muslim Personal Law', *Modern Asian Studies*, 42 (2), 489–518.

Vervenioti, Tasoula (2002), 'Charity and Nationalism: The Greek Civil War and the Entrance of Right-Wing Women into Politics', in Paola Bacchetta and Margaret Power (eds.), *Right Wing Women: From Conservatives to Extremists Around the World* (New York: Routledge), 115–26.

Yuval-Davis, Nura (1997), *Gender and Nation* (London: Sage).

3

The Legal Structures of Kinship: Re-Working Affinity, Residence and Entitlement in the Kolkata Family Court

SRIMATI BASU

This paper is in conversation with three principal aspects of Sylvia Vatuk's work. First, Vatuk (1971) has investigated the ways in which kinship norms are affected by the context of urbanization, where 'traditions' of kinship practices are both evoked and transformed—more generally, kinship and residence norms in urban contexts, and the interplay between discourses of the extended family and conjugality. Second, Vatuk's research on discursive categories for delineating the family, and particularly attempts to interpellate such categories within law is explored in the context of courts (2004). Third, a few years ago, Sylvia and I both began extended ethnographic projects on Family Courts in India. We have since then followed linked but distinct trajectories, Sylvia focusing on Muslim women's experiences with family law and I tracking questions of governance and jurisprudence in the management of family law and family violence (Vatuk 2001 provides one of the early examples of this body of work). In this paper, these themes intersect as I focus on evocations of kinship norms in the Family Courts, and the ways in which they serve to mediate the distribution of resources such as income, space and intimacy.

I am of the generation that grew up in India watching the idyllic family drama *Hum Log* on Doordarshan long before I knew the slightest thing about anthropology; Hindi and Bangla fiction and films trained us to understand that a narrative was incomplete till a conjugal couple had been satisfactorily reconciled within an extended family setting, often requiring an ocean or two of pathos in the process. This intergenerational patrilineal joint family, attached to a common core of property, a shared household, and a web of choreographed relationships, is often seen as iconic of the family form in India in sociocultural accounts (to say nothing of mainstream fiction and film), despite the existence of a vast array of kinship and family forms in the region. This paper centers around the mythic patrilineal joint family as imagined through yet another lens, that of legal institutional discourse: it traces 'the family' as evoked in contemporary 'Family Law'. This discursively produced version of the 'family' determines the economic and cultural terms for marriages (and hence families) in crisis, and ultimately comes to define marriage and family even more broadly through the homogenization and normalization of law. Drawing on my ethnographic research in the Family Court, I argue here that courts and related organizations which undertake to manage matters of marriage and family work within a number of contradictory discourses. They evoke both the economic and emotional entitlements of the joint family as the inevitable backdrop to marriage, and contrarily emphasize conjugality as the prime legal criterion of marital expectations.

In the contemporary nation state, categories of kinship are rendered 'legal' through particular mechanisms. The subfield of kinship studies has weighed biological and cultural factors in kinship in various energetic debates, e.g. in Veena Das' evaluation of Punjabi kinship 'as a dialectic between the rules deriving from nature and the rules deriving from culture' (1994, 198). Beyond the question of how important shared biological substance is to kinship, anthropological studies emphasize cultural roles as foundational to notions of kinship, with the transmission and exchange of rights and responsibilities, labor and space, serving to anchor these roles. Such customary forms of entitlements or responsibility (such as common-use land or usufructuary rights or division of labor) are, however, not just transformed in legal negotiations in the modern nation state. More accurately, new notions of kinship are constituted through legal maneuvers. Subjectivities are created and validated in legislative debates and courtrooms by evoking custom, norms and varied understandings of legal text, and they result in a remapping of the entitlements and privileges within which kinship practices are framed.

This is not to argue that the family and kinship are reconstituted through law only in the post-colonial nation state. Indrani Chatterjee (2004) persuasively argues in the introduction to her anthology *Unfamiliar Relations: Family and History in South Asia*, that molding kinship through governance is not a post-colonial or even colonial phenomenon: many precolonial attempts to categorize family and kin, often undertaken for purposes of justifying asset distribution or lines of succession, were cast in terms of relational rhetoric, or the rhetoric of cohesiveness or status. Emphasizing the lack of evidence for a discrete separation between familial and political realms, she asserts that 'there has been no 'family' in South Asian history that was not simultaneously a political, economic, social and juridical entity. Only by bleaching the family and the household of its multiple meanings and functions could a discrete and private site be produced for both contemporary experience as well as for scholarly recuperation' (Chatterjee 2004, 35). Research on matrilineal communities (Arunima 2003; Saradamoni 1999) and levirate marriages (Chowdhry 1994) has also provided ample evidence of the encoding of customary law by the colonial state that transformed kinship and brought into being new modes of sexuality and entitlement.

This paper dwells on that great anthropological staple, the patrivirilocal joint family, and its inscription in contemporary Hindu family law. Despite its innumerable variations by region, caste and ethnicity (Gough 1994; Kolenda 1984), the Hindu patrilocal 'joint' family is often represented by anthropologists as a grand normative phenomenon, iconic of cohesion and mutual dependence in kinship relations. A familiar example in North American classrooms might be the film *Dadi's Family*, a documentary about an extended farming family in Haryana (Camerini et al. 1988): I for one am drawn to it as a teaching tool because of the ways in which it ethnographically captures space and life-cycle rituals and multiple social relationships. The film attempts to recuperate the rationale of the joint family that everyone benefits by pooling resources, living together and sharing everything, even though it does gesture to potential fracture points such as the educated urban son who is starting a nuclear household, and the dissatisfactions of daughters-in-law who feel alienated by nexuses of power, having to be surrogate daughters while never quite able to be one.

The patrilocal extended family form is invoked as a weighty, ubiquitous trope in everything from Indian film to colonial/post-colonial legislative and developmental discourses, positing the 'joint family' as the most significant of economic units for agrarian families, which adapts flexibly to industrialization, urbanization and entrepreneurial work, 'joint family property' as the primary route for intergenerational property transfers, and a benevolent altruistic head of household as arbitrator of the distribution of resources (Madan 1994; Vatuk 1972; Wadley 2002). Debates around property during the Legislative Assembly discussions over the Hindu Code Bill in the 1950s provide a case in point (Agarwal 1994; Parashar 1992). In counterpoint, radical visions of social change target the joint family as being central to gendered hierarchy, violence and oppression, such as the *Towards Equality* report prepared for the UN Decade for Women, which asserts that 'It is not the fact of patriliny by itself but its association with joint property, and joint household and certain rules and patterns of marriage which lead to greater constraints over women and affect their position in an adverse way' (CSWI 1974: 58). This paper deals specifically with urban contexts, where joint family living carries a different set of valences as well: alongside normative discourses of joint family living and resource sharing (often troubled in ways delineated above) are the strategic difficulties of finding affordable residential space, and managing eldercare expectations and domestic violence.

The most significant factor to trouble the solidity assigned to the joint family has arguably been the discourse of conjugality that occupies a parallel trajectory in defining post-colonial legal subjectivity. As historians have argued recently (Majumdar 2004; Sreenivas 2008; Sturman 2005), notions such as the rise of the individual legal subject interpellated by market forces and conjugal intimacy within the safe haven of the nuclear family emerge in certain strands of nationalist discourse, affecting the milieu within which post-colonial marriage law is constructed. A disjointed map of entitlements emerges within Hindu family law, in which succession/inheritance of property is solidly grounded in, and draws institutional benefits from, joint family property, whereas marriage/divorce law posits an autonomous conjugal unit grounded in notions of romance and nuclear intimacy. Marital property is primarily negotiated in the context of alimony and divorce, there being no legal notions of joint property in a marriage (other than through individual decisions to own jointly).

This paper examines ongoing challenges to and reinscription of the joint family in legal and quasi-legal settings. The research draws on my fieldwork in Kolkata in 2001 and 2004–5. I conducted participant observation in the Family Courts, the Women's Grievance Cell associated with the Kolkata Police, and several other organizations that informally undertook mediation and counseling related to Family Law. I also worked and traveled with and interviewed related personnel, and briefly visited other Family Courts in India as well as Dhaka for comparison. The project started as an ethnography of the Family Court and expanded to include an exploration of the management of Family Violence. Names where used have been altered for confidentiality. Translations are my own.

Using ethnographic observations from the Family Courts and related non-governmental organizations in Kolkata, the paper delineates both litigants' attempts to challenge and solidify shifting meanings of family, as well as judicial constructions of changes in the joint family and the judicial process of Family Courts as a form of kinship. I focus on the ways in which problems of urban space and constructions of desire and romance are used to work through issues such as the cohesion of the patrilocal family and the role and status of extended family members. Courts are simultaneously engaged in transforming understandings of the extended family and reestablishing ideas of its contribution to economic and social structures, thus recognizing generational contracts as well as, contradictorily, expanded notions of companionate marriage.

THE COURT AS FAMILY

My primary field sites, the Family Court in Kolkata and associated agencies that undertook Family Law counseling, mirrored these fractures and assemblages around kinship categories. In India, the establishment of Family Courts is explicitly tied to demands arising out of the feminist movement of the 1970s and 1980s. *Towards Equality: Report of the Committee on the Status of Women in India* (1974), the comprehensive documentation and policy analysis on women's status produced in preparation for the 1980 UN Conference, as well as numerous women's organizations and social work organizations in India, strongly urged that the model of Family Courts be adopted (The Family Courts Act 1984). Family Courts were also championed by legal scholars who favor 'Alternate Dispute Resolution' (ADR) methods to counter bureaucratic complication, delays and corruption in the courts, and were seen as parallels to other new legal ventures such as Consumer Courts, Traffic Courts and Lok Adalat or People's Court (specifically focused on rapid resolution of cases). The Family Courts Act (1984) decreed that special courts were to be created for the disposal of divorce, maintenance, adoption and custody cases 'with a view to promote conciliation in, and secure speedy settlement of disputes related to marriage and family affairs' (1984: 1). These were to be courts where litigants would express their concerns to judges in 'plain language', thus supposedly overcoming the alienation of legal processes. Clients were to work first with 'counselors' (paralegals or social workers, not lawyers): they were to help negotiate settlements, try to bring the parties back together, and advise about legal issues.

Alternative legislative styles and processes are thus integral to the ways in which these courts are imagined, as the self-reflexive statements of its members indicate below. While a detailed analysis of slippages in this radical vision of a court is beyond the scope of this paper, suffice it here to indicate that there have been substantial difficulties in transforming modes of institutional power, legal process and the cultural assumptions embedded in marriage. Most relevant for understanding the cases that follow is the ambivalence in interpreting family in case law mirrored by these lower-level courts, as well as the keenly felt sense of Family

Courts as a different mode of legal adjudication that mirrors and even improves upon dispute resolution within families.

By definition, the court existed to mediate contested kin entitlements and behaviors, even as it frequently validated hegemonic norms of kinship. Court personages self-consciously saw themselves as instituting new forms of law and kinship, using legal reform to enforce perceived kin/conjugal responsibilities, and the language of fictive kinship to soften the contours of legal authority. An exemplar of both of these processes comes from my very first visit to the courts, where a little girl's custodial visit to her father in court occasioned gifts of candy from the judge and counselors, sweets to the judge from the girl and her mother, the singing of 'Happy Birthday' and 'Baa Baa Black Sheep' in the judge's chambers. The judge persuaded the estranged couple to go out with their daughter for a meal. She advised the husband to honor his wife's desire to work, especially during unstable marital times, adding that she was asking him to make up with his wife, 'saying what your elder sister should but hasn't'. She appealed to him as an ex-schoolteacher who believed that children lacking fathers always felt out of it, then asked him whether the court visitation felt formal or like a relative's house (*attiyor bari*). He mumbled the latter (perforce?), and she said: 'that's why I was promoted over others to this place, to make Family Court different, because I'm a mother and a woman, otherwise it would have been another male judge'.

The judge's inscriptions of her role typify the ways in which court personnel drew clients into webs of kinship. She appeared to draw on the language of kinship in order to create comfort, but also to enable the authority of interference in the most intimate of issues, to render her disciplining palatable, indeed to inhabit the familiar in order to carry out an unfamiliar and unwelcome sanction. The self-interpellation, however, is not just to be 'like' family but to claim being the 'better' family, in that she focused on the litigants' broader interests rather than the 'real' family members' own stakes in the conflict which often vitiated their advice. While male judges had their own paths of establishing connections, here her gender (as mother, teacher, judge) was repeatedly invoked to justify essentialized notions of empathy and nurturance deemed critical to this new legal process. Performances of kinship such as gift exchange, birthday celebrations and meals were critical to creating the spaces in which such authority could be enabled. The Kolkata court has had one female and one male judge for the last eight years—the gender distribution embodies the spirit of the Family Courts Act and subsequent pressure from women's groups to have more women judges. Whether women's styles of judging are substantially different is up for debate.

Similarly, 'counselors' frequently used, and were themselves hailed by, kin categories in order to facilitate legal processes and speedy outcomes. For a case where the 'counselors' sought to ascertain a man's home address in order to serve him with his court papers, Manavi took along a friend and went to the man's brother's house, saying they were aunts (*mashi*) of the bride and wanted to meet the new groom. She reported that the brother and his wife treated them very well and promised to produce an address for their brother, who was not living there then. In the next phase, after she had indeed been given an address, I accompanied Manavi and another counselor to the man's rural home a few hours from Kolkata. Upon meeting the young man, to whom she was to deliver a notice to appear in court (with a criminal sanction if he didn't appear), she greeted him warmly, saying how much she had liked his face when she first saw his picture, how handsome and gentle he seemed. She established an easy familiarity with him and his mother, talked about his brother's hospitality, and told his mother that her daughter-in-law spoke of her fondly. We drank tea with them and met their extended family and neighbors, then toured the neighborhood. After a while, Manavi suggested 'as an aunt' that it would be good if he came to court on the assigned date and talked to the judge himself, thereby softening the non-negotiability of the legal summons. The family responded cordially and brought all their documents out from a high shelf for us to peruse, immediately sensitive to the empathy; the counselors were able to explain the urgency of the summons and the nature of the appearance, to make it clear to the young man that it was not a summons under the Dowry Prohibition Act as he feared. As he walked us back to the railway station, he talked about his dreams of starting a small business and his passion for Hindi movies. This account should indicate the informal styles through which legal directives and summons were conveyed to people in this alternatively styled court. Specifically, discourses of kinship were deployed both instrumentally and strategically to convey ease, approachability, and the availability of familiar registers of emotional response. The necessary actions were achieved through counselors performing as 'aunts' rather than officers of the law.

In a parallel account of kinship being used by the litigants to achieve optimal results, Manavi told me about recognizing a woman who was in court for a divorce, the wife of the Principal of a renowned college, as a former school and college classmate. The former classmate was in court for a divorce, and had received the paltry sum of Rs. 500 as maintenance despite her husband's income. When Manavi introduced herself, she was delightedly taken home to meet her classmate's 95 year old, acutely ill mother. The mother, Manavi narrated, recognized her as well, held on to her hands and pleaded with her (and the other counselor who was with her) for a better outcome, saying she would not die in peace until the case was resolved, and that she was counting on them (*'tomra koriye dao'*, translatable as 'you can make it happen'). When the maintenance order was tripled in a subsequent court hearing (not necessarily through the counselors' intervention), her classmate's mother asked one of her other daughters for some cash and put it in two envelopes, then sent those on and died the next day. Manavi and the other counselor received a small cash amount from her classmate's mother—it was not the amount but the thanks which touched her, she claimed. This narrative demonstrates the circumstances in which counselors work through kinship ties and fashion their own, and despite its dramatic elements, was in fact more typical than not, in that litigants sought out connections with such court officials through relatives or neighbors or friends and then hailed them through kinship categories.

Thus, the court gets enmeshed in the simultaneous disentangling and entangling of kinship ties. Court officials consciously place themselves within familial positions even as they are involved in undoing or refashioning family ties in the course of their work. They thereby cast themselves as embodying, and modeling, 'better' families.

CONJUGALITY *VS.* EXTENDED FAMILY

Susan Wadley's staunch defence that 'the Indian joint family is built upon the idea and reality that power comes through numbers, and that those who seek to be the most powerful, especially in India's village communities, should remain in joint families in order to successfully sustain a family's honor and position' (2002: 11) is representative of the work of numerous anthropologists who have sought to map the continuing relevance of the joint family in India. Similarly, T.N. Madan argues that 'the sentiment for joint family living has remained generally undiminished irrespective of the kinds of household the respondents themselves lived in' (1994: 433). In counterpoint to these generally Functionalist arguments, other scholars have contended that discourses of conjugality, embedded in the workings of modernity, nationalism, class and caste, regularly interrupt notions of the extended family, and are constitutive of policy and practice.

Several historians locate conjugality within nineteenth century social reform movements that seek to re-vision marriage and women's role within the polity and civil society. Rochona Majumdar argues that 'Western ideas of domestic management were combined with Indian ideals of hierarchy and devotion to produce the dyadic couple form by the turn of the century in urban, Indian life' (2007: 437). Looking to Calcutta of 1875–1940 (viz. the same city as the location for the courts in this piece) as a 'teeming urban metropolis' with an 'expanding and diverse population', Majumdar uses the example of marriage negotiations to point to the emergence of a diffuse middle-class *bhadralok* culture where men's status no longer depended so much on caste as on 'participation in public life and civil society', and where individual characteristics of the couple thus fell under much greater scrutiny (2004: 912, 924). Notable for the later analysis of cases here is Majumdar's observation that while women's education began to matter more as social capital in the marriage market, these were characterized as the skills of an expert homemaker inhabiting a traditional caste household role with grace and harmony, 'a new model and aesthetics of womanhood identifying women as harbingers of the auspicious in the new, urban, middle-class Hindu home' (2004: 926); that is, women's achieved status had to be located within the affinal family. Mytheli Sreenivas' recent book maps several registers in which colonial 'debates about the family' in the Tamil region including 'affective and property relations' served as a diagnostic of 'the formulation and contestation of Tamil social relations', a site of imposition of colonial authority as well as of resistance of caste, gender and class categories (2008: 3). Sreenivas depicts the emergence of discourses of conjugality as being central to nationalist resistance: the phenomenon of 'self-respect marriages' not only resisted Brahmanical hegemony but posited 'contractual conjugality' grounded in 'compatibility, equality and companionship in marriage' as the cornerstone of reform, also 'Tamil individual subjectivity' as critical to the modernized national self (2008: 86). Sreenivas' reading of Tamil women's magazines from 1890–1920 traces the inscription of a privatized domestic sphere where 'companionate domesticity' was the 'heart' of 'marriage ideals', located in 'a fixed residence, rooted in the conjugal relationship', women active roles in marriage and childcare serving as an 'anti-market' foil for increasing urbanization and commercialization (2008: 99, 101, 105). In these instances, the conjugal couple, particularly in urban contexts, is central to the constitution of the modernized nation state.

A related line of argument foregrounds the transformation of economic conditions in the nineteenth century as the driving force for the emergence of notions of the individual subject, conjugal responsibility, and the loosening bonds of the joint family. Rachel Sturman traces the cracks in the seemingly inviolable colonial administrative notion that the 'property based nature of Indian family structures were axiomatic' based on 'a combination of ancient textual prescription and contemporary evidence of customary practice'—cracks were wrought by claims to shares of individual property and goods, deemed as part of a process of 'configur[ing] autonomous legal subjecthood' and 'reshaping . . . material and symbolic debt' (2005: 616, 619). Both extended family capital and individual enterprise were critical economic imperatives at this time: '[P]atterns of colonial adjudication need to be seen as attempting simultaneously to secure the jointness of the joint family in order to protect the security of creditors and debtors, *and* to increase the independence of family members in relation to each other in order to promote market transactions' (Sturman 2005: 623). In Sreenivas' analysis centered on the Madras Presidency, individual property ownership began to be associated with national modernity, and coparcenary joint property with tradition, in initiatives such as the Gains of Learning Bill which sought to separate men's professional earnings from the joint property of their families (2004: 944). Invocations of conjugality figured prominently in these claims alongside invocations of capital: 'opponents of joint property linked individual ownership with both capital and conjugality. On the one hand, they emphasized that men's individual ownership of property was necessary for capitalist development; on the other, they argued that the property relations of the conjugal couple and their children superceded the rights of the male coparcenary' (Sreenivas 2004: 942). In both these accounts, thus, the male legal subject is called upon as having privileges and responsibilities to the joint and the conjugal family; female economic entitlement becomes the rationale upon which this separation is wrought.

Despite the ongoing prevalence of the extended family, several anthropologists and sociologists have argued for hidden scripts of conjugal emotion from women, often embedded within caste, class, ethnic and kin hierarchies. Pervez Mody's ethnography of 'love-marriages' maps some convoluted trajectories through which couples' romantic relationships have to be reconciled within a community's inscription of appropriate marriages, such that the couples themselves refuse to describe either desire or rebellion as playing a role in their elopements, and deny marrying for choice or love (2006: 344; Puri 1999: 140 also argues for the ways in which love marriages are reconciled within 'arranged' categories). In contrast, Gloria Raheja looks to Uttar Pradesh women's songs to signal resistance to the cultural norm that men's primary loyalties are to their natal families—themes such as the truer love of wives compared to mothers, husbands' misguided attachments to their natal families, obstacles to conjugal intimacy from in-laws, men's public avowal of ties to their natal families but private subversion of them, and men's attachment to the notion of the *jori* or couple foreground wives' desires as well as tensions in extended patrilineal households (Raheja & Gold 1994: 124–36). Raheja argues that these songs do not imagine a world without 'marriage and the family' but rather that 'marriage ought not to deprive a woman of intimacy or reduce her to the status of a passively submissive and powerless interloper in a household of patrilineal kin', that women believe it to be morally valid that 'a diminution of the strength of those patrilineal relations [is] a valid resolution of conflicting kinship expectations' (ibid.: 123). Jyoti Puri's study of urban middle-class women captures women living under very different conditions, but her findings are remarkably similar: married women describe realizing their goals of having 'understanding, caring husbands and mutual, companionate and egalitarian marriages' but tension and constraint with other family members in the extended household (1999: 147, 151). Like Raheja, Puri contends that these women do not reject marriage, but rather imagine themselves to be entitled to 'marital intimacy and companionship', and strategically use the space of marriedness to 'set standards of gender-egalitarian and mutual married relationships' and 'negotiate deep-seated inequalities' in their structural positions in the patrilineal household (1999: 153). That is, while potentially marginal practices such as 'love-marriage' have to be recuperated, the 'traditional' space of the daughter-in-law in an extended patriarchal family can become a site of negotiation by using discourses of conjugality.

The legacy of these historical trajectories, and a public site for these cultural contestations, is well illustrated in the two contradictory discourses about conjugality and kinship that lie at the heart of divorce, custody and maintenance cases. First, marriage law for various communities, as initially reformed in the 1930s-50s and then through the end of the century (Agnes 1999), envisions individual subjects who have contractual economic obligations towards each other: alimony, child support, household and reproductive labor, monogamy as the favored norm (even implicitly for Muslims), and more recently (since the 1980s) the right to be free of violence. The right to maintenance exists whether or not spouses (most often husbands) are employed, and defaulting on maintenance may be punished with jail time and fines. Second, however, marriage laws are implicitly framed within a cultural norm that individuals, almost always men, are financially responsible for their extended families, that the extended family household is the default living situation, and that daughters-in-law are to deliver competent domestic labor and eventually be integrated within the family.

The following case provides a typical script for daughters-in-laws' labor and liability for maintaining domestic harmony. In a 2004 hearing of a 2001 case, the husband sought divorce on grounds of desertion and cruelty, alleging that within three days of the wedding his wife 'caused problems'. He pled that the way she talked was 'a bit abnormal', that she threw utensils (at someone?), and '*barir kajkormo korey na*' (did not do domestic work), and that she left and began living with her parents, agreeing to return only on condition that her husband got a separate residence. Articulations of the husband's position here—'I did not want to separate my parents and therefore did not agree to the proposal', 'she did not behave properly with the inmates [*sic*] of my house', that she made his mother ill and that the household members were in constant tension—were framed squarely within a discourse where harmonious life in the extended family was the only possible location of conjugality, and attempts to separate the unit were a threat to social cohesion. The wife's response, in turn, echoed a set of strategic positions that complied with her role in the extended family. She submitted that she wanted to stay but could not, that her in-laws wanted Rs. 50,000 and their behavior changed when they did not get it, and that she did not object to staying with the in-laws. This scenario stands for a vast number of cases (also echoed in my previous research on property cases (Basu 1999), showing that normative scripts of femininity were likely to be validated judicially. These were the discursive terms upon which conjugal roles were most frequently challenged in court, where being a good wife depended upon a seamless, willing, self-effacing harmony with the extended patrilineal household.

Women's 'adjustment' to family 'tensions' was frequently touted as the most skillful, capable response to these inevitable constraints, whereas provisions for separate residence indicated a failure of such resolutions and introduced the heavy-handed mark of law in the family. Manavi, the counselor whose kin negotiations are described earlier, narrated to me her intervention with a young woman in her neighborhood who had suddenly gone back to her parents' home while her husband was out of town. The woman said her mother-in-law fussed at her about household work, like whether the potatoes had been cut properly, and had once said in an argument 'one day I'll burn you to death' ('*ekdin puraiya marum*'). She also implied that the father-in-law had made sexual overtures. Thus, her complaints fell within the common script of extended family tensions, and the counselor's advice about adjustment and eventual empowerment also reflected these ideologies:

> I told her her mother-in-law had a lot of health problems like high blood pressure and blood sugar and had been laid up, and that a lot of problems crop up in the domestic realm. When I would leave for my Master's courses, my own mother-in-law would say 'off dancing again' ('*oi je nachtey berochchey*'). I told her [the young woman], 'in five months, you haven't yet put down roots in this family's soil yet' ('*e poribar-e tomar shikor mati obdhi-i pounchoyni*'), you'll have to make space here, establish your influence ('*adhipotyo sthapön*').

Significantly, the counselor's mediation emphasized the value of extended family living, and establishing a long-term presence within the family, awaiting a transformation in the balance of power while waiting out conflict.

The wider financial commitments of husbands to their families were also used to negotiate neglect, cruelty and maintenance claims. Responsibilities to the extended family were depicted in husbands' legal claims as culturally normative, and served to mitigate economic obligations to the conjugal unit. In a child support case, the father proffered that about a quarter of his take-home pay as a professor was going to repay a loan for his sister's wedding. That is, familial obligations for pooling resources for daughters' weddings was cited as normative—such contributions are not necessarily ubiquitous, but neither is it extraordinary for a brother to do this. Once the assertion had been put forth, the judge would need to consider this diminished amount as the base for child support, or to challenge its validity as a strategic sidestep.

The ideological valuation of the extended family was almost

inevitably woven into the fabric of the argument, even when the family was quite evidently in shambles. Note the judicial reification of a particular form of the 'Indian family' norms and the demonization of 'the West' in the following admonition to facilitate visits for a non-custodial father and the paternal family. In response to the wife's attempt to include as a condition for custody that there be no contact with the mother-in-law, the judge scolded:

> Indian Hindu family means connection with family. After marriage, the primary family is the husband's family, the wife's family is secondary after that. In a Western country children move far away from their parents (*chchelemeye boro holey baba ma'r thekey durey jan*). Where on earth have you learned these things, don't you have parents? (*kothay e shikkha peyechchen, baba ma nei*?)

In response to this assault, the litigant just mumbled in a low voice: I had parents (*baba ma chchilo*), while the judge continued, 'A mother can't keep her kids away from their grandparents'. The husband chimed in that he had an objection relating to his in-laws' home when he visited his kids there, but the judge sternly reminded him he could only 'have a "problem", not an "objection", when they were trying to get back together (*milmish*)'. These comments exemplify the ironic terrain family courts judges must negotiate: while the very fact of public legal dispute over custody, visitation and separate residence destabilized the notion of a monolithic stable tradition of patrivirilocal family cohesion, ideologies of the centrality of the paternal family, the role of a woman's natal family in training her to value patrilocal preference, or a husband's reluctance to visit his in-laws' home were asserted as self-evident cultural practices that must be incorporated into emerging legal positions, always to be part of the context in which conjugal rights were to be negotiated.

However, discourses of conjugality thrived within the very same legal environment. Failure to meet the affective standards of the nuclear unit could also be deemed as legal grounds for cruelty, to be mediated by judges. The following case for restitution of conjugal rights case demonstrates some markers of conjugal expectation: the wife alleged that her husband got rid of her because she had two daughters and did not want to give her medical attention, that he never took her out anywhere or spent time with her, and that he neglected the children. In his response, the husband countered with evidence of doctor's prescriptions, 1,200 pictures of vacations in Mumbai and southern India, and pictures of birthday parties held each year for each child. They had been ordered by the judge to find housing for the couple and children away from the extended family (where there appeared to be problems with interference and violence), but the deal fell through when the wife objected to the size of their individual dwelling. In the legal strategy for restitution he filed in response, the husband had to construct himself as one whose final responsibilities lay with the nuclear unit, the vacations and birthday parties symbolizing commitments to this individualistic entity, and he had to legally efface his joint family ties; the amount of his long-term alimony payments rested on this determination. It is of course impossible to evaluate the truth of such claims that are framed as well-worn legal strategies, but the point is that both these discourses—extended family obligations and conjugal responsibilities—could be simultaneously, or alternatively, inhabited within the current legal nexus.

Women's legal strategies sometimes incorporated notions of traditional entitlement and sought to frame their grievances within those parameters, but also introduced other registers of conjugality. In the cases cited earlier in this section, allegations invoked troubles within the extended family, often in terms of violence against daughters-in-law, an issue with public visibility and hence a strategically strong space from which women can speak. While the truth of any of these legal narratives is impossible to ascertain, the National Crime Records Bureau and numerous other organizations provide ample evidence of the widespread prevalence of domestic violence, and this was a prominent focus of criminal prosecution at the time. In the case where Manavi counseled the young woman, it seemed likely that the problems articulated by this young woman would culminate in a demand for a separate residence. Significantly, the initial negotiating space often invoked extended family tensions (real or strategic) as a culturally valid discontent of marriage, and one meriting legal redressal.

In contrast, other women articulated desires for romance and conjugal space as a normative expectation of marriage, a double-edged move which claimed wifely power but could often be the source of suspicion and ridicule. These claims were more consistent with the legal apparatus of restitution of conjugal rights and economic rights within marriage. Women could often validly propose separate residences as a condition of continuing the relationship, given the provenance of the Family Courts to focus on reunion and reconciliation of couples, not extended families, as envisaged in marriage laws. In a 2004 case with the couple on the verge of reconciliation, the judge declared (to the husband, but with an implicit lecture for the wife as well):

> you can't abandon your mother and father and have a family/household (the translation of *sansar* here does little to capture the sense of stability and auspiciousness of the term), you have to have a *sansar* along with your parents. If you had a lame or disabled sister how could you abandon her? It so happens that your sister is independent and has a job.

Moral imperatives of joint family residence were called upon here, even as autonomous possibilities for single women's survival outside the extended family were presented, and the conjugal unit was granted preferential legal sanction.

These contradictions are exemplified in the extended account which follows, where representatives of an organization were mediating marital conflicts and hoping to effect a reconciliation, by asking both partners to manage and balance their roles. The wife had complained about feeling harassed by the mother-in-law about domestic tasks and help with childcare, and by the husband's maternal uncle's wife, who she suspected of having an affair with her husband. She alleged particularly that everything the couple talked about between each other, or what she said to him on the phone, was repeated back to her sarcastically: for example, that she told him she felt like eating an egg roll, that she said on the telephone that she missed him. Her husband demurred feebly that the family members just heard things because they lived close by. Counselors reprimanded her for her expressed expectation that she wanted him to understand what she wanted without her saying it: she was told she should not expect her husband to read her mind and ought to be explicit, and that she needed to learn not to hear a lot of things and to help her mother-in-law as well she could. This advice mirrored that of Manavi's in the earlier case, that adjusting within the extended family while sublimating conjugal expectations represented the most successful resolution. However, the husband too was admonished to keep certain things about his domestic life private, to not run to relatives with everything, and to negotiate with his mother to get domestic help for his wife—the conjugal sphere and his obligation to speak in support of his wife's well-being were validated here. In response, he claimed that he usually told his wife she needed to deal with her own stuff, and ignore what others said (which allowed him to avoid addressing her treatment as well), but he added that he could not agree to a mediated solution whereby he would leave his residence or have his old mother live by herself. These conditions related to finding affordable urban residential space but also the social and economic responsibilities of eldercare by sons. The counselor immediately agreed, saying 'of course not, we would never ask that', and made arrangements to meet with the mother without the couple to clarify matters. Both discourses of conjugal intimacy and gendered kinship roles had to be negotiated here, alongside considerations of limited economic and spatial resources. Each discourse thereby had to be modulated, and the axis of resolution lay in ironing out their differences in expectation in meanings of marriage.

During my fieldwork in the courts, I observed numerous mediation sessions with a variety of organizations—state, party-affiliated, independent feminist—where complicated arrangements had to be made so that separate nuclear and extended households could be established, often within the same space because separate rental space (let alone ownership) was unaffordable and unsatisfactory. Cases of marital discord thus provided vivid flashpoints to examine the instability of household forms, distribution of emotional and affectional ties, and deployment of and resistances to power. The central issue often was a woman's unwillingness to return to the joint family, and family abuse was commonly cited as a ground (Basu 2006). It seems fair to say that a fair amount of family violence did exist, but also that it provided one of the optimal legal strategies for women to seek separation without appearing selfish or alien. In adjudicating about violence given the legal statutes governing domestic abuse, judges often willy-nilly recommended separate conjugal space if possible—otherwise, what would be a good reason for a woman not to live with her in-laws? However, extended family living was seen as necessary in other cases, especially when caregiving or financial obligations were an issue. These legal interventions exemplified the disarticulation between discourses of marriage law and property law, between marital obligations and generationally grounded entitlements, and between modern notions of intimate conjugality, customary norms of gendered domestic space, and the material difficulties of achieving both given the limitations of income and urban residential space.

CONCLUSION

Sylvia Vatuk's ethnographic evidence thirty years ago (1972) that kinship was re-configured in the urban context while retaining its nexuses of power is borne out by the contemporary data from Kolkata Family Courts. The courts themselves mirror and construct kin relations in the process of mediating family disputes. The patrilocal extended family continues to assert great ideological dominance, even as its existence as a viable economic and residential unit is challenged in marital disputes—it comes to stand as an unquestioned site of economic pooling and social strength, or oppressive violence and zone of tension, depending on the framing of the litigants' claims. While conjugal compatibility appears to be foregrounded in marriage law, it is often covertly claimed through optimal legal strategies, and inevitably pitted against the daunting hegemony of the ideal that society thrives best through women's harmonious, skillful melding into the conflicted space of the extended family.

REFERENCES

Agarwal, B. 1994. *A Field of One's Own: Gender and Land Rights in South Asia*, Cambridge South Asian Studies, Cambridge, England; New York: Cambridge University Press.

Agnes, F. 1999. *Law and Gender Inequality: The Politics of Women's Rights in India*, New Delhi: Oxford University Press.

Arunima, G. 2003. *There Comes Papa: Colonialism and the Transformation of Matriliny in Kerala, Malabar, c. 1850–1940*, New Delhi: Orient Longman.

Basu, S. 1999. 'Cutting to Size: Property and Gendered Identity in the Indian Higher Courts', in *Signposts: Gender in Post-Independence India*, ed. R.S. Rajan, New Delhi: Kali for Women.

—— 2006. 'Playing Off Courts: The Negotiation of Divorce and Violence in Plural Legal Settings in Kolkata, India', *Journal of Legal Pluralism and Unofficial Law* 52, 41–75.

Camerini, M. and R. Gill, Public Broadcasting Associates & PBS Video. 1988. *Dadi's Family*, Boston: PBS Video.

Chatterjee, I. 2004. *Unfamiliar Relations: Family and History in South Asia*, New Brunswick, N.J.: Rutgers University Press.

Chowdhry, P. 1994. *The Veiled Women: Shifting Gender Equations in Rural Haryana, 1880–1990*, New Delhi; New York: Oxford University Press.

CSWI. 1974. 'Towards Equality: Report of Committee on the Status of Women in India' (trans.) G.o.I. Ministry of Education and Social Welfare. New Delhi.

Das, V. 1994. 'Masks and Faces: An Essay on Punjabi Kinship', in *Family, Kinship and Marriage in India* (ed.) P. Uberoi, Delhi: Oxford University Press.

Gough, E.K. 1994. 'Brahman Kinship in a Tamil Village', in *Family, Kinship and Marriage in India* (ed.) P. Uberoi, Delhi: Oxford University Press.

Kolenda, P. 1984. 'Woman as Tribute, Woman as Flower: Images of "Woman" in Weddings in North and South India', *American Ethnologist* 11, 98–117.

Madan, T.N. 1994. 'The Hindu Family and Development', in *Family, Kinship and Marriage in India* (ed.) P. Uberoi, New Delhi: Oxford University Press.

Majumdar, R. 2004. 'Looking for Brides and Grooms: *Ghataks*, Matrimonials and the Marriage Market in Colonial Calcutta, circa 1875–1940', *Journal of Asian Studies* 63, 911–35.

—— 2007. Review Essay: Arguments within Indian Feminism. *Social History* 32, 434–45.

Mody, P. 2006. 'Kidnapping, Elopement and Abduction: An Ethnography of Love-Marriage in Delhi', in *Love in South Asia: A Cultural History*, ed. F. Orsini. Cambridge: Cambridge University Press.

Parashar, A. 1992. *Women and Family Law Reform In India: Uniform Civil Code and Gender Equality*, New Delhi: Sage.

Puri, J. 1999. *Woman, Body, Desire in Post-colonial India Narratives of Gender and Sexuality*, New York: Routledge.

Raheja, G.G. and A.G. Gold. 1994. *Listen to the Heron's Words Reimagining Gender and Kinship in North India*, Berkeley: University of California Press.

Saradamoni, K. 1999. *Matriliny Transformed: Family, Law, and Ideology in Twentieth Century Travancore*, New Delhi: Sage; Walnut Creek CA: Altamira Press.

Sreenivas, M. 2004. 'Conjugality and Capital: Gender, Families and Property under Colonial Law in India', *Journal of Asian Studies* 63, 937–60.

—— 2008. *Wives, Widows, Concubines: The Conjugal Family Ideal in Colonial India*, Bloomington: Indiana University Press.

Sturman, R. 2005. 'Property and Attachments: Defining Autonomy and the Claims of Family in Nineteenth-Century Western India', *Comparative Studies in Society and History* 47, 611–37.

Vatuk, S. 1972. *Kinship and Urbanization: White Collar Workers in North India*, London: University of California Press.

—— 2001. 'Where Will She Go? What Will She Do?': Paternalism Toward Women in the Administration of Muslim Personal Law in Contemporary India', in *Religion and Personal Law in Secular India*, ed. G.J. Larsen, Bloomington: Indiana University Press.

—— 2004. '"Family" as a Contested Concept in Early-nineteeenth-century Madras', in *Unfamiliar Relations: Family and History in South Asia*, ed., I. Chatterjee. Delhi: Permanent Black.

Vatuk, S.J. 1971. Trends in North Indian Urban Kinship: The 'Matrilateral Assymetry' Hypothesis, *Southwestern Journal of Anthropology* 27, 287–307.

Wadley, S.S. 2002. 'One Straw from a Broom cannot Sweep: The Ideology and Practice of the Joint Family in Rural North India', in *Everyday Life in South Asia*, ed. D.P. Mines and S. Lamb, Bloomington: Indiana University Press.

4

Marital Intimacy: A Four-Generation Study of Change among Havik Brahmins

HELEN E. ULLRICH*

Respect and intimacy reflect different power dimensions in human relationships. One Totagadde girl showed her respect for her neighbor's wisdom by remaining silent in his presence. Such respect precludes an intimate relationship. Totagadde Havik Brahmin marital relationships historically codified respect for the husband, as his wife's personal deity. This left little room for intimacy. I analyze changes in marital intimacy over four generations in the village known pseudonymously as Totagadde, where I have worked closely with the Havik Brahmin community of some thirty households.[1] Before presenting the four generations, I will describe the setting and provide some ethnographic background. The oldest generation consists of people in their eighties or nineties; the second generation includes their children and daughters and sons-in-law; the third generation consists of their grandchildren; and the fourth generation includes the great grandchildren of the first generation. The second generation consists of those in their sixties and seventies; the third generation, those in their forties and fifties; and the fourth generation those in their twenties and thirties. To illustrate particular points I will provide details from Totagadde Havik Brahmin families.

Now women expect involvement as partners in marital life; many men also expect their partners to have opinions of their own. This was not always the case. When I arrived in Totagadde in 1964, husbands in their twenties and thirties rarely consulted their wives. Mothers-in-law told me that their daughters-in-law needed no education because their sons would make all the decisions. Although these wives wished their husbands would consult them, their reality was otherwise. There has been a cataclysmic change in marital intimacy since the 1960s. Erikson's explanation of intimacy as the sixth stage of psychosocial development follows:

> Intimacy, that is, the capacity to commit himself to concrete affiliations and partnerships and to develop the ethical strength to abide by such commitments even though they may call for significant sacrifices and compromises. (Erikson 1985: 263)

In this paper I use marital intimacy to reflect a companionate relationship. To the extent that a couple considers each other's needs and wishes one may infer intimacy. The change in sexual practices includes consideration of the other and an expectation of mutual satisfaction. When women married before puberty, they had yet to mature to intimacy in the Eriksonian sense. Some did mature to marital intimacy; others had experienced such emotional trauma at the time of their marriage that they cloaked their emotional vulnerability in passivity. Now that women marry in their twenties, they have the maturity requisite to develop intimacy. The expectation of marital intimacy is part of the cataclysmic change in which the man and the woman have the determining say in whether to marry. Moreover, there may be mutual respect, but wives no longer regard their husbands as their personal deity. For those unable to tolerate a spouse, divorce and marriage to another has become an option.

During the period from 1964 to 2008, residents in the village Totagadde have experienced much change. Previously for all practical purposes women were secluded (Vatuk 1982: 70). They required someone to accompany them whenever they left Totagadde. Men had thought women afraid to travel alone, but when bus transportation in the 1970s provided access to nearby towns, they believed their daughters were competent to travel alone to college. These daughters accompanied their siblings and mothers to physicians in the nearby town. Women of the first two generations have rarely traveled alone. They have told me they would get lost if they went unaccompanied to the nearby town. Moreover, they reported that they lacked the skills to shop alone or to find their way. Their urban-dwelling children reported embarrassment over their mother's passivity and inability to function autonomously beyond the family environment.

In 1964, Havik women had no financial independence. Some expressed the view that only with economic resources would they be free to express their own opinions. As one woman in a good marriage stated, 'If I disagree with my husband, that might escalate into a quarrel. He could throw me out of the home. How would I survive?'

In 2008, I overheard the same woman instructing her granddaughter in grammar school to state her opinions. The granddaughter had complained that a server overlooked her when serving seconds at a feast. The grandmother asked whether her granddaughter had requested more. When the reply was negative, her grandmother told her the server had no way of knowing her wants without her asking. A married granddaughter is working as a software engineer in the United States. Originally her family had restricted the choice of groom to India, but after three years, this same grandmother commented that her granddaughter had neither a groom nor the work experience of her classmates. She was behind professionally. When her grandfather permitted the search for a groom to include men working in other countries, she quickly found a groom in the United States and an opportunity to work and to advance professionally. From a background of socialized passivity this grandmother now prepares her granddaughters for appropriate assertiveness.

Factors which led to a companionate marriage include increasing levels of education, professional opportunities for men and women, marriage at an older age usually after finishing one's education, the option to determine whom one will marry, and women supporting women. Vatuk (1994) emphasized the importance of education as well as female solidarity in her multigenerational study of a Hyderabad family. Other works (Vatuk 1980, 1982) emphasized the dependence of women on the family combined with restrictions on women within the Indian family. My hypothesis is that all these factors have led to the change. However, the primary factor has been education. The change in ideal family structure from a joint family to a nuclear family and a decrease in the number of children have further allowed for close marital relationships. Through four generations—from mother to daughter to granddaughter to great-granddaughter—the increased expectation of marital companionship has enhanced marital intimacy. Though the setting is a multicaste Karnataka village, I focus on the Havik Brahmin caste. My impression, however, is that similar changes have occurred among other Totagadde castes.

FIELD METHODS

From my first research visit to Totagadde in 1964 I have always lived with the same family. Its members, along with all the other Totagadde Havik Brahmins, taught me the Havik dialect of Kannada and encouraged me to participate in their festivals and ceremonies. The entire village has extended its hospitality. During the first two visits when my focus was on linguistics I had designated informants. At times when they had no other work, the rest of the Haviks served as my informants. My approach included participant observation, unstructured interviews, and also more formal questioning to elicit linguistic data.

After the first two visits, my focus expanded to depression, anxiety, and the impact of cultural change on health. For this I have used formal questionnaires that served as a basis for many to discuss their perceptions in depth, as well as participant observation. I collected the data on intimacy in numerous ways. Spontaneous comments illustrated changes over time. For instance, one woman who was criticized as too forward in her relationship with her husband and too outgoing in 1964 and 1974 was pointed to as a role model in 1985. One woman who would have been a role model for her passivity in the 1960s was said to be insufficiently assertive in the 1980s. Some openly praised my formal questionnaires, while others balked, responding that I already had the information. I included the entire adult Havik population. As one never knew when there would be other visitors, finding a time to interview in private was a challenge. Even when someone would tell me to come at a particular time, I might have to wait until other visitors left. The biggest challenge was to interview those who were rarely alone. Often I would interview women while they prepared food, an otherwise solitary activity for them.

ETHNOGRAPHIC BACKGROUND

Totagadde is a Karnataka village located about 200 miles (306 km) from Bangalore. The pseudonym refers to the major crops—areca nut plantation (*to:Ta*) and rice paddy (*gadde*) [I use a capital to indicate retroflex phonemes; a colon to indicate vowel length, and *sh* for the palatal sibilant]. In 1964, only Havik Brahmins owned land. Tenant farmers tilled the Brahmin or temple-owned land. With land reforms in 1961, 1966–7, and 1974, non-Brahmin tenant farmers in this multi-caste village gained ownership of land which they had farmed for more than two consecutive years. Members of all castes now own land.

In spite of losing land to tenants who had farmed the same land for more than two years successively, Havik Brahmins regard the late twentieth and twenty-first centuries as a more prosperous age. This is apparent in the quality of clothing, quantity of gold jewelry, educational achievement, professional skills, and elaborateness of ceremonies. This population has produced bankers, lawyers, doctors, and hardware and software engineers. Both women and men work in the various professions.

Brahmins and non-Brahmins have built separate houses for nuclear families and more elaborate homes attest to the new found prosperity among all castes. Although members of all castes have sought advancement outside of Totagadde, the focus of this paper is on the Havik Brahmins. The Havik Brahmin caste has traditionally been the economically, judicially, and ritually dominant caste of Totagadde. Educational and employment achievements illustrate economic dominance. Although non-Brahmins have traveled and worked in different areas of India, none has worked in other countries, while employers have sent Brahmin sons and daughters to conferences and to training programs in other countries. To retain dominance, Havik Brahmins have encouraged members of other castes to use modern farming techniques and to take advantage of educational opportunities. Haviks attribute the respect and the lack of intercaste conflict within Totagadde to their cooperating with non-Brahmins. They point out that non-Brahmins in nearby communities show more strife.

Non-Brahmins in college proudly volunteer which Totagadde Brahmins are in their class. On the other hand, Brahmin students are reluctant to indicate which non-Brahmin classmates come from Totagadde. In contrast, these same college students socialize and personally extend wedding invitations to their Brahmin and non-Brahmin classmates from other villages. Moreover, Haviks from other villages socialize and attend Totagadde non-Brahmin weddings. This suggests Brahmin college students are uncomfortable with caste ranking within Totagadde. Outside of Totagadde Havik Brahmins pay less attention to caste ranking. An indication of this transition is the comfort with which Brahmin grade school children socialize with and invite their non-Brahmin Totagadde classmates to their homes. This is a marked difference from the 1960s when Havik Brahmins did not socialize with non-Brahmins.

Since 1986 the Havik Brahmin population has declined from 152 to 132. There are 39 households with a mean of 3.3 people in a household, a median of three, and a mode of two. Of thirty-nine households all but four have children or siblings in an urban area. Until recently, within the past fifteen years, one son would stay in Totagadde to manage the land and to assist his parents. Then a decade or so ago a dutiful son responded to his father's request for his return to Totagadde to help with agriculture. He, his wife, and son had been happy in Bangalore where he had a teaching position at the university. His parents boasted of his accomplishments and enjoyed visits with him in Bangalore. When they asked him to return to Totagadde to assist his father, he resigned his job. What had been two nuclear families became a joint family. His father was used to directing his son; however, his son had had special training in agriculture. Neither listened to the other. His parents' pleasure and pride in his accomplishments have been replaced by mutual resentment. This case has served as an example for Totagadde residents of the importance of encouraging one's children, even if one has only one son, to follow their own career pursuits. In the future with migration of an only child for work, there is likely to be a further decrease in the Totagadde Havik Brahmin population.

Nine castes reside in Totagadde. There are thirty-nine Havik Brahmin households. There is one Lingayat family and one barber family. There are several potter families. Members of the elder potter generation are concerned that their children and grandchildren are abandoning the traditional profession. Although the caste profession pays poorly, some elders insist that their children at least know how to make pottery. But they know a career working with computers is both more prestigious and better paying than pottery and farming. Vokkaligas, Divarus, and Shetterus primarily farm. Their children also attend college. The barber is more prominent on ritual occasions, as many villagers choose to use the barber in town. Hoslurus, Holerus, Divarus, and Shetterus may work for others. Those elders who have opposed their children's education find themselves the object of criticism among their own caste. (This was the situation of Havik Brahmins in the preceding generation. Parents determined the amount of education their children received.) This denial of educational opportunity has ruptured family relationships and some sons who have been so denied have left the joint family. The Dalits (Holeru) and scheduled tribe (Hosluru) in Totagadde have also benefited from education, as have the Shetterus who originally came as migrant laborers. They have stayed and number college graduates among their ranks. The more recently developed hamlets may include potters, Vokkaligas, and Divarus. The Brahmin and Dalit hamlets are the only groups which have not incorporated other castes in their hamlets.

Over the past forty years the Havik Brahmins have reinterpreted their practice of religion. Whereas their home as a sacred space was limited to Havik Brahmins in 1964, members of other castes may now enter their homes. This includes one's children's friends, servants, and other guests. Marriage alliances may include other Brahmin castes. In the 1960s one Havik woman in a love match married a Brahmin other than Havik and found herself banished from her parental household; her brother's wife now denies this. Education has expanded horizons, ritual is less important than preparation for a profession. Few women continue to observe menstrual taboos, and those who do so observe them only in Totagadde itself. Those in school, in a profession, or in an urban area report that observing the taboos would be inconvenient for other family members. With increased prosperity from a primarily agricultural society to one in which professional children earn more in a month than their father earns in a year, Havik Brahmins are giving priority to their profession over their religious practice.

THE FIRST GENERATION

The elders when I first worked in Totagadde are now in their eighties, nineties or deceased. Women generally married before puberty (Table 4.1). The first sight of their spouse was at the wedding ceremony. A marriage at that time involved an alliance between families. The bride's duty was to fit into the joint family. She had to do her husband's bidding and learned that her husband was her personal god. But her husband had a higher power, his father. The eldest man in the household was the *yejma:nru* 'household head'. He had lifetime tenure in this position. His wife, the *yejmanti,* retained power as long as her husband was alive. The proverb *atte wand ka:lu, sose wand ka:lu* 'there is a time to be a mother-in-law and a time to be a daughter-in-law' was salient for this generation. The young daughter-in-law entered her husband's household as a visitor until

TABLE 4.1: AGE AT MARRIAGE

	Generation One	Generation Two	Generation Three	Generation Four
Age at Marriage				
Women	N=21	N=8	N= 29	N=16
Women Range	8–15	12–21	14–33	20–29 (limited data)
Mean	11	15	21	23
Mode	13	14	21	21
Median	12	15	21	23
Age difference with spouse				
Range	5–30	3–14	2–10	3–11 years
Mean	12	9	5	6.3
Mode	10	4	6	none
Median	10	6	6	7
Men	N= 7	N =10	N=24	N=13
Men Range	16–44	17–28	20–34	25–36 (in progress)
Mean	24.5	24.8	26.5	28
Mode	None	25	27–28	29
Median	25	None	27	29

Source: Adapted from Ullrich 1987, pp. 618–19.

puberty. Her mother-in-law taught her and occasionally abused her.

Spirit possession for this and the next generation (Ullrich 1993: 647–9) provided a bride with an opportunity to adjust. This necessitated trips with one's husband to healers. Other members in the household did the possessed woman's work. At times her husband did this work. When I asked one woman who had a history of spirit possession whether she was depressed when she was first married, she responded with the comment, 'I could not be depressed. My being depressed would upset the joint family'. The following year when I again talked with her about depression, she surprised me by saying, 'What do you think? Of course I was depressed'. She talked with her youngest daughter-in-law, a woman with a college education, about her difficulty in adjusting to marriage. Her mother-in-law's experiences as a bride shocked and saddened the younger woman, as members of different generations hold such diverse views of marriage. Differentiated by generation and by education, she and her mother-in-law experienced different cultures.

In the 1960s beating one's wife for her mistakes was common. Moreover, women now in their seventies and above believe that this is a husband's right—if his wife 'does him wrong'. The definition of wrong has been reinterpreted over time in this generation from a husband's being dissatisfied with the way his wife polished the silver or went somewhere without his permission to —and this was left to my imagination but I think that adultery meets the criteria for 'grave error in judgment'.

Just being able to take refuge at one's parental home is a major change for an abused wife now. In 1964, an abused wife who sought refuge at her parental home was denied protection. Her parents returned her to her husband's household. Others in Totagadde avoided involvement, although his parents partitioned the land and arranged for the troublemaker son to build a house located on the distant end of the hamlet. Men had the opportunity to give free reign to their anger. The age difference between husband and wife (Table 4.1) and the cultural respect for the husband gave a woman few options. The difference in age between husband and wife ranged from five to thirty years for the twenty-one women of this generation (Ullrich 1987b: 618).

Women's realm was inside the house. When a visitor came, the women retreated to the inner part of the house. They stood when entertaining male guests. Indeed, some have apologized to me for standing on their own porch and explained that they showed visitors respect by standing in their presence. Should they wish to express an opinion which contradicted their husband, they talked to the wall. Men provided the connection to the outside world.

Birth control in the 1960s was abstinence for members of the first generation. The number of children a couple had ranged from 2–13, with a mean of 5.6 children, a mode of 3, and a median of four–five (Ullrich 1987: 623). Their daughters and daughters-in-law have added abortion, IUDs, and tubal ligations to the birth control repertoire. One needed two sons for the ritual involving death ceremonies—an heir and a spare. Women who had one child were described as *ka:ge banje*, 'crow barren'. Members of the current college-education generation are unaware of this term. Indeed, many choose to limit their family size to one child. The number of children range from 0 to 3 with a mean of 1.3, a mode of 2, and a median of 2.

The life stories of two women of the first generation illustrate their time. (Totagadde residents gave me permission to relate their life stories, agreeing that pseudonyms or initials provided sufficient anonymity.) One woman, J.G., married before puberty. She had a difficult adjustment to marriage, which manifested itself in spirit possession (a *pishaci*). Her husband took her to many healers, but religious healers were unsuccessful in their treatment. When her husband took her on a pilgrimage and taught her a mantra and meditation, she recovered and maintained meditation with the mantra for her entire life. J.G. had a respectful relationship with her husband. According to tradition, she never said his name and he never said her name. When she disagreed with him, she spoke to the wall. In that way he heard her opinion, but she could never be said to argue or contradict him. In this relationship there was affection and love. However, she maintained a deference and respectful distance from him. He taught her to read, so both were literate. They had four sons and five daughters who survived to adulthood. She also lost three infants.

The second woman, T.S., married before puberty. Her husband beat her. As a result, she left the room whenever he entered the room. She never spoke to him and referred to him as *muduka* 'old man'. He had a village-wide reputation for anger. His daughter-in-law commented that he swore at people, including the gods. 'If he dropped a (statue or picture of a) god, he might say "let it rot, let it be destroyed, whore, or son of a widow". He talked like that about my husband and his wife when they were not present', the daughter-in-law said. T.S. had six children—three sons and three daughters—who lived to adulthood. She had also lost six infants. Both T.S. and her husband were illiterate.

J.G. reflects the early marriages in which the joint family provided the core. The husband-wife relationship was less important. However, through her spirit possession she gained a close relationship with her husband. Her respect for him was paramount. She ate from his plate after him, as she believed men should eat before women. In every possible way she honored him with respect. T.S., however, had no respect for her husband whom she ignored. She most certainly had her own plate. She slept with the grandchildren, whereas J.G. always slept with her husband. Many years after their husbands died, J.G.'s respect and T.S.'s bitterness remained palpable. Those who grew to love and respect their husbands focused on their husband's positive qualities, whereas those who experienced physical and verbal abuse remembered their husbands with contempt.

THE SECOND GENERATION

Marriage for women of this generation varied from a pre-pubertal marriage at age twelve to marriage around age twenty-one (Table 4.1. Age at Marriage). When some women expressed dissatisfaction with the fiancé chosen for them in the first clash of wills with their fathers, their fathers went so far as literally to whip their daughters into submission. Others out of respect for their fathers refused to state an opinion after a prospective groom came to view them. Many women in this generation had a primary school education followed by their marriage.

Although women were confined to the house and the village,

they wished for wider horizons. Husbands regarded their wives and daughters as afraid to do anything on their own. Opinions went unstated. Wives believed that their husbands took credit for any successes and blamed their wives for any failures. One example was a husband who went to have new clothes made for the children. He forgot that the children had grown over the past year and held his wife accountable when the new clothes were too small for their children.

J.G.'s oldest daughter had a pre-pubertal marriage. However, her second daughter, J.A., married at age nineteen and had a primary school education. Neither her oldest daughter nor J.A. expressed any opinion about her future husband. However, J.A. experienced so much strife in her marriage that her father let all his succeeding children choose their spouses. Moreover, J.A.'s husband rarely sent her to visit her parents. This infuriated J.G. who raised J.A.'s children so they could attend Totagadde schools. J.A. told me that with her family's limited resources, her brother's education was more important than hers. However, all of her younger sisters who belong to the third generation have college degrees. J.G.'s third daughter married a Havik Brahmin, her tutor. Her fourth daughter had an inter-caste marriage to one of her non-Brahmin college classmates after she had graduated from college. That this match met with her father's approval shows how rapidly change occurred in this society. This father was the same person who in the 1960s believed religious purity prevented his sitting on the same bench with non-Brahmins and despite the protest of his children insisted that only Brahmins could dine inside his home. By the 1970s he reflected on how much he had changed and stated that hospitality to his children's friends had priority over ritual purity.

T.S.'s daughters married before puberty. Her daughters-in-law married around age eleven to age thirteen. One daughter-in-law, S.P., married at age twelve, but had already attained menarche. S.P., a second generation woman, indicated that parents with an unmarried daughter who attained puberty were supposed to abandon their daughter in the forest, but I have no case histories of this practice. She reported that in reality they quickly arranged their daughter's marriage and on the day before the wedding performed a ritual to atone for a woman's marriage after menarche, *stri: samska:ra*. By the third generation this had been incorporated into the marriage ritual, because women of succeeding generations have all married after puberty. This includes all of T.S.'s granddaughters and her great-granddaughters.

S.P. reported that her wedding night proved traumatic for her and her husband. She ran from the bedroom in fear; he was furious. As she reflected on this in 2008, she reported that sexual relations for a twelve-year-old is tantamount to physical abuse (*himse*). She observed respect for her husband, but never developed intimacy. She observed the practice of sleeping without a blouse, as she believed that her husband's touching her blouse while they were sleeping would shorten his life (Ullrich 1987: 619). Throughout her marriage she emphasized his god-like features, her obedience, and her worship of him. However, she avoided his company and was very much a silent partner. When she felt depressed, she was unable to hear his supportive comments. Although she wanted a companionate relationship, she was unable to transcend her own anger at her father for arranging this marriage necessitating the painful renunciation of her indulgent father who represented her childhood. Kaker pointed out that Indian fathers tend to withdraw from their daughters at puberty (2007: 32). She frequently reported that her husband was too good for her. Her attributed his good fortune and prosperity after his marriage to her.

Women of this second generation visited each other frequently in the village. However, when there were visitors from outside of the village, they retreated into the kitchen and their husbands spoke for them. Wives who made decisions without asking their husbands risked physical abuse. If a wife was unexpectedly absent from home when her husband returned from town, he might beat her in anger. Husbands felt that women were afraid to do anything on their own. Their bragging about how good the lives women had because they needed to make no decisions denied the anger they felt when wives did make decisions. With spousal abuse in this generation as in the preceding generation, no one interfered. Wife abuse was less common in this generation than in the preceding generation and it was the last generation in which others silently tolerated wife abuse.

Birth control became an option for the second generation.

Some used abortion, although the elders in the family disapproved. Several men obtained vasectomies. The first man to obtain a vasectomy waited until he had two sons; the second, his brother, decided upon a vasectomy after the birth of one son. Vasectomy was the method of choice until a happily married couple had a negative experience with vasectomy. At that time there was no post-vasectomy follow-up, and the wife became pregnant. After much marital conflict, the couple discovered that his vasectomy had been unsuccessful. After that, tubal ligation became the non-reversible birth control method of choice. Women in this generation also tried intrauterine devices. Wives often initiated consideration for birth control. The priest's wife boasted that she was the first to have a tubal ligation. She and her husband discussed this and told her father after the operation. He was furious, but another couple had consulted her father who had disapproved. After that, the wife was unable to persuade her husband to disobey his father-in-law and allow the tubal ligation. Although culturally people stated that two sons were necessary, some wives felt that their land holdings were insufficient to support two sons. Vatuk (1980) emphasized the requirement of a son to care for his parents in their old age. However, in Totagadde the rhetoric was on the need for a son to conduct one's funeral rites. One woman without the requisite two sons but with many daughters suffered a life-threatening miscarriage. However, her parents urged her to have the requisite two sons— or else, her husband might 'become crazy—' as his father had suffered from schizophrenia. (Her children have limited their family size to one or two children. Two of her children have two daughters each, one has one son, the others have both a son and a daughter.)

Women in this second generation longed for their husbands to consult them. This is the last group of women who viewed their husbands as their personal gods. Some ways in which women illustrated their respect included always sitting with their head lower than their husband, standing when relatives were visiting, serving their husbands, and eating from their husband's banana leaf or plate. Ideally the husband would leave some food on his plate, which would serve as a 'gift' to his wife. During this generation wives began to challenge the belief that women were inferior to men and that husbands were a wife's personal deity. While women of the third and fourth generations may respect their husbands, their husbands have descended from their pedestals.

Marital intimacy for wives in this generation had an element of fear and the necessity for obedience. Some wives harbored a lifelong anger at their fathers for arranging their marriage against their wishes. They may have gone on to describe their marriages as happy, but the women of this generation all regarded marriage as traumatic. The time immediately after marriage posed many difficulties to the bride. Adjustment to marriage proved difficult, with depression a common phenomenon. The first year of marriage involved frequent visits to the woman's home. Some men of this second generation attributed this custom to aiding a woman's adjustment to marriage.

This second generation also seemed the most idealistic. Its members wanted to choose their grooms believing that love marriages were preferable to arranged marriages. They, unlike their husbands, would accept intercaste marriages. Education was also a key to economic independence and then personal independence. They were curious about American sexual practices. However, they hoped their husbands would not 'bother them a lot about sex'. They idealized the occasional woman political leader and the woman with a job. But these remained ideals which members of this generation had no opportunity to realize. Since they knew that these were not choices available to them, they could maintain the ideals and try to provide opportunities for their daughters.

During this generation, husbands shifted from an ideal of passivity for wives to one of assertiveness, an ideal generally applied to the next or third generation. However, in this second generation one woman acted to save the family land from her husband's gambling debts. There was no formal divorce, but after the courts awarded her control of the land, he moved out. She also had control of his portion of the land because he was ruled incompetent to manage the land secondary to his gambling problem. Her saving the land for the next generation, her children, illustrates the strength of the intergenerational ties and the preservation of the land for her sons. Initially, when she took over the land, Havik Brahmin sentiment censured her for taking management control from her husband, yet at the time of her death there was only praise and respect for her courage.

While there was a strong patriarchal tone to the second generation, the second and third generation Havik women often discussed the 'best marriages in town'; both of which belong to the second generation. The women assessed these husbands as the most caring. I walked in on one of the couples during an intimate display of affection. Unnoticed, I quietly left. Yet both these husbands and wives always shared with each other, at times making decisions which relatives considered unfair to the husband. In one case when the time came for their children to attend college, the wife moved with her children to the college town so she could 'cook for them'. Since she was a woman who hated cooking and was consequently a poor cook, her real role was as a chaperone. The husband remained alone in Totagadde. The son has stayed in the college town where he developed a business selling Totagadde produce, while the wife moved back after the children completed their education. The other couple featured a wife whose serious illness in her twenties made obvious her husband's devotion. Since her recovery he has consulted her in decision-making and encouraged her participation in his business enterprises.

THE THIRD GENERATION

Marriage for women in the third generation occurred upon completion of their education, from a high school education or college. Those women who failed their high school examinations kept this a secret; some retook the examinations so that they would have a degree. Fathers arranged marriages for those who failed high school as quickly as possible. The fathers of this generation thought they would have difficulty arranging a marriage for a daughter with a master's degree. Between generations the emphasis shifted from the importance of a pre-pubertal marriage to educational qualifications. Some mothers-in-law boast about their daughter-in-law's educational achievements. If the daughter-in-law has one degree level above her husband, that serves as an indication of intelligence. A gap of more than one degree level moves a woman into a pool of more highly educated men.

In one case, a beautiful high school graduate had a suitor, but she wished to delay her marriage. When he came to see her, she was conveniently absent from her home. Older fathers thought that her father was a fool to delay his daughter's marriage into a wealthy family, advising that after marriage the suitor would stop his philandering. Other fathers whose daughters had recently graduated from high school empathized with the girl's youth, advising that she was definitely too young for marriage. There was widespread awareness that marriage for a girl under eighteen and a boy under twenty-one was illegal. The Sharda Marriage Act of 1929 and the Hindu Marriage Act of 1955 both set the minimum age for marriage for a man at twenty-one and for a girl at eighteen. Obviously, this had long been disregarded, but in the third generation some parents used it as a justification for delaying their daughter's marriage. All knew that as long as nobody brought a legal case, there was no problem with an underage marriage. (One non-Brahmin bride told me that she was fourteen. Her eavesdropping mother-in-law immediately came forward and contradicted the bride, saying that she was eighteen and that she did not know her own age; she hustled the bride away from me.)

In past generations fathers and male relatives made the marital decisions, consulting neither bride nor groom. By the third generation, physical force had given way to psychological force. Fathers expressed their anger at no longer pliant daughters. Certainly father's sisters empathized with their brothers when their nieces refused all suitors who failed to meet their qualifications. The father needed to locate the groom, but the daughter had veto power. This was the first group of women to articulate what they wanted in a husband. The general search list included a husband with a profession who lived in a nuclear family apart from his parents, and had a certain income. I was surprised at how fathers eventually found suitors who met a daughter's qualifications. The pleasure with which some of these women told me that they assented to the marriage evidenced the perceived degree of choice. For instance, one bride wanted to work but had no clear profession and her groom requested that she remain at home. She decided that the cost of insistence would have been at the expense of her happiness. She ended the conversation with the comment, 'I chose to marry him'. This woman had refused some of her father's favorite choices, but her father also valued this son-in-law.

One woman in the third generation expressed concern that her household might gain a reputation for women who become depressed upon marriage. She focused on her mother's and grandmother's depression at marriage. Her failure to realize just how widespread depression was at marriage in her mother and grandmother's generations suggests that this was no longer the case in the third generation. Yet unlike her mother and grandmother, she had chosen her husband. She was grateful to her father for supporting her choice and therefore kept her distress hidden. Her husband expected her to do the housework and cooking, whereas she had expected they would share. Both had careers. Moreover, she criticized her husband for providing insufficient private time with her in a joint family setting.

One woman married after her pre-university degree, assenting to the marriage. However, after the marriage she repeatedly commented in her husband's hearing that she had wanted to finish college but her father had insisted that she marry (Her younger sister completed college before her marriage and is employed in Bangalore). Her mother-in-law finally told her that her complaints were upsetting. After this daughter-in-law had her children, she attended college and earned her degree. (Her husband lacks a degree, so if this daughter-in-law had finished college before her marriage, she would have been too highly educated for the man who became her husband.)

To the mother-in-law's distress, her son and daughter-in-law argue. But in spite of the arguing or perhaps because they feel free to express their opinions, they have a strong marriage and consult each other. Women in this generation express themselves and argue with their husbands. Mothers-in-law may worry, but also notice that their sons and daughters-in-law have closer marital relationships than they had.

Women in this third generation demand to be heard. Whereas their mothers were silent perhaps out of self-preservation, these women generally have no fear of their husbands. They may pick their arguments, or they may choose silence as a judicious decision. They may ask their husband whether they can go to town with their friends. If the husband denies permission and his wife wishes to go, she will disregard her husband and go anyway. Such disobedience seems irrelevant in this generation. In the prior two generations this disobedience was likely to precipitate a beating.

These third generation women have discovered that they can talk with other women about how their religion might discriminate against them. Discretion is important, as each household decides what practices to observe. Those in urban areas report that their family would suffer if they observed the traditional taboos. This has co-occurred with secularization and urbanization (Ullrich 1992). Education has become more important than segregation of women because of menstrual taboos. Women in this generation observed the taboos when at home, but when attending high school and college they felt no need to specify their ritual status. Some avoid Totagadde in a ritually polluted state; some Totagadde women continue to observe, while others tactfully avoid drawing attention to their cessation of menstrual taboo observation.

With increased education women may have an opportunity for economic independence. Those who lack such skills or lack education are at greatest risk for abuse. To my knowledge, four Havik husbands abused their wives in this third generation. One endured the abuse in silence. There were no screams to hear, because as a neighbor surely I would have heard them. He pinched her and bruised her. Finally she had endured all the abuse she could tolerate. So she ran for refuge into the house where I was staying. She felt her options were to leave or to commit suicide. Her husband tried to follow her into the house to beat her and drag her back, but my host forcibly ejected him. She stayed and we talked until her parents came to take her home. Embarrassed about her limited education, she said that she had only completed the seventh grade. The Havik men of Totagadde gathered and marched on the husband's house with plans to give him a dose of his own abuse. However, he hid in the kitchen where his mother latched the door. This husband abused his wife to get at the joint bank account, which her father had opened upon her marriage. He put the account in his and his daughter's names. After awhile a panchayat, consisting of two male relatives which the husband chose and two which the wife's father chose, and one on whom both agreed, met and she was returned to her husband. Her father provided money for house repairs. Through this abuse the husband did gain access to his wife's money. This woman has remained reticent to talk with others and appears depressed.

In the third generation there were three cases in which women managed the family land. The first case also involved a woman who had a dysfunctional husband, an alcoholic who had actually sold the land to satisfy his craving for alcohol. His wife went to court and got the land returned to her. She still manages the land. While he was alive, she chained up the furniture so he was unable to sell it for alcohol. A second case also involved a woman whose husband was dysfunctional. She remained passive. Men of the second generation commented that she was too passive for her own good. The husbands in these two cases and in the second generation case above all physically abused their wives. However, the third case in the third generation involved a woman who managed the land so that her husband could pursue a banking career. He chose to limit his career, so he could help with the land, but at times when his work commanded his time, she managed it. Initially such assertiveness among women was because of the need to survive, but now women's assertiveness expands a couple's resources.

Two of the women in this generation who received beatings had married alcoholics. The assertive one has an eighth grade education; the passive one has a high school education. The assertive woman obtained control of her husband's land and moved to town where she worked. She maintained her Totagadde ties and is proud of how she managed a difficult situation. She sent all three of her children to college. The other women remained passive and endured his beatings, although her husband's parents partitioned the land so that they lived separately from them. This wife remained in Totagadde in isolation. Both of her children have college degrees and have found success in their chosen professions. Since her husband's death, her successful sons take her on trips and help her manage the land.

The fourth beaten woman of this generation has an iron will. She disliked her mother-in-law, so she returned to her parental home. This assertive woman told her husband she would return after he had a house built separate from her in-laws. He did so. She has told me that getting what she wants is worth a beating. She demanded her share of her father's land. Her decision to go to court for that alienated her from her brothers. She believes she acted appropriately and seems oblivious to others in Totagadde who criticize her aggressiveness.

Family size has dropped to one or two children in the third generation. The couple makes the decision about family size and in-laws and parents rarely comment directly. One mother commented to me that she wished her son and his wife would have a second child, but she knew that they planned to limit their family to one child. Tubal ligations, vasectomies, condoms, and oral contraceptives are all means of birth control for this generation. Parents are aware of the expenses associated with private English medium schools, colleges, and a modern lifestyle. One couple stated that they wanted to be able to send their son abroad to study. They had planned to limit their family to one child from the time of their marriage. Factors in determining family size include the wife's health, whether the wife works, and whether the first child presented great difficulties. When I asked about the need for sons to perform funeral rituals, my questions were ignored. Couples having a second child wanted a child of the opposite sex from the first child. One daughter-in-law had failed to realize that she might have a second daughter. She was so depressed at the birth of a second daughter that her mother-in-law told me that her daughter-in-law's psychiatric health had higher priority than bearing more children. When one Totagadde man's sister's had four daughters and her husband wanted to continue to try for a son, his brother-in-law told him he was crazy to keep having children, since his wife had high-risk pregnancies. Such interference is rare but may be effective, as this sister has had no more children.

In this generation the health of the mother (or one's wife) may take priority over having children. This third generation is the first to have prenatal care and hospital births as a matter of course. Women in preceding generations occasionally had hospital births for reasons of health or status. Women of all generations now fear home births. The Havik midwives, all of the first generation, are deceased. Traditions around pregnancy have also changed. Women choose to stay with their obstetrician until delivery. Mothers or mothers-in-law now come to the couple rather than the wife going to her parental home for the delivery. After the delivery, the wife now spends several months at her parental home. Just as pregnancy practices have changed, the treatment of a new mother may change.

In this generation concern with high risk pregnancies initially prompted prenatal care. This was extended to prenatal care for all. Women who have had high risk pregnancies may insist that one child is sufficient. But if the husband wants another child, the woman's parents tell her to obey her husband. These women have prenatal care and frequent monitoring. Those of the first generation who had sisters die in childbirth are not only vigilant about their granddaughters' care but also angry at those husbands who failed to obtain prenatal care for their wives.

Sexual intimacy has become more open with this third generation. Despite a mother-in-law's disapproval of a daughter-in-law's obvious interest in sex, women now expect fulfillment in this arena. The mother-in-law understands the husband who 'leaves his wife alone' and thinks this proper. Upon marriage, a newly married couple has its own room. If there is no extra room in the house, the household head has one built for a couple before the marriage.

THE FOURTH GENERATION

Although marriage for women generally occurs upon completion of their education, some complete their education after marriage. Some have chosen to pursue advanced degrees after marriage and then take up jobs. Before giving a horoscope, intermediaries ask what qualifications a suitor wants in a wife. Some now include a 'double degree' (master's degree), a bachelor in medicine, a law degree or a dental degree. As before, the groom needs to be taller and older than the bride and a light skin color indicates beauty. Some suitors want wives who plan for employment; others request educated wives who stay at home.

In contrast to the first and second generation where fathers arranged their daughters' marriages before puberty, twenty-three is now regarded as a good age for a bride (Table 4.1). When an unmarried woman is older than twenty-five, relatives and parents worry about finding a suitor. Initially, the girl's father distributes her horoscope to suitors whom he has selected. Before giving out his daughter's horoscope, he determines the suitor's earning capacity and the quality of the in-laws. Although the couple usually resides as a nuclear family, still the extended family's reputation is important. The daughter only learns about a prospective suitor after the preliminary investigation, and if she and he are both interested, relatives arrange a meeting for the couple to talk in private. After this talk they each may make a decision. Most frequently the suitor telephones or indicates to kinsmen his decision. If this is a love marriage—whether within the Havik Brahmin caste or outside the caste—, there is no comparison of horoscopes. When a man and woman agree to marry, relatives of both sides meet and this meeting precedes an engagement ceremony at the fiancée's home.

Sons often ask their mothers to come with them to look at a prospective bride, and these mothers feel honored to be included. One commented that she wondered whether her son would agree to marry such a plump woman, but she said nothing about this to her son. The decision was his, as he would live with her. The mother had liked everything else about her son's prospective bride. (They did decide to marry.) In the first two generations, marriages had occurred within a month of the decision. In Generation Four, from the time of the decision to marry the man and woman correspond and telephone each other. Relatives take note of whether the suitor is considerate, as well as whether the man and woman enjoy each other's company. The wedding can be broken off any time before the *mangalasu:tra* (wedding necklace) is tied. Elders believe a couple's engagement will not survive if the period is long, but the length of engagements is increasing.

Havik Brahmin marriage patterns now include an elaborate separate engagement ceremony, whereas previously the engagement was announced concurrently with the decision to marry. In 2003, when I asked what brides received at marriage, one bride's mother informed me that I forgot to ask about the 'welcoming of the groom' *wara upaca:ra*. This recent addition of the bride's family giving wedding presentations to the groom is optional. Originally the wedding involved a four-day celebration. Now the wedding is one day; the entry of a bride into her husband's household may be on the same or another day. However, inviting all the relatives for the announcement of the decision to marry and then relatives plus villagers for the engagement ceremony are recent innovations. Increased prosperity and extended engagements provide the background for these changes. Now both bride and groom see each other and talk before the engagement. The period after the formal engagement is a time for the couple to continue talking and to become better acquainted. This is often by phone or with a chaperone. The groom's side has priority over the bride's side as to the choice of marriage date. In the case of arranged marriages this is the accepted ritual. When the groom comes from abroad for the marriage, all participants accommodate the bridegroom's limited time away from graduate school or work.

All Brahmins in Totagadde receive an invitation to engagement ceremonies. Relatives on both sides also come. Engagement ceremonies have been held without the groom if he is studying or working abroad. Cumin seed and jaggery are given to all the guests. At this ceremony the priest determines the auspicious day and time for the wedding (*muhurta*). The elaborate engagement party had its origin in this generation. Previously only the bride and groom, their parents, and a priest were present for the engagement before the gods and the determination of the *muhurta*. Beginning with the elaborate engagement ceremony is an extended engagement period. In one case, the formal initial decision to marry was followed after several months by the engagement party and then months elapsed before the wedding. The couple wanted to prepare for life together. The girl had an impressive job in north India; the groom, in Bangalore. The bride and groom had to obtain time off from their jobs for the engagement and then for the wedding. The bride needed time to find a job in Bangalore and the groom wanted to find appropriate housing there.

When those of the second generation heard about the plans

for a long engagement, they assumed that neither side was serious about marriage. Although they were uncomfortable with the shift from engagement to marriage within a month to extended engagements, their real discomfort may be that allowing a couple to become better acquainted before marriage introduces the possibility of a sexual relationship. Some women in the fourth generation forbade their fiancés from visiting because they have feared for their reputations. Aunts and grandparents have worried that girls would find themselves pregnant and abandoned. To my knowledge unless parents have intervened to separate the couple, premarital sexual relationships have resulted in marriage. Some women assumed that love marriages have involved premarital sex. In cases where both families are supportive of the couple's decision, this has not apparently been a concern.

During my 2008 visit, Havik women informed me that now no woman marries without her own consent. When I asked daughters about their marriage choices, some said that they trusted their fathers to make good decisions for them. This seemed to be the politically correct response to my question, as some have gone on to make love marriages without consulting either parent. On the other hand, fathers take their responsibility seriously and worry about finding grooms with whom their daughter will be happy and who will provide well for them.

One woman of this generation became upset when the initial phase of marriage failed to meet her romantic expectations. She was vociferous in her disappointment. Indeed, she wished a separation. Her father, stepmother, and husband remained supportive, but obtained a psychiatric evaluation for her. She received psychiatric treatment for depression. Some older men accused her of being a demonness for making such demands of her husband. Their wives remained judiciously silent. This was the first time a bride openly discussed her disappointment in marriage and openly considered divorce. After some time passed, she adjusted to the marriage and developed desired intimacy, and a good marriage. The strongly expressed feelings among the Totagadde Havik Brahmin men, as well as the bride's expressed feelings, illustrated that a marked change had occurred among the different generations with regard to marital expectations.

Many brides are eager for the wedding night. The room is

decorated with flowers. Lamps are lit from the lamp in front of the household gods (*de:varu mane*). After dinner the bride and groom sit before the gods. The groom blindly breaks four coconuts and puts them in his wife's sari. If the eye of the coconut comes, then a son will be born. If the half of the coconut which the bride draws out is smooth, the child will be a daughter. If the coconut break is smooth, there will be no need for a cradle the first year. If the edge is jagged, a child will be born the first year. Those present sing when the couple goes to their room. Then they ask the groom, 'Do you want gold or a woman?' (*honnu be:ka: heNNu be:ka:*)? (Another version is 'Do you want fruit or a woman? *(haNNu be:ka: heNNu be:ka:*)? A recurring pattern is for the couple to wait for another night to consummate their marriage. They discuss this and whether they are tired. Honeymoons are increasingly common but may occur several weeks after the marriage. While many brides and grooms appear to have good adjustments, some return from their honeymoon uncomfortably silent. In some cases the brides have returned home; in other cases the dissatisfied grooms have returned the bride to her parental home. In some cases with apparent marital difficulty immediately after the marriage the couple have reconciled.

One wife whose husband recently beat her for leaving an umbrella on the porch received support from her mother who came and took her back to her parental home. A year has passed and she has yet to return. None of the women with whom I discussed this believe that she was at fault. The young women think that a divorce would be the most appropriate action, as they think her return would result in further physical abuse. Older people pointed out that she was poorly educated and her family was poor and they think she should return. Others, fearing her husband would follow his father's pattern of wife abuse, had told him to treat his wife with consideration and to avoid his father's example. Should there be a divorce, many predicted that no father would give his daughter in marriage to a family now known for wife abuse in two generations.

Many women of this latest generation are professionals and reside in urban areas. Married women have become college professors, software engineers, elementary school teachers, agricultural officers, telecommunication officers, and bankers. The men have become college professors, software engineers, school teachers, agricultural officers, lawyers, doctors, bankers, and pharmaceutical researchers. For success in these professions assertiveness is essential. While intelligence (*curuku*) is important for members of all the generations, assertiveness (*jo:ru*) is newly important. The women in the first two generations consider assertiveness a negative quality. Members of this fourth generation proclaimed their assertiveness. Those of all generations are proud of the accomplishments of the third and fourth generation. They comment that a month's salary for some women as well as men is more than a year's income from Totagadde crops.

With economic independence and culturally endorsed assertiveness, divorce has also become an option. One professional woman in Totagadde initiated a divorce. Her husband pleaded with her to stay, but she insisted that she wished to resume her career. A woman from a nearby town became a banker after her husband divorced her. One has remarried. Some village women wonder why the other has yet to remarry. Others in the fourth generation wonder whether sexual incompatibility was the reason behind the divorce. The husband who divorced his wife gave as the reason for the divorce that she was not a woman. Some wonder whether he failed to treat her with consideration and so she avoided sex with him. Both women have good reputations and are attractive. When I go to functions now, the men inform me that the courts are now filled with divorce cases. Remarriage has recently become a possibility.

In the prior three generations widows were stigmatized. In this generation elders think a woman needs a companion. A marital companion is preferable to a bad reputation from men who might take advantage of a woman.

There is less visiting among women in the village, although at the same time women are more adept as hostesses in a wider range of settings. These women travel by themselves, those in the United States have often flown alone back and forth to India. They also may travel by themselves throughout India. In one case a family regarded their daughter as so beautiful that they were afraid to send her to college, but after her marriage she has traveled from north India to Karnataka alone to attend family functions. Even without formal education, women in this fourth generation have learned to manage on their own.

CONCLUSION

'Silence is golden' may have been appropriate for the older generations of women in Totagadde. This silence may have prevented abuse; but it also limited intimacy and hid wifely resentment and bitterness. Women of the first two generations avoided arguments with their husbands out of fear that their husbands would desert them. Although I know of no such cases of desertion, the insecurity of economic dependence often led to a wife's fear and resentment of her husband. Wives did not like to ask for things, even things they needed. The silences that circumscribed marital intimacy decreased with each generation. Even women of Generation Four felt that yelling at and arguing with their husbands was inappropriate. However, they do so and the importance of having their say overrides prior socialization. This has produced compromises and increased intimacy within marriages.

The age at the time of marriage has increased with each generation. Even without the accompanying education, an older age at marriage gives greater maturity and a sense of one's self. I know of no woman in Totagadde of any generation who believes this is bad. They praise the changes and even associate them with greater prosperity. With an increase of age at marriage from pre-pubertal years to the mid-twenties, women have developed clear senses of their own worth and value system. They are less likely to be intimidated and more likely to expect a companionate marriage. Divorce and remarriage have even become options.

Many couples live in urban areas. Their attachment to their families—parents and in-laws—remains a factor in some choosing where to settle. Husbands and wives who have lived abroad may decide they prefer to return and live near parents and in-laws. Even those who reside in the United States have frequent visits from relatives. Although the family residential patterns have changed from joint to nuclear, they may become joint when Totagadde parents are no longer able to work the land and reside on their own. Many parents plan to live with a son in an urban area.

Education, increased age at marriage, and professional opportunities have increased openness within marriage. The marital couple has become the focal unit of family organization. This is a marked change from the time when the couple was subservient to the elders in a joint household. Best of all this evolution has had the support of all generations in the Totagadde Havik Brahmin community.

NOTES

*I am grateful to the American Institute of Indian Studies which funded my research in 1964–6, as well as in 1975–6, 1986–7, and 1994–5 as well as to the American Philosophical Society which funded my research trip in 1985. I returned for a six-week preliminary study of depression in 1964. I have funded my visits to Totagadde since 1998. This has provided me with a way of maintaining the Kannada language as well as my relationships with Totagadde residents. In addition, I telephone my host family for specific questions about facts and to maintain relationships. I thank the editors Ann Gold, Karen Leonard and Gayatri Reddy, as well as Toby Feibelman, Doranne Jacobson, Barbara Ramusack, Charlene Smith, and Rob Stuart-Vail for their constructive comments on context and editorial assistance. I am responsible for any flaws in data or interpretation.

1. I started research in Totagadde, a village approximately 200 miles northwest of Bangalore, as a linguist. Later I trained as a psychiatrist. My research has a multidisciplinary approach with anthropological, linguistic, and psychiatric dimensions.

REFERENCES

Erikson, E.H. (35th Anniversary Edition) (1985). *Childhood and Society*, New York: W.W. Norton and Company.

Kakar, S. (1996, rpt. 2007). *Indian Identity*, New Delhi: Penguin Books.

Ullrich, H.E. (2000). 'A Thirty-Year Perspective on Hindu Marriage and the Law: Cultural Confirmation of Change'. *With This Ring Divorce, Intimacy, and Cohabitation from a Multicultural Perspective*, ed. R. Robin Miller and Sandra Lee Browning, Stamford, Connecticut: Jai Press Inc., pp. 5–18.

—— (1994). 'Asset and Liability: The Role of Female Education in Changing Marriage Patterns among Havik Brahmins', in *Women, Education, and Family Structure in India*, ed. Carol Chapnik Mukhopadhyay and Susan Seymour, Boulder: Westview Press, pp. 187–212.

—— (1993), 'Cultural Shaping of Illness: A Longitudinal Perspective on Apparent Depression', *The Journal of Nervous and Mental Disease*, 181 (10): 647–9.

—— (1992). 'Menstrual Taboos among Havik Brahmin Women: A Study of Ritual Change', *Sex Roles*, 26 (1/2): 19–40.

—— (1987). 'Marriage Patterns among Havik Brahmins', *Sex Roles*, 16 (11/12): 615–35.

Vatuk, S. (1994) 'Schooling for What? The Cultural and Social Context of Women's Education in a South Indian Muslim Family', *Women, Education, & Family Structure in India*, ed. Carol Chapnick Mukhopadhyay and Susan Seymour, Boulder: Westview Press: pp. 135–64.

Vatuk, S. (1982). 'Purdah Revisited: A Comparison of Hindu and Muslim Interpretations of the Cultural Meaning of Purdah in South Asia'. in *Separate Worlds: Studies of Purdah in South Asia*, ed. Hanna Papanak and Gail Minault, New Delhi: Chanakya Publications, pp. 54–78.

—— (1980). 'The Aging Woman in India: Self-Perceptions and Changing Roles', in *Women in Contemporary India and South Asia*, ed. Alfred de Souza, New Delhi: Indian Social Institute and Manohar, pp. 280–309.

5

Family Strategies in Khalapur, UP, Over the Twentieth Century: Asha Ram Teacher and His Khandan

PAULINE KOLENDA

INTRODUCTION: BACHELOR—SONS AND INFANT AND CHILD DEATHS

The concept of the stem family is common in the study of European peasantry. Originated by Frederic Le Play, a French nineteenth-century sociologist, it refers to the practice of only one child inheriting the family farm from his forbears. In Conrad Arensberg's study of the Irish family (Arensberg 1940), it was the youngest child in a sibling-set who was supposed to remain at home to care for his or her parents and eventually to inherit the farm. A non-inheriting brother could choose to become a priest or a seaman; a sister could marry or become a nun. Many such siblings emigrated to other parts of the UK or to the USA. The stem family was found to be common in Sweden, Spain, and other parts of Europe, as well as Japan. Sometimes the heir was the eldest son, sometimes the youngest; sometimes a daughter could be the heiress. It seemed to be the last stage before peasants in Europe 'were no more' (Lopreato 1967).

The stem family is not characteristic of Indian kinship systems, but Sylvia Vatuk found something like it among the middle-class families in parts of Meerut, UP in the 1960s. Many of the men who headed these families were in-migrants from villages or other towns, residing in Meerut because they had found white-collar jobs there. She wrote:

> Traditionally, all a man's sons would be expected to remain either in the parental household of close by, but because urban conditions often make this arrangement impracticable or impossible, in the mohallas, at least one son is expected to remain with his parents until their death. . . . This situation suggests the emergence of the stem family pattern in the urban setting. (Vatuk 1972: 70)

A trend toward stem family also appeared in the western UP village of Khalapur. In north India generally, only sons can inherit their father's land—not daughters—but all sons are supposed to inherit equally. This means that inherited land is sub-divided by one man's multiple sons, and individual holdings over a number of generations can become too small to support a family. This is especially true where there is a shortage of uncultivated land into which to extend cultivation or where it is difficult for other reasons for a farmer to increase his land-holding. I see the practice of keeping one or more adult sons unmarried, rather common in the north Indian village of Khalapur in the first half of the twentieth century, as a move toward the eventual adoption of the stem family. While a bachelor son inherited his portion of land from his father, he lacked sons to whom to pass his land. Usually, the bachelor officially adopted one of his married brother's sons who, after his death, inherited the bachelor's land. A bachelor in one generation prevented the sub-division of his portion of land for at least a generation. That keeping some sons as bachelors was a purposeful strategy on the part of Khalapur landed villagers was confirmed to me in 1984 by a Bania woman, herself the mother of four as yet unmarried sons, when she said,'It used to be if one had four sons, one married off only two, but now, one married off all four.'

Research by others in India, as well as my own in Khalapur (Kolenda 1998), indicates very high infant and child mortality rates through most of the twentieth century. For example, in the khandan of Brahman Asha Ram Teacher, an account of which appears in the second half of this essay, his wife, born in 1918 and married in 1935, bore six children, of whom only two sons lived to adulthood.

In Khalapur, as in most of north India, there was a strong preference for sons over daughters (Miller 1981). Excess daughters, meaning more than one or two for a married couple, were rare in Khalapur family genealogies for much of the twentieth century, and all who reached adolescence were married, while unmarried adult sons were fairly common. The usual explanations for son-preference in India held true for Khalapur. Daughters married into other families and did not stay to care for their parents, while sons stayed, worked, earned and helped support their parents. True in Khalapur also was the requirement that a family give a dowry with a daughter in marriage, while a son's wife brought in a dowry. In Khalapur, there was a further explanation—the need for self-defense. The Rajputs, who made up almost half the population, and owned almost all the agricultural land, had had to fend off raiders right up through the nineteenth century as the remains in the front of the village of a fortress testified (Hitchcock 1956: 69, 177). In short, sons were needed until recently for defense of village, clan and family. Girls were less necessary as a single fertile woman could produce a number of sons for her husband's lineage.

Parents and grandparents could strategize with respect to marriages because they arranged the marriages of children. Whether blood relatives or not, boys and girls of the same caste within the same village could not marry, as all in the same village were considered kinsmen. To a son of the village, all the daughters of the village were his sisters or father's sisters or daughters. Wives came from other villages just as local daughters were married into other villages. A young girl's life changed, often traumatically when her bridegroom and his male party took her away to his village and home. This pattern of village exogamy was practiced by all castes in Khalapur and, for the system to work, by all the villages in the region.

I. RESEARCH

Anarkali, an unschooled Rajput, who had given birth to eleven children and supported education for the four sons and two daughters who had survived, asked about my work. After my reply, she said it was about *bhara* (increase) and *ghatra* (decrease).

Indeed, I was gathering the information that would make it possible to assess whether the families that composed a khandan were getting better off or worse off. Eventually, I could compare the khandans.

Khalapur was a very large village (about 5000 people in 1955 and almost double that in 1984). I lived there for 16 months in 1954–6 and returned again for four months thirty years later in 1984, and was there for a few weeks in 1985, 1986, 1997 and 1998. Between 1953 and 1956, Cornell University had a team of social scientists residing there and studying it. Each of us specialized in some aspect of village life. I focused on the untouchable sweepers and on the topics of caste, religion, kinship and family, while others studied economics, politics, language, child rearing, and governance. (A few of the published works emanating from the study of Khalapur include Dube 1958; Hitchcock 1956; Kolenda 1958, 1982, 1989, 1990, 1998, 2003; Minturn 1993; Minturn and Hitchcock 1966; Retzlaff 1962.) Upon my return in 1984, I was on my own, accompanied by a team of three women assistants. Fortunately, another anthropologist, J. Michael Mahar, aided by a local teacher and educated young men of the village, had finished a census of Khalapur in 1983. Their enumerations were made by khandan or minimal patrilineage, a social unit in terms of which villagers divided and identified themselves and their fellows. Essentially, a khandan was composed of the adult men who had a common grandfather plus their wives and children. To get a reasonably fair and complete view of a village with such a large population, I took a sample, drawing from the census every twentieth khandan, or 32 in all. A research assistant, Indira Sapru, and I visited the residences of all of these khandans in the spring of 1984, filling out questionnaires covering the amount of land owned, the crops sown and raised, material objects owned, cinema and TV-watching, and so on. I kept full notes of conversations and made genealogical charts and diagrams of living quarters for each khandan. In 1985 and 1986, we visited all the khandans again to do maternal histories with the women. Again in 1997 and 1998, we visited the khandans, and the khandan history in this paper, representing one out of the 32 khandans studied, compares two time periods—1984–6 and 1997–8.

Below I describe in detail a khandan in which three members were school teachers. In my sample of 32 khandans, there were eight male teachers and three female teachers living , suggesting that there might be 160 or more male teachers in Khalapur in 1983 (8 in a 5 per cent sample, then 160 in the population). I have chosen a khandan with teachers because teachers appeared to have been highly motivated both to become educated themselves and to educate their children. The increased availability of schooling and higher education was one of the greatest forces for change in Khalapur and in India generally in the last half of the twentieth century, and awareness of educational opportunity figured in family strategies.

To speak of family strategies, there must be a strategist. Indira Sapru and I talked with Brahman Asha Ram Teacher at length, and he voiced some of his intentions and the obstacles he encountered in trying to achieve his goals. He was a strategist. We talked less to other men of Asha's khandan, but I assume that what each accomplished, he intended to do—such as building a new house or tilling fields. I have had to speculate about the intentions and actions of dead men of the khandan and about those of some absent married daughters and their marital kin. I infer the strategy from actions that had to be planned for and thus were intended. When it comes to schooling of children, I assume the father of the children in question made the final decision about children attending, especially since there was considerable expense involved, but opinions and actions of mothers and the children themselves and possibly others entered into the success or failure of particular children.

There were two advantages to taking the khandan as the unit for interpretation and analysis. First, each khandan census record included four or five generations of male descendants of a single apical ancestor. We visited all those the census listed as in the khandan. Through interview and observation, we learned how single families grew into multiple families, and how brothers and cousin-brothers divided their households over generations. I could then compare the strategies of different households within a khandan and evaluate their successes and failures. Second, the men of the khandan in their prime, those in their forties or early fifties, had lived through the same decades and were to a certain extent responding to the same conditions in their environment, even though each had different material and human resources.

The kinship term 'cousin-brother' in English referred to male cousins. In the Hindi of Khalapur, all of a person's first cousins were called '*bhai*' (brother) or '*behan*' (sister). North Indians speaking English commonly refer to male cousins as 'cousin-brother' and I do that in the account of Asha's khandan later on, using the term 'cousin-brother' to mean the referent's father's brother's son.

Birth certificates or birth records were not customary in rural India. People undoubtedly varied in their degree of accuracy in giving their own and others' ages. For many individuals, I have had to estimate year of birth using whatever clues I had, and I have consistently included those estimated birth dates, so that the reader can have a sense of the time when the person lived and acted.

II. MILESTONES IN KHALAPUR HISTORY

An important factor that influenced a Khalapur khandan's struggle to survive and better itself was the caste to which it belonged. Asha's Brahman caste membership greatly influenced his and his khandan's life-chances.

The village traditional history held that the village was taken from some Jat caste occupants in the sixteenth century by the ancestors of the present-day Pundir Rajputs (Hitchcock 1956: 60), the dominant caste of Khalapur. The Rajputs composed about two-fifths of the population of Khalapur. The other three-fifths were composed of people of thirty-one other castes, mostly Hindu, a few Muslim (Hitchcock 1956: 23–4). Some of those invited to settle in Khalapur were enticed or rewarded with some land to till. This was probably the case with the Brahmans who were even in the mid-1950s one of the larger of the thirty-one other castes, composed of about 300 people (Hitchcock 1956: 24). The Brahmans were valued for their religious expertise. As household priests, they performed religious rites within the homes of Rajputs and others on scores of annual Hindu holy days. They read almanacs to determine auspicious and inauspicious days and times, and horoscopes to see if a proposed bride and groom's fortunes were compatible, and they performed Hindu weddings. They were respected for their purity and could thus cook for all other castes, since the food they prepared was pure.

Khalapur is just across the Jumna River from the Punjab, and in the Punjab in the last quarter of the nineteenth century, a Hindu reform movement, the Arya Samaj, developed. The Arya Samaj was anti-Brahman, and its influence over time may partly explain why the rich ritual life that was so much in evidence to me in the 1950s had declined by the 1980s. As Asha commented to us in 1984,

> He [grandfather Mamraj] used to do *puja*s (ritual offerings)—the Lakshmi puja at Diwali, the Saraswati puja at Dashera, and did *katha* (religious reading) from the *Ramayana* and *Sat Narayan*. Now that system [he used the English word] is gone. *Dharam kam hai.* [religious duty has diminished]. The *jiijman*'s [clients, here clients of the Brahman household priest)] have no time for this. They are busy with cultivation and selling crops and business. The celebration of the festivals goes on but not on a big scale.

Asha himself never did purohit work. 'After my education, I went into service.'

Various other milestones in the history of Khalapur affected family strategies. Elderly men born in the nineteenth century told me in the 1950s that until the 1920s, the Rajput dominant caste men of Khalapur were primarily herders. They were settled in a nucleated village, but their herd-boys took their animals daily to the plentiful pasture around the village. Especially important to each khandan was its *gheer* (compound) where cattle, water-buffaloes and horses were kept at night. The adult men and older boys of a khandan slept in a *chaupar* or men's house near the gheer and *bagar* (the women's quarters) to protect their animals, women, girls and small children from intruders.

In the latter part of the nineteenth century, the Rajputs of Khalapur were known for being cattle-raiders, stealing cattle from smaller villages across the district border from them. Since the police of the district to the south could not pursue criminals who had crossed over into the district to the north, the Khalapur raiders usually succeeded in their depredations. In the late nineteenth century, British officials believed the Rajputs of Khalapur to be so guilty of female infanticide that a contingent of soldiers was stationed nearby for a few years to try to stop the practice (Hitchcock 1956: 78).

Some Rajput elders had served as soldiers during World War I; some had gone to fight in the British Indian army in the Middle East. In the early decades of the twentieth century, the most likely alternative for a Rajput man to supervising the cultivation of his family's land or husbanding his family's animals was to serve in the military. Then, in the 1920s, a canal from the Ganges River was extended eastward to Khalapur, making possible the more adequate irrigation of crops (Retzlaff 1962: 13). The growing of wheat, pulses, and rice became more extensive. Farmers also grew small stands of sugar cane to supply themselves with *gur* (brown sugar). In the 1930s, sugar mills were erected, one to the south of Khalapur in Muzaffarnagar, and one to the north in Deoband (Minturn and Hitchcock 1966: 4), encouraging the growing of sugar cane as a cash crop. Dirt roads to facilitate the bullock carts carrying cane from the cane fields of Khalapur to the mills were established. The building by many landed khandans of fired-brick women's houses marked the increasing prosperity. The unit of such houses was typically a row of three or more rooms, fronted by an arched portico. The most elaborate had three such rows around a rectangular courtyard. The whole compound was surrounded by a mud-brick wall. In earlier times, the women of a khandan all shared one room in an adobe house for sleeping in inclement weather and for storage; in the new brick houses, each married woman usually had her own room where she stored her grain and goods and where she and her unmarried daughters and small sons slept in cold or wet weather. In dry warmer weather, they slept outside in the courtyard. The men of the khandan continued to sleep communally in a men's *chaupar* or *baithak* outside the women's quarters and in or near their *gheers* (cattle compounds).

Around 1906, a primary school for boys was founded in Khalapur; it went to the fourth or fifth grade or 'standard'. In the 1920s, a *pathshala* was founded with eight grades, offering a Hindu religious education; in 1954, it had 25 male students, all of high-caste rank (Hitchcock 1956: 27). Asha Ram Brahman attended the primary school in Khalapur in the 1920s. I do not know whether his father, Dhuuli Brahman, a teacher during the 1910s, also attended the Khalapur primary school as a child. In 1954, the boys' primary school had an enrollment of 174 students. The Kanya Pathshala or girls school, founded in 1949, had 60 students in 1955 (Hitchcock 1956: 27). When I returned in 1984, there were eleven primary schools in Khalapur, most of them teaching both girls and boys.

After Independence in 1947, some prominent Rajputs of Khalapur organized to donate land and resources to build a high school. Opening in 1952, the new school at first went from sixth to eighth grade and gradually ninth, tenth or 'Matric' (for matriculation) were added, and later, eleventh and twelfth or 'Inter' (for Intermediate) were added. In 1953, the high school enrolled 425 male students from Khalapur and nearby villages and had eighteen teachers (Hitchcock 1956: 27–8). Astute farmers valued an educated son who could deal with government officials, and they gradually recognized that educated sons might get jobs outside the village.

In 1952 , Khalapur was chosen as a village to be improved by a government-sponsored Community Development Project (CDP). Assigned to work with villagers on agricultural and other improvements was a Village Level Worker. The sugar mills and the CDP encouraged the farmers of Khalapur to use improved seeds, fertilizer, pesticides and other inputs to have more bounteous harvests. The Green Revolution with improved wheat took off in the nearby Punjab in the mid-1950s, and Khalapur adopted this innovation as well.

The 1970s in India are especially remembered for the years of the Emergency declared by Prime Minister Indira Gandhi in 1975. During that period, Mrs. Gandhi's son, Sanjay Gandhi, spearheaded efforts to require government servants to limit the numbers of their children. Those with 'enough' children were required to subject themselves to vasectomies, and other birth control programs included traveling health units that set up camps where rural women could quickly have tubal-ligations. Some camps were held near Khalapur and some women had 'the operation'. A Primary Health Care Center, a small medical resource, was established in Khalapur in the mid-1950s.

In the years between 1956 and my return to Khalapur in 1984, the growing of sugar cane increased enormously and with it, the prosperity of the landed. The enrollment of the school increased. In 1968, the first girls attended the high school. Parents had finally learned that their educated sons wanted to marry educated brides, so they had begun to send their daughters to school beyond the fifth class in primary school. In 1984, there were 1,200 students in the high school. More than half were Rajputs, and about half were girls. About half came from Khalapur; about half, mostly of the Jat caste, came from villages around Khalapur. There were very few low or middle-ranking caste students.

What struck me first upon my return in 1984 was the spread of dwellings and cattle yards into what had been the pastures around the village. Indeed, there seemed to be very little pasture land anymore. Most farmers, rather, brought fodder to their animals in the *gheer*s. In place of mud houses, many cultivators had built large fired-brick houses, most nicely finished with stucco.

Some castes were dis-employed. The Watercarriers were no longer needed, as high caste women now had pumps in their courtyards and did not need watercarrier servant women to carry pots of water from the village wells into their courtyards. Many watercarriers now worked on local brown sugar making operations (*kaleshyar*s). The potters, the goldsmiths and shoemakers likewise were dis-employed, as people preferred the wares available in the nearby towns. The potters, used to having horses or donkeys to carry clay or pots, had taken to running horse-drawn *boogie*s (platform on wheels) back and forth to the nearby towns in a kind of taxi service (one *boogie* could easily carry eight or ten persons). The laundrymen (*dhobis*) had mostly left, as women preferred to launder their own (new since the 1950s) nylon saris. Life had become easier for women, since electricity meant that there were at least a half dozen local mills where wheat could be ground into flour, and rice could be husked, so they did not have to spend hours in the early morning grinding grain in heavy hand mills in preparation for the morning chapattis. Some houses also had electricity. A number of village sons had become trained to be Ayurvedic, Homeopathic or Unani doctors and served in the village, mostly prescribing over-the-counter 'Western' patent medicines and giving injections. There were many more shops than in the 1950s, some traditional—selling grain, soap and spices—, but some selling medicines. One shop rented and repaired bicycles, and buses came once a day on a paved road connecting the village to the nearby towns. A Bank of India had been erected in the pasture near the bridge.

Most significantly I felt the orientation had changed from inward-looking to outward-looking. In the 1950s, a sufficient and satisfying life could be led within the village. Artisans made shoes, wove cloth, made dishes, and made jewelry for village daughters to wear as brides. Over 30 Hindu holy days had to be celebrated, lavishly if possible, with special foods and elaborate home altars and rituals presided over by the family Brahman. One felt sorry for the lone son who worked outside in some town or city.

By the 1980s, brides brought television sets in their dowries. Enormous escalation had occurred in the content and costs of dowries as consumerism took hold in India generally. Cinema theaters in the nearby towns were attended especially by the older schoolboys, and enterprising young men brought movies to the village via a VCR. Radios and wrist watches were widespread. Fathers who could afford the high cost of the required dowry wanted to arrange marriages for their daughters with educated young men who, preferably, worked in a city. The city way of life beckoned.

Of course, all females in Khalapur still covered their heads. In the 1950s, married women covered their faces with the ends of their saris when on the pathways outside their houses. They were also supposed to crouch and freeze if a man passed them when they were outside. These customs, however, had disappeared when I returned in the 1980s. Women were still in purdah, and, indeed, married women seldom went out of their courtyards, but school girls were complaining about having to cover their heads. After all, they were daughters of the village; only the in-married women should have to cover their heads.

To help to understand Asha's khandan-history, I should mention various aspects of women's lives. First, there were two parts to wedding rites in the Khalapur area. The first part was the *shadi* that took place at the residence of the bride. The bridegroom and his all-male party came from his village to be entertained by the bride's people and for the wedding rite itself, involving Sanskrit recitation by a Brahman priest and the circling of a fire by the bride and groom. The day after the wedding rite, the bride was taken by the groom's party back to his village, where she stayed with his mother and other related women for a few days before her brother or some other male relative fetched her home. The second part of the wedding was the *chala* that took place months or even years after the shadi, when the bride had matured and presumably was ready for sexual intercourse and the bearing of children. Again the groom and his party came, were entertained for a day or two, and brought the bride back to the groom's village. Usually, the couple consummated their union after the chala. The bride might be brought home after a few weeks. In the early years of marriage, indeed, she might be at her parents' as much as she was in her marital home. The time between shadi and chala has grown shorter for Khalapur brides during the second half of the twentieth century as brides have married at later ages; by the 1980s, some mature brides had the shadi and chala *on* the same day.

A woman was expected to give birth at her *sasural* (the home of her husband's parents). She was aided in delivery by her mother-in-law and other females at her sasural and by a low-caste *dai* (midwife). The government had a trained midwife in the village since 1952 who some families called in to help, although she would not touch the birthing baby or the accompanying polluting bodily fluids; only a low-caste dai would do that. Village doctors might also be called to give injections against tetanus and to stimulate labor, and hospitals, nursing homes and doctors were increasing in the nearby towns of Muzaffarnagar and Deoband, so that Khalapur families could turn to them if they were in crisis and could afford the expense.

From the maternal histories, we gathered from the women in our 5 per cent sample, we learned of certain patterns. New mothers often had difficulty breast-feeding, and resorted to goat's or cow's milk; and babies were not introduced to solid food until the age of two. When a rare couple suffered an incapacity to conceive, the difficulty was solved through treatment of the wife. It was common for there to be years between chala and first pregnancy, and it was common for a woman's first child to die.

The four stage process I saw taking hold by the end of the

twentieth century as landed families adjusted to the inadequacy of the amount of land owned to the number of members of the family is as follows:

1. Stage one. Families limit the numbers of daughters to no more than two, and try to maximize the number of sons, but allow only one or two to marry, the other or the rest remaining unmarried .
2. Stage two. Families send at least one son to school so that he can qualify for a job located other than on the farm, preferably in town or city. Families try to get a good dowry with the bride of the job-holder, making it possible to give a good dowry to one's daughter or daughters.
   Families try to arrange marriages for daughters with educated men, preferably with jobs off the land. It may be necessary to send one's daughter or daughters to school as an aid to attracting an educated son-in-law. Families also try to buy additional land and to build additional housing, as needed.
3. Stage three. If the above strategy has not worked—that is, the educated son can not get a job and must work on the farm, one may still try to get a good dowry when he marries, but the couple may try to limit the number of children to three—two sons and one daughter.
4. Stage four. Families limit the number of children a couple bear to one or two.

BRAHMAN ASHA RAM, TEACHER

One of the most successful khandans in shifting male members off the land and into other occupations was one that started the process early, that of Asha Ram Brahman. Asha Ram's grandfather, Mamraj, (b.1866) was a *purohit* (household priest) with many *jajmans* (clients). Although Mamraj was an only son, he had only 60 bighas of land. He must have decided that 60 bighas were insufficient to support his three sons, none of whom became purohits like himself. Perhaps Mamraj in the early twentieth century could see that demand for purohit services declining as the teachings of the Arya Samaj—anti-idolatry, anti-ritual, anti-Brahman-priest—spread from the Punjab and became accepted by many in Khalapur.

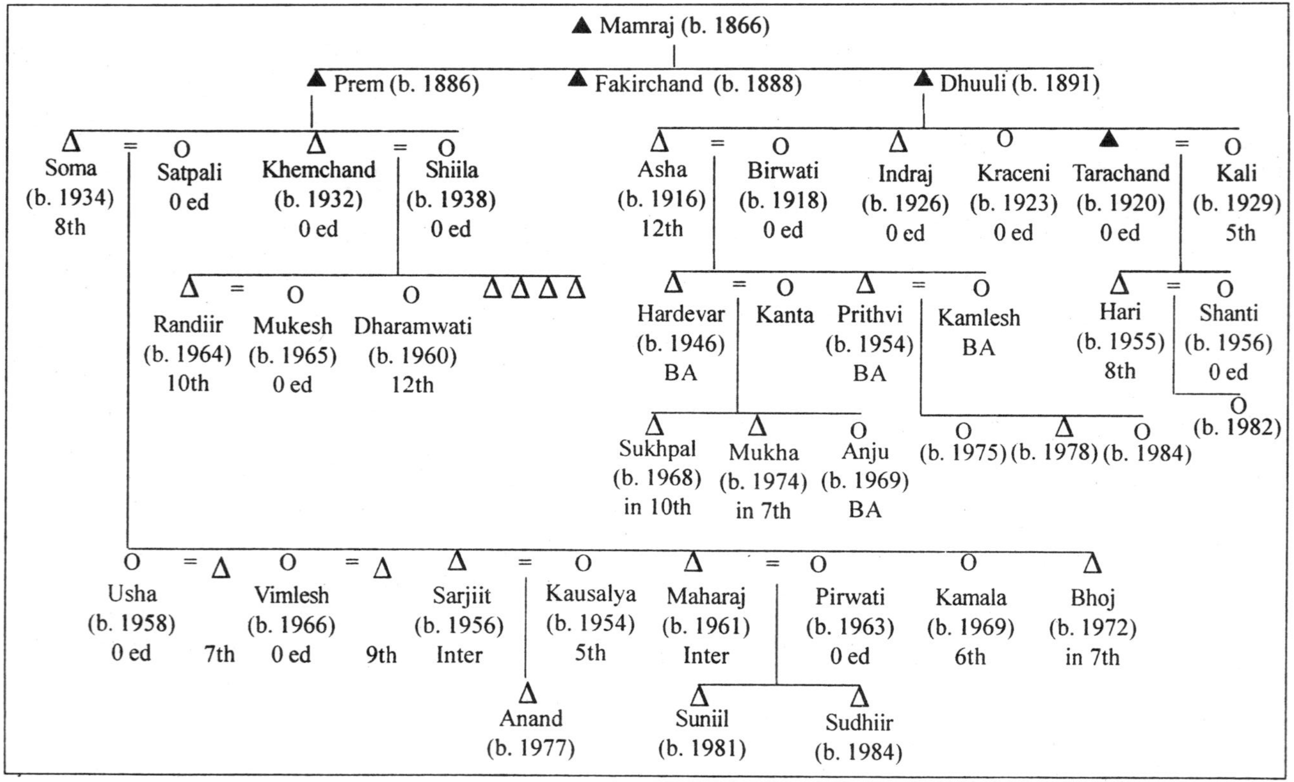

Figure 5. 1: Asha Ram Brahman's Khandan in 1984

Legend: Δ: male ▲: dead male; O: female; —: siblingship; | : parentage; =: marriage

Of his three sons, Mamraj kept two, Prem (b.1886) and Fakirchand (b.1888), on the land, and he sent the third, Dhuuli (b.1891), to school. Fakirchand remained a bachelor; Prem was married, as eventually, was Dhuuli. Dhuuli, who was Asha Ram's father, attended four years of school in Khalapur and became a primary school teacher in the neighboring village of Guloli. 'He used to walk the mile between [Khalapur] and Guloli each day. He earned 3 rupees per month', commented Asha Ram. Dhuuli must have been teaching in Guloli during World War I and thereafter.

Dhuuli had three sons and one daughter. The pattern was repeated as two sons, Tarachand (b.1920) and Indraj (b.1926), were kept on the land, with only the former married. The third and oldest, Asha Ram (b.1916), was sent to school and was married after he finished in 1934. Following the rule of village exogamy, Dhuuli's one daughter, Kraceni (b. 1923), with no schooling, was married into Antwara village, Saharanpur District. Perhaps the dowry or dowries that one or both of her older brothers' brides had brought in served to enrich the dowry Kraceni took with her.

Asha's explanation for why his brother, Indraj, was not married was, 'No one liked him due to his lean appearance'. The 'no one' seem to be the elders of potential brides, none of whom approached Indraj's elders with a proposal of marriage. Possibly, it was not just his 'lean appearance' but such elders' awareness that Dhuuli had only 30 bighas to divide among three sons.

Asha Ram's career as a teacher started with four years of primary school in Khalapur, followed by middle school and the HAV Intercollege in the nearby town of Deoband. He probably studied for 12 years. The language Asha read and wrote with facility was Urdu. When I asked him to record his expenditures on his family's agricultural activities, he wrote rapidly in Urdu. He liked to listen to Muslim *qawwalis* (love-songs) on the radio (he did not like film music) and he had enjoyed the Urdu films *Mughal-e-Azam* in Delhi and *Pakeezah* in Saharanpur that he had seen some years ago. He could also read and write Hindi and knew some English. He was one of the few persons in Khalapur who had a cupboard of books from his student days, some in Urdu, some in Hindi. He did not subscribe to a newspaper, but went to a Rajput ex-village headman's, to read the newspaper.

Asha Ram enjoyed a teaching career of 42 years. Between 1934 and 1945, he taught third and fourth grades for two or three year stints in five different villages in Saharanpur district, varying in distance from Khalapur from over 60 to 5 km. Between 1945 and 1956, he was district inspector for physical education, a job that required him to travel over the district by bicycle, bus and train. From 1956 to 1961, he was on deputation to the HAV Intercollege in Deoband, teaching political science and Urdu. For a brief period, he was at the District Board Office as inspector. Then he became headmaster of 3 different junior high schools one after the other—in Govardhanpur, 63 km from [Khalapur] from 1961 to 1963; in Miragpur, 3 km from Deoband, from 1963–73; in Ambetha, 2 km away, from 1973–6. He retired in 1976 at the age of 60, with a pension of Rs. 125 per month.

By 1984, the 30 bighas that Dhuuli had inherited had dwindled (for reasons unknown to me) to 27 bighas. His three sons, Asha, Tarachand and Indraj, had each inherited 9 bighas. Tarachand had died in 1980 at 60, having been sick since 1949. His only son, Hari (b.1955), although only 29 years old, had arranged for the 9 bighas he inherited from his father to be tilled by his father's cousin-brother, Khemchand, on a half-and-half basis. Khemchand (b.1932) and his brother Soma (b.1934), sons of Dhuuli's brother, Prem, had inherited Prem's 30 bighas. Cultivation of their land was largely managed by Khemchand, while the retired Asha Ram helped by keeping accounts, ordering fertilizer, seed and other necessary inputs. Khemchand's brother Soma was chronically ill; he drank and took opium; he was only able to help with the work some of the time. Asha's brother, Indraj, was able to work but also indulged in opium and alcohol. Hari, Tarachand's only son, who had studied through eighth grade, had had a job at the tin factory in Deoband, but quit after a short time and did not work. Asha considered Hari a wastrel. Asha Ram complained,'Over the past four or five years, Indraj has taken up drinking, because he associates with bad company, both Rajputs and Brahmans. Many of them drink *shraab* (country liquor). Now I am afraid he will lose his land due to his bad habits. All my life I worked to hold on to our land, but between Hari's bad habits and Indraj's, the land may go'. He seemed to suggest that land would be sold by his nephew and brother to pay for the costs of liquor and opium.

The cousin-brothers sowed 36 bighas (out of 57 bighas) in cane, producing about 900 quintals of sugar cane. About a quarter of their crop they sold to *kaleshyar*s (small-scale sugar-making operations), because it was in excess of that required by the Deoband sugar-mill. They kept 2 quintals of *gur* (brown sugar) for themselves. They sowed 15 bighas of *gehon* (wheat), then *munji* (rice). They had 4 or 5 bighas in *chera* (fodder) for their two *bel*s (bullocks) and one *jyota* (water buffalo). They both sold and ate *munji* and *gehon*.

The copy of a year's accounts that Asha Ram kept for 1983-4 suggested that his costs for cultivation of his and Indraj's land totaled Rs. 5,441 to which must be added Rs. 300 for feed for the bullocks. His gross income from the sale of sugar cane, rice, and wheat was Rs. 9,492, so their profit was Rs. 4,041. For the four cousin-brothers, their total profit appeared to be over Rs. 12,000. They had no tube well or pump in the field, because their land was close to the canal. They had no tractor, but rented one for plowing, as well as using their own pair of bullocks. Khemchand, aided by Indraj and sometimes Soma, depended for sowing, weeding, harvesting and so on upon a team of Harijan laborers, each paid Rs. 10 per day. Other costs were for fertilizer, land tax, irrigation water, seed, and insecticide. On the day (12 May 1984) we interviewed Asha Ram, he had instructed Indraj to go with the *muzdur* (laborer) Harjiit Harijan to cut the rest of the wheat.

During his long teaching career, Asha's wife, Birdevi, remained with her husband's family in Khalapur. Depending upon the distance, Asha either resided in his place of work, coming home briefly every ten days or so, or lived in Khalapur and commuted to his teaching posts when they were nearby.

Asha's wife Birdevi (b. 1918) I remember as a tiny frail being, sitting on her heels, curled around her *hooka*, 'very old and toothless' (say my notes). Birdevi had grown up in Salempur village, Muzaffarnagar district, and had no education. She said that she had been married 50 years, that she had had her shadi at age 15 and her chala at age 16. Of her six children, two survived to adulthood. Birdevi had her first child seven years after her chala, at age 23. Her first son died of fever at three months. Her second child, a daughter; a fourth child, a son; a fifth child, a son, all died at '5 or 7 days'. Her third child, her son Hardevar (b.1946), and her sixth child, her son Prithvi (b.1954), survived, and both, in 1984, lived in Delhi. She had her children at her sasural and had been served in birthing by the village dai (midwife). 'I had no trouble breast-feeding. I had nice healthy children, but they died of fever,' she commented.

As fathers, the four cousin-brothers, Soma, Khemchand, Tarachand and Asha Ram all took advantage of the presence in Khalapur of the Intercollege, established in 1952, in their common strategy to educate sons so they could take up jobs off the land. Asha's elder son, Hardevar (b.1946), graduated from the Intercollege in Khalapur and attended the Rajput College in Agra where he did well and won prizes for track races. Hardevar's BA was in English, Political Science and Hindi. He applied to the police department in Delhi and was selected. In 1984, Hardevar was a bodyguard to the prime minister. He lived in government quarters in the Police Lines, but owned a house in Shalimar Bagh, Delhi.

Asha's second son, Prithvi (b.1954), eight years younger than his brother, studied in Khalapur through seventh class and then went to Delhi to live with his brother. There, he attended Vijayanagar Higher Secondary and Ramjas College on the University of Delhi campus, where he took a BA. Prithvi was in the Police Vigilance Department as an inspector in 1984. He owned a house in Jahangirpuri, Delhi.

Tarachand's wife, Kali, gave birth to eight infants, but only one survived, a son Hari (b.1955), who studied to 8th grade and, as mentioned, lacked employment. Asha's cousin-brother Soma had three sons. Two had already finished the 12 grades at the Intercollege by 1984. The eldest son, Sarjiit (b.1956), worked in the office of the sugar-mill in Deoband, writing assignments for farmers for the amount of cane to deliver. Soma's second son Maharaj (b.1961) was a printer at the tin factory in Deoband. In 1984, Soma's youngest son, Bhoj (b.1972), was studying in seventh class.

Asha's cousin-brother, Khemchand, had five sons. All attended the Khalapur Intercollege, the oldest son, Randiir (b. 1966) had already finished Inter (12th) by 1984 and had joined his older cousin, Maharaj, at the tin company in Deoband as a printer. Khemchand also had four unmarried sons, three of whom were studying in 1984—Satpal (b.1969) in eighth class, Natpal (b.1972) also in eighth, Satendar (b.1977) in first at the Khalapur Montessori School. His youngest son, Jiitpal (b.1979) was too young to go to school.

The khandan seemed to have Rs. 12,000 per year or Rs. 1,000 a month to live on and cover their children's school expenses. Asha also had a pension of Rs. 1,500 per year. Khemchand's son Randhiir, and Soma's sons Sarjiit and Maharaj were working in jobs in Deoband. I do not know what each earned, but probably at least a few hundred rupees per month. Despite their seeming prosperity in 1984, the khandan seemed to be coming through a struggle as it recently had to increase its housing facilities (see Figure 5.2). The women's quarters were on one side of a pathway and consisted of an old house with six rooms, a fired brick one-room hut and a two-room nicely stuccoed new house with a title over its verandah, 'Tara Chand 1984'.

A khandan decision seem to have been made to reserve four of the six rooms in the old house for the newly married sons of Khemchand and Soma. On the left margin of the long rectangular courtyard were two rooms one beside the other. Across the top of the courtyard were a pair of double-rooms, one pair beside the other. One pair belonged to Khemchand's wife, Shiila (b.1938). In it was a cot, brass vessels and a dried-clay grain storage vessel. Her daughter-in-law Mukesh (b.1965), wife of her one married son, Randhiir (b.1966), had the other pair of rooms. The recently married couple's possessions, including two bicycles, a radio, a tape-recorder, a fancy electric lamp, the last three items probably part of Mukesh's dowry, were kept here. The room on the margin of the courtyard closest to the top rooms was Soma's son Maharaj's (b.1961) wife Pirvati's (b.1963) room. She shared it with her two baby sons, one aged 3, the other six months. There were dowry items in this room also, including a coffee table, two upright handsome chairs, a fancy electric lamp, pictures and decorative pottery. As one came in from the street, the room on the left was either being constructed or re-con-

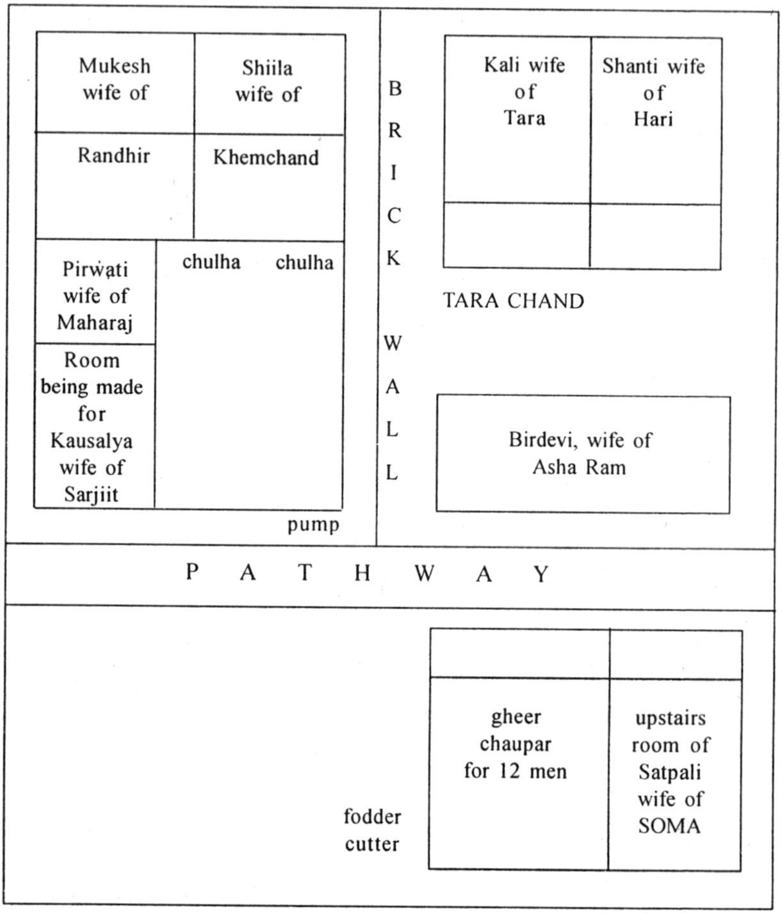

Figure 5.2: Living Quarters of Asha Ram Brahman's Khandan

structed. It was to belong to Soma's married son, Sarjiit. Until it was finished, Sarjiit's wife and small son, Anand (b.1977) aged 7, in second grade, were staying in a room rented from a neighboring 'uncle'. The necessity of renting a room until a new room was finished appeared to to be a desperation measure being taken as the sons of the khandan married and had families.

In the courtyard of the old house were two *chulhas*, one belonged to Khemchand's wife. She cooked for Khemchand, herself, their four unmarried sons and their married son, Randhiir and his wife (8 persons). The other belonged to Soma's married son Maharaj's wife. She cooked for Maharaj, herself, and two babies (4 persons).

A wall had been erected in July or August of 1983 between two sides of the women's compound. On one side was the old house described above. On the other side were two small buildings, a one-room house where Asha Ram's wife slept and kept her possessions, and a new stuccoed fired-brick house with two rooms side by side, fronted by a verandah. Tarachand's son's wife, Shanti (b.1958) said it was called 'Tara Chand 1984' because 'it was built with his money and belonged to him', although Tarachand had died in 1980. One of the two rooms in the new house belonged to Hari's wife, Shanti; the other room belonged to Hari's widowed mother, Kali (b.1929).

According to Asha Ram, the decision to make the wall was his. He had the carpenter Prakash make it. Asha explained that the women of the two branches of the khandan used to abuse each other using vulgar language he could not bear to hear, so he had had the wall erected to hush them. Khemchand's son Randhiir, was more specific in his explanation. He said, 'Tara's son Hari is an only child and my wife [Mukesh (b.1965)] is an only child and she could not adjust to having so many people around.' The wall did, of course, separate Hari's and Randhir's women, whatever the nature of their clash.

On the other side of the path was the *gheer* with a *chaupar*, a one-room men's quarters where all the men and boys slept except for the five-year-old Jiitpal, the youngest son of Khemchand. These included Asha, Indraj, Hari, Khemchand, Satpal, Natpal, Satendar, Randhiir, Soma, Mahendra, Sarjiit and Bhoj—12 in all. It is only on the men's chaupar that they had *bijlii* (electricity).

On the roof of the *chaupal*, a room and a verandah had been built. This belonged to Soma's wife Satpali. She slept here with her unmarried daughter Kamala. They cooked there for Soma, Bhoj and themselves (4 persons). Building atop the chaupar seemed to be another desperation measure. While Tara's son, Hari, had been able to build a new two-room house, and Atma Ram had a one-room house built for his wife, Soma had only managed to build on the roof of the men's chaupar.

Although Asha Ram had retired in 1976, there was a sign in front of the house announcing the presence there of a teacher for the JTC Basic Refresher Course. Asha did not admit to us that he ever had any students to tutor. Asha's wife and his nephew's wife earned by spinning. At the branch of the Gandhi Ashram in Khalapur, they exchanged the thread they had spun for cloth.

The families in the khandan had various conveniences. There were five radios, four bicycles, three sewing machines, one tape-recorder, one iron, a number of wrist watches. There was no television set, nor sofa-set nor dining-set, items becoming popular in some new brides' dowries in 1984. Other evidence of increasing prosperity was the family travels. In 1982, Hardevar had taken his family and his parents, Asha Ram and Birdevi, to Kashmir on a holiday; they had seen Vaishnodevi, Srinagar and Jammu. Earlier, in 1953, Asha Ram had gone to Benares.

When we visited the khandan in 1997, we learned that two more of Khemchand's five sons had completed their schooling. Satpal, aged 27, and still unmarried, had finished Inter as well as a BSc in Agriculture; he worked at a computer company in Delhi. Natpal, 25, and also unmarried, had finished Inter and taken both an MA and an MBBS degree. He had set up a medical clinic in the home of his married sister, Dharmvati, who lived in Modipur, near Deoband. Khemchand's two youngest sons were still studying. Satendar, 20, was studying in 12th, and Jiitpal, 18, was studying in tenth. Note that as yet, four out of five of Khemchand's sons were unmarried.

By 1997, Soma's youngest son, Bhoj (b.1972) had finished 12th and had become a quality controller in a carpet factory in Panipat.

To summarize, out of the eleven sons of the four married cousin-brothers in Asha's generation, all were educated through eighth grade or beyond, and eight managed to find work off the land, 3 locally in Deoband, one near Deoband, 3 in Delhi, and one in Panipat. Two were still studying, their futures yet unknown. Only one, the least educated, with eight grades of school, depended entirely on income from his land.

While the four married men of the khandan of Asha's generation had altogether 11 sons, they had only 4 daughters. Khemchand had educated his one daughter, Dharamwati (b.1962), through Inter, and she had married an Inter who was a cultivator. Soma had educated only one of his three daughters, Kamala, who studied through sixth; she married in Panipat to a *boogie jyatra* (platform drawn by a water-buffalo) driver who had studied to the seventh standard. Soma's other two daughters who had had no education married men who has studied till 10th.

As for the education of wives, three had had no education—Mukesh, wife of Randiir (who had studied till 10th); Shanti, the wife of Hari (who had studied till 8th); Pirwati, wife of Maharaj (who had studied till 12th). One wife had studied till fifth class—Kausalya, the wife of Sarjiit (who had studied till 12th). While Khemchand and Soma had seen to it that their daughters married men who were as educated as the daughters themselves, they had not been so intent on getting daughters-in-law of equal education for their sons.

Between his retirement from teaching in 1976 and his death in 1992, Asha Ram and his wife spent part of the time in their village home and part of their time with their sons in Delhi, Asha Ram with his eldest son, Hardevar, and his wife with their younger son, Prithvi. Asha Ram liked to watch TV when visiting. Otherwise, he said he felt like a prisoner in Delhi—even though his sons were good to him—because he did not know anyone there. When we returned in 1997, we realized that he and his wife had stayed in the village, continuing to visit the sons from time to time.

It is very unlikely that Asha Ram's grandchildren, will ever live in Khalapur. In 1997 when I visited, Asha Ram was dead (he died in 1992). His wife was still living in Khalapur; she died in November 1997. All three of the children of Asha Ram's eldest son, Hardevar, were settled in businesses in Delhi then. The two sons had both earned MA degrees and both worked in private businesses. The one daughter, Anju, had earned a BA degree at Daulat Ram College in Delhi, and was married to a man who owned a factory. Hardevar's elder son, Sukhpal, was married, but his younger son was not. The two sons, one married, the other unmarried, lived with their parents.

Asha Ram's second son, Prithvi, died in 1988 when his scooter's petrol tank burst into flames. His widow, a BA, continued working as a clerk in the office of Hamdard University in Delhi.

Prithvi's eldest daughter had earned a BA degree and, still unmarried, worked with her mother at Hamdard University. The other two daughters and a son were all in school—the one son in 11th grade, a daughter in 9th and a daughter probably in 6th. Prithvi's wife had a tubal-ligation after the birth of her last child, a daughter. She had waited until after the fourth child, a girl, because she had been hoping for a second son. Kanta, Hardevar's wife, also had had a tubal-ligation after having three children, two sons and one daughter.

Among the 23 grandchildren of Asha's two younger brothers, only one boy had finished his education in 1997—Anand, the son of Soma's son Sarjiit. He had finished Inter at the Khalapur Intercollege, but he did not want to study further and perhaps could get into the police. Soma's daughter, Usha, married into Hatwara, had a fifteen year old daughter, already married, who had had no education. Otherwise, 17 of the 21 other grandchildren were in school, while 4 were too small to attend school yet.

In one generation, there had been a great change in the experience of child-bearing for some of the women of Khandan 3. Asha's wife had given birth to six children, of whom only two reached adulthood. Three sons and one daughter had died in infancy. Asha's elder son, Hardevar, and his wife had two sons and one daughter. Asha's younger son Prithvi and his wife had three daughters and one son. The two couples had lost no children to early death; the wives had given birth in Delhi hospitals. Asha's wife, Birdevi, had her last child when she was 34. Both the wives of Hardevar and Prithvi had their tubal-ligations at the age of 30.

Asha's brother Tarachand's wife, Kali (b.1929), had borne 8 children, of whom only one survived to adulthood. This son, Hari (b. 1955), and his wife, Shanti, followed the pattern of his parents. In 1997, they had lost three sons and one daughter at early ages but had two young sons, aged 9 and 11. Like her husband's cousins' wives, Shanti seems to have had her last child when she was 30 years old, although she seems not to have had a tubal-ligation. Shanti's experience with motherhood contrasts with that of her husband's cousin-brothers' wives in Delhi. Shanti lost four children, while Kanta and Kamlesh lost none. The difference in education and probably income of the rural couple as compared to the urban couples, and the greater access to hospitals and medical care that there was in Delhi probably help account for the differences in child survival.

In 1984, Dharmvati, Khemchand's only daughter, had been married for five years and had no children. In 1997, she had two sons and two daughters. We were told that she had had a combination abortion and tubal-ligation some time after having her last child in 1990. Khemchand's eldest son and his wife, Randhiir and Mukesh, had four daughters, the youngest born in 1994. There was no question of Mukesh having a tubal-ligation, we were told. 'They will try for a son. They must have a son.'

Among Soma's children, Vimlesh had had a tubal ligation after having had a son and daughter. Vimlesh's married sister Usha, aged 39 in 1997, had had two daughters and three sons, her last born in 1990. While she was not reported to have had a tubal-ligation, there was some speculation that possibly she used some other form of birth control.

Among the children of Asha, his brother and cousin-brothers, ten couples had completed their families by 1997. The number of living children a couple had varied from one to five. The total number, 30, gave an average of 3 children per couple. Of these 30 grandchildren, 17 were boys; 13 were girls. As suggested in Prithvi's wife's disappointed hopes for a second son and the requirement that Randhiir and Mukesh must keep trying for a son even after having four daughters, the desire for a son or sons was great. The birth order of the children for Randhiir and Mukesh, for Pritam and Dharmvati, Ramkumar and Usha, Vishnu and Vimlesh suggests that they waited through one or more daughters in order to have one or two sons.

One of the three women teachers in my 5 per cent sample was the widow of Asha Ram's brother, Tarachand, Kali (b.1929). We asked how she had become a teacher. Asha Ram told us that while he was the district inspector for physical education between 1945 and 1956, he found himself in debt to the tune of Rs. 4,000. Asha's superior asked, 'Is there anyone in your family who can work?' His brother Tarachand could not. 'Not only was he sick but he took *dode* (opium), *shraab* (country liquor) and *bhang* (marijuana)'. The superior said, 'Is there any woman who can work?' 'Yes', said Asha. 'My younger brother's wife.'

So the superior appointed her as a teacher with a school in her own home. Thus, she could draw a salary and presumably get Asha out of debt. Since Asha Ram was the inspector, he explained, no one would question her qualifications to be a teacher. In fact, she was uneducated and could just barely read Hindi. After some years, Asha, with his son Hardevar's help (Hardevar was probably a middle school student in the 1950's), taught Kali enough so she could be a teacher. In 1984, she was teaching in a primary school in Talheri Bazarg village.

A factor in a family's regress is not only the death of children and of adults in their prime, but also the difficulties connected with disabled children and adults. In Asha's family, his nephew Hari's only daughter in 1984, age two, could not walk nor speak. Never becoming normal, she died at the age of 11. Asha's cousin-brother, Soma, had an adult daughter, Vimlesh (b.1962), who was mute but not deaf. In 1984, she had been married for three years to a man educated till the tenth standard who owned a small factory. In 1997, we learned that Vimlesh had a son and daughter, but her husband, now a mechanic in the Khatauli Sugar Mill, had taken a second wife, with whom he had three sons and three daughters.

In 1997, not only was Asha Ram deceased, but his brother Indraj had left Khalapur to go live with his widowed sister, Kraceni, in Antwara village, Saharanpur. She had three sons living in Delhi; two were in the police and one had a shop there. She had a married daughter living in Mirzapur, near Deoband. Another married daughter had been deserted by her husband; was reported to be somewhat deranged; and lived with her mother. Given the isolation of Kraceni and her daughter, she probably needed Indraj's help. He supervised the cultivation of her dead husband's land and gave his own land and Asha's out on contract to two men of the Muslim Rangar caste of Khalapur. Tarachand's son Hari continued to do nothing, giving out his land on contract as before.

Thus, Asha Ram's khandan is one that succeeded in preserving its land over five generations. In early generations, the elders limited the number of sons who were to work the land to two and required that only one of these marry. Other sons became educated and were able to find work off the land, either in factories in Deoband, in the police in Delhi, or, in Dhuuli and Asha Ram's cases, as schoolmasters. Some members of the family endangered the preservation of the land through their addictions to both opium and alcohol and to illness (both of Asha's brothers, Indraj and Tarachand, and Tarachand's son, Hari; and his cousin-brother Soma), or they limited their capacity to move off the land through their limited educational accomplishment (Tarachand's son, Hari).

This khandan began its movement off the land and out of Khalapur early. Dhuuli, Asha's father, was already a teacher most probably by the late 1890s. Asha Ram began his teaching career in 1934. In contrast to other families, this one seems not to have been cursed with the disappointment of having educated unemployed sons. Of the four brothers left on the land (Tarachand and Indraj, Asha's brothers; and Soma and Khemchand, Asha's cousins), only one, Khemchand, seems to have avoided debilitating addictions to opium and alcohol. Education did indeed serve as a means to get jobs off the land for the grandsons of Dhuuli.

Eventually the land became irrelevant to Asha's descendants. Asha arranged that his bachelor brother's 9 bighas should be inherited by Asha's grandson—namely Hardevar's eldest son, Sukhpal. However, Asha Ram came to regret this gesture of generosity, because Sukhpal was precluded from receiving a scholarship of Rs. 350 a month at his Delhi school because he was no longer a dependent of his father, Hardevar. Asha said Sukhpal berated him for having made it impossible to get a scholarship 'all for 9 bighas'.

Note three of this khandan lived in Panipat—Soma's daughter, Usha (married to a cultivator who later worked in an iron factory); Soma's daughter Kamala (married to a man who had a *boogie jyota*, a wheeled platform drawn by a male water-buffalo used as a kind of taxi or bus) and Soma's son Bhoj (an accountant in a carpet factory). This suggests that one helped the other. Similarly, one of Soma's sons and one of Khemchand's sons worked as printers at the JJ Enterprise in Deoband. And Asha's two sons and his sister's two sons were all policemen in Delhi. It seems likely that cousin helped cousin in getting jobs.

Looking at the fourfold process, we see that in Asha's father's generation and his own, one brother out of three was expected to remain unmarried. In Asha's sons' generation, advanced degrees were the key to leaving the village and living comfortably in the city; both his sons had BA degrees. His elder son's sons in Delhi had MA degrees. Asha's cousin-brother Khemchand had one son with a BSc, working in Delhi, and another with both an MA and an MBBS degree running a probably lucrative medical clinic. The wives in Asha's sons' generation were limiting their families through tubal ligations and other forms of birth control.

For this khandan, education had been a way for the men to get jobs, so they were no longer dependent on the land. In 1997, Khemchand was still alive, though aged 67, but still looking after the land cultivation. It was not clear who would take charge of tilling the land after his retirement or death—possibly one of Khemchand's younger sons studying in Inter and tenth in 1997; possibly his brother Soma's grandson Anand who had finished 12th and did not want to study further. Between the two brothers, Khemchand and Soma, there were six sons working in Deoband or elsewhere. Possibly one of these might be willing to give up his job and/or devote at least some of his time to tilling the land.

The strategy of getting sons off the land had been successful. Khemchand's 15 bighas divided among five sons would give each only 3 bighas. Soma's 15 bighas divided among three sons would give each 5 bighas. Asha's grandson Sukhpal was to inherit his great-uncle Indraj's 9 bighas, and Asha's two sons would presumably divide his 9 bighas, so each got 4.5 bighas, definitely uneconomical holdings.

IV. TEN CARD LIFE

From the sketch of Teacher Asha Brahman's life, we can identify the important elements in a family strategy in Khalapur. I shall call it Ten-Card Life. I use the word 'card' and make the analogy to the game of poker in order to bring in the element of luck, both good and bad, very important to how one can play the hand, or live one's life.

There is, first, the time and place where one is born, and second, one's sex. Third, comes the caste into which one was born and what its work was. Fourth whether one's family was landed or landless, and if landed, how much land it owned and its quality. Fifth, the number and qualities of siblings, children, and others whose lives impinged on one's own—all the members of the khandan including both those born into it and those married into it. Sixth, whether one was sent to school and for how long and with what success. Seventh, whether one married and whom one married. Especially important with respect to marriage was the dowry a bride brought and whether she was fertile and bore children, especially sons. Among younger people, the bride's education became increasingly important. Eighth, addiction or non-addiction to drugs, alcohol, gambling of oneself and significant others. Ninth, catastrophic happenings as they impinged on oneself and significant others. Tenth, the general economic, political and social environment of one's times and places.

Teacher Asha Ram Brahman's Ten-Card Life showed that he was lucky in having been born early, in 1916, when being educated was rare and there were fewer people competing for available resources and available jobs. Second, he was lucky to have been born male and to have survived infancy and childhood, because in the early twentieth century, few females born survived to adulthood, although many male children also died. Third, he was lucky to have been born, as a Brahman, into a high-ranking caste even though the demand for the services of household priests, the traditional work of Brahmans in Khalapur, was in decline. Fourth, his khandan had land but only a medium amount of it. Neither he nor others either found the wherewithal to buy or chose to buy more land. One of Asha's brothers was credited with building a house for himself, his wife, his only son and the son's family. Fifth, since Teacher Asha Ram Brahman's father had two brothers and Asha himself had two brothers, the land had been sub-divided, so while Asha's father's father had had 60 bighas of land, Asha himself had only 9. He lived with two brothers and three cousin-brothers with whom he had to try to cooperate in the cultivation of the land and in sharing *bagar*, *gheer* and *chaupal*. He had these brothers' and cousin-brothers' wives and children, and children's children along with his own wife and sons and grandchildren to contend with. Sixth, Teacher Asha was sent to school, the only one of his brothers and cousin-brothers to do so, and he spent enough years in school to be qualified to be a teacher. Seventh, while one of Teacher Asha's brothers was kept unmarried, as had been one of his father's brothers, Teacher Asha married. When Teacher Asha and his wife married in 1935, not much was required for a Brahman girl's dowry, although she seemed to have a sewing machine that had perhaps been part of her dowry. Asha's wife bore six children, of whom only two sons lived to adulthood. Eighth, Teacher Asha did get into some difficulty with debt in the 1950s but he was lucky to have been helped by his superior at work. One cousin-brother, two brothers, and one of his brother's sons all seem to have become unable or unwilling to work due at least in part to addiction to opium and alcohol. Teacher Asha feared his brother's son would have to sell his land to pay debts he had for opium and/or alcohol. Fortunately, one of his cousin-brothers, seemingly unaddicted, took responsibility for cultivation of their land. Between Asha's salary as a teacher and his income from their land, Asha was able to educate his two sons. The sons were able enough both to have attained BA degrees, and his eldest son's sons both took MA degrees, and his daughter took a BA degree. Both sons and grandchildren married educated and healthy spouses. Ninth, there were catastrophes—old ones such as the high loss of children born to his wife, but also new ones such as the death of his younger son, a policeman in Delhi, at age 35, when the petrol tank on his scooter caught fire. Tenth, from the 1930s the agricultural economy of Khalapur became more and more prosperous as farmers grew more sugar cane as a cash crop. This had led to the building of the local high school and additional elementary schools in the village. In Delhi, Teacher Asha's sons and their wives learned about birth control and took advantage of the opportunities to have a form of contraception. The increased popularity of education even for women had resulted in Teacher Asha's younger son's wife being well enough educated, with a BA degree, to support herself after her husband's death.

REFERENCES

Arensberg, C.M. (1940), *Family and Community in Ireland,* Cambridge, Mass: Harvard University Press.

Dube, S.C. (1958), *India's Changing Villages: Human Factors in Community Development*, London: Routledge and Kegan Paul.

Hitchcock, J.T. (1956), 'The Rajputs of Khaalapur: A Study of Kinship, Social Stratification and Politics'. A dissertation in Anthropology submitted to Cornell University.

Lopreato, J. (1967), *Peasants No More*, San Francisco: Chandler Pub. Co.

Kolenda, P.M. (1958), 'Changing Caste Ideology in a North Indian Village', *J.Social Issues* 14: 53–65.

—— (1982), 'Widowhood among "Untouchable Chuhras"', in A. Ostor, L. Fruzzetti and S. Barnett, eds., *Concepts of Person: Kinship, Caste and Marriage in India*, Cambridge, Mass.: Harvard University Press, pp. 172–220.

—— (1989), 'Micro-Ideology and Micro-Utopia in Khalapur: Changes in the Discourse on Caste over Thirty Years', *EPW*, 12 August 1989, vol. 24, no. 9, pp. 1831–8.

—— (1990), 'Untouchable' Chuhras Through Their Humor: Equalizing Marital Kin Through Teasing, Pretense and Farce', in O.M. Lynch, ed., *Divine Passions*, Berkeley, Ca.:University of California Press, pp. 116–53.

—— (1998), 'Fewer Deaths, Fewer Births: Decline of Child Mortality in a U.P. Village, Manushi no. 105, March–April, pp. 5–13.

—— (2003), 'Preemo, Innocent at Home', in K.C. Mac Kinnon (ed.), *Behind Many Masks: Gerald Berreman and Berkeley Anthropology 1959–2001, Kroeber Anth. Soc. Papers*, nos. 89/90, pp. 24–40.

Miller, B.D. (1981), *The Endangered Sex: Neglect of Female Children in Rural North India*, Ithaca, N.Y.: Cornell University Press.

Minturn, L. (1993), *Sita's Daughters: Coming out of Purdah*, New York: Oxford University Press.

Minturn, L. and J.T. Hitchcock (1966), *The Rajputs of Khalapur, India* New York: J. Wiley & Sons.

Retzlaff, R.H. (1962), *Village Government in India*, Bombay: Asia Publishing House.

Vatuk, S. (1972), *Kinship and Urbanization: White-Collar Migrants in North India,* Berkeley, Ca.: University of California Press.

6

Degrees of Diasporic Separation: Family Narratives of Continuity

KAREN ISAKSEN LEONARD

This essay was originally titled 'Six Degrees of Separation', because my multi-sited ethnography focused on six sites in which emigrants from Hyderabad, India, had settled since the mid-twentieth century and made new lives for themselves: Pakistan, the UK, Australia, the US, Canada, and the Persian Gulf sites, Kuwait and the UAE (Leonard 2007). However, there were really eight sites, as the last two are separate countries, although they are quite similar, and my study also included Hyderabad itself. In any case, such a title helps us understand that this was not only multi-sited research but research about multi-sited lives. While the emigrants from Hyderabad negotiated separations from and connections with each other and their homeland in ways strongly shaped by their new contexts, they lived their lives with several contexts in mind simultaneously, creating family narratives that stressed continuities.

The emigrants I studied were rooted in Hyderabad, India, and not only that, they were rooted most firmly in the former Hyderabad State, the native state ruled by the Nizam until 1948. Because of my own initial work in Hyderabad city in 1966, relatively soon after the state's forcible 1948 incorporation into independent India, and my historical work on longtime Hindu nobles and servants of the state, the diaspora I researched from 1990 to about 2000 was that of the 'old Hyderabadis', those who termed themselves *mulkis* or countrymen in the Indo–Muslim Hyderabad State with its Persian and Urdu official languages.

These Hyderabadis moved, putting down new roots, and relatives and friends of theirs also moved and put down new roots, in not just one but several places, and people kept in touch. My research involved, then, not a field of bounded sites but a field of relations, relations across sites and across time too, as the project went on for more than ten years.

Sylvia Vatuk has done similar work. In 1990, Sylvia published a masterful analysis of the cultural construction of family identity by a Nawayati Muslim family that experienced ruptures and reorientations in 1855, when the British refused to recognize a successor to their employer, the Nawab of Arcot, in Madras. Comparable perhaps to the seizure of Hyderabad by India in 1948, this earlier event sent a branch of the Madrasi Nawayati family to Hyderabad. We do not have Sylvia's complete account of this *khandan* yet, but we do have that fine piece on its collective identity and her 2004 analysis of the life story of Zakira Ghouse (1921–2003), showing how this woman worked within her family and societal culture to achieve her goals. Sylvia mentions women's increased educational and work opportunities in Hyderabad after 1948, and Hyderabadi women emigrants have found opportunities abroad too, especially after the 1960s.

Here, I want to examine family and life histories, choosing just a few examples of families stretched across countries, to argue that those left at home feel the degrees of separation more and are called upon to reconceptualize their notions of self and family more than those who go abroad. Those in the homeland have created family narratives that stress continuities in the face of change, recognizing and incorporating a field of multi-sited or transglobal families in different ways. Rather than emphasizing the futures envisioned for and by younger family members in the new sites, narratives that often stressed new beginnings, I want to highlight the ways in which family and life histories strove to connect those futures to the past. The family narratives were constituted jointly by those at home and abroad, but I argue that those still living in the Hyderabadi homeland had greater incentives to emphasize continuities yet faced greater difficulties in doing so.

For citizens of Hyderabad city and state, Police Action in 1948 and the creation of Andhra Pradesh in 1956 were major ruptures; they struggled to find places in independent India and the new Telugu-speaking state. Life for the residents of Hyderabad city changed after 1948 in ways that go far beyond new architectural styles, new road names, rising population density, and new administrative and street languages. Families moved from the old city to the new and young men took up new careers; more women began to work and have careers. However, globalization has meant another level of change altogether. Since the 1960s, almost every family has members overseas. Aging parents who once welcomed opportunities abroad for their children now face painful and possibly permanent separations. Family histories rooted in Hyderabad and India have been replaced by new narratives oriented toward the new places, yet family members try hard to see continuities rather than completely relinquish the past. A few grandmothers' laments serve to illustrate the point that those left behind in Hyderabad had great difficulty adjusting to the multi-sited family networks.

Two sisters, Miriam Bilgrami and Khadija Mehdi, talked to me in a Banjara Hills home in Hyderabad, women with most of their grandchildren in the US and Canada. One sister said:

> All my children are abroad, all my grandchildren are abroad; we didn't want it this way, we could never think it would be like this. But providence. . . . My eldest sister is in Lucknow, she married there, and my mother was so upset, sending her all that way out of Hyderabad. But look at us.

The other sister reported that all her grandchildren dislike India and hate to come to it. She has visited them in Los Angeles, but she tells them, 'India is my home, you must respect it, you must visit me here'. A third grandmother, Pushpa Umapathi, talked unhappily about her visits to Texas, where her daughter and son-in-law had just bought a house although 'of course they are planning to return to Hyderabad'. There, her granddaughter anxiously asked her not to wear a sari when walking her to school. When I asked if her grandchildren there identified as Hyderabadi in any way, she burst out: 'Hyderabadi? They're not even Indian'.

Political changes in Hyderabad and the economic and social changes brought by India's development and globalization have altered the opportunity structure for successive generations of families based in Hyderabad, alterations detailed in my recent book. Most family histories started with memories of government service with the Qutb Shahis, Mughals, British, and Nizams. In the nineteenth century, Western-style educators, engineers, and doctors pioneered modern livelihoods not dependent on the state, although in old Hyderabad these professionals were often part of the ruling elite or close to it. Then in the mid-twentieth century, those who worked for political and social change in Hyderabad, like those in India's nationalist movement, were often lawyers. After 1948, and especially before 1956, some district-based Hyderabadis gained political power and a few Hyderabadi administrators and politicians rose to the all-India level. Women joined modern professions, particularly as educators and doctors, and then still newer professionals, computer scientists, physicists, chemists, academics, businessmen and women, moved to study and work abroad.

Settling and taking citizenship abroad, Hyderabadis bought property there. Thus property and women, the two 'possessions' held precious and thought to bring the emigrant students and workers back home, both moved abroad. Property could be bought in the new sites, rendering family property back in Hyderabad less important. Women could be taken along or could go on their own, with significant consequences for family dispersal. Jobs, careers, educational and social activities, even marriages, divorces, and remarriages undertaken by Hyderabadi women abroad have had positive but also often disruptive impacts back in Hyderabad.

Against this background of shifting occupations and timings, and despite differences of class, occupation, religion, and gender, the numerous family accounts I gathered revealed striking similarities when it came to the feelings of abandonment and separation of those left behind. It was one thing for the young emigrants to carve out positions and acquire properties in new places, discarding their ancestral roots, properties and positions inherited from the days of the Nizams as they looked hopefully to the future. It was quite another for the people in Hyderabad to have relatives and friends moving out of Hyderabad and India in large numbers, probably permanently, producing deeply-felt ruptures within families. The parents and grandparents in Hyderabad still drew inspiration from the past achievements of family members, still saw themselves and the family narratives rooted in the familiar past. Although sometimes given the choice, aging parents chose to stay in Hyderabad rather than live abroad with their children. As one of the grandmothers above (Khadija Mehdi) said, 'in the homes of my children, I have no identity, I'm just a glorified servant, and there's no way of getting around. Here, within one mile I have all my family and friends and social work activities, and a car and driver.'

For this paper, eight family narratives illustrate how strongly the degrees of separation were felt by those left in Hyderabad and how people developed narratives of self and family identity that continued to tie together their now multi-sited families. The eight narratives are those of three Hyderabadi Hindu families whose transitions to Indian Hyderabad and Andhra Pradesh were relatively easy, three Hyderabadi Muslim families whose transitions were less easy, and two Hyderabadi Anglo Indian families who eventually relocated to Australia. All of these narratives stress the continuities in the evolving family identities.

Two Hindu Hyderabadis talked about their families and their children abroad, relating them to concepts of Hyderabadi culture and citizenship in the time of the Nizams. These two, B.N. Raman and B.P.R. Vithal, were young men in 1948 when India incorporated Hyderabad State. They joined the Indian Administrative Service, the elite IAS, but they still retained strong *mulki* Hyderabadi identities. B.N. Raman, a Brahman whose ancestral village was near Madras and Karnataka, graduated from Nizam College in 1948 just before Police Action and wanted to continue his family's tradition of service: his uncle, a Superintendent of Engineering, and his father, a Medical Officer, were both in the Nizam's service, the latter doing pioneering medical work in rural areas. Raman was schooled in Karimnagar district to the sixth standard and then in Hyderabad city. As Hyderabad fell to India, Raman did well in three sets of competitive exams, the Hyderabad Civil Service (HCS), the Indian Foreign Service, and the Reserve State Bank. However, the IAS superseded the HCS and he ended up in that; like his father, he worked in the districts. His memories of the educational, health, and medical services of his father's time and his own were vivid. Raman spoke of Major Naidu, Sarojini Naidu's husband and the Nizam's Chief Medical Officer, and his organization of the medical services and the 'Walker style' of rural hospitals; about famine, drought, and influenza work in the early twentieth century in conjunction with Catholics, Methodists, and the Madras government; about the French-built dak bungalows on the road from Vijayawada to Nandir; and about Meadows Taylor's still-standing *Manzil* (residence) in Shorapur.

Raman spoke with appreciation of Hyderabad's cosmopolitan culture. He stayed in touch with Muslim friends who went to Pakistan, UK, and the Gulf States, although unsigned Id Mubarak cards sent to him after an Indian/Pakistan conflict by his friends Hamid Ali of Pakistan's Reserve Bank and Qayyum of the Pakistani Navy drew the attention of Indian Intelligence. Yet the next generation was leaving Hyderabad and even India: Many of the children of Raman and his three brothers and four sisters were in Canada, the US, and Bahrain, where they were members of Karnatak Associations and Hyderabad Associations. Raman's own two sons worked in computer and medical careers in the US. Raman's wife spent time away from him, cooking in the US for the younger, unmarried boy. The older son had married a woman of his own choice, and Raman spoke proudly of this daughter-in-law's social service work with the mentally retarded in a school near Sacramento, California, as proudly as he spoke of the two colleges he had established in Nizamabad as District Collector and of his younger son's ambition to come home and work as a doctor in rural or tribal areas. In the fast-changing family landscape, Raman valued old Hyderabad's traditions of service and cultural tolerance but saw their applicability elsewhere, positively envisioning the family's transglobal future by emphasizing this continuity.

Another Hyderabadi who joined the IAS was B.P.R. Vithal. He and his wife came from families formerly in Rajahmundry, in the Telugu-speaking districts of the Madras Presidency. Both their fathers, however, had shifted to Hyderabad and Vithal's father had been Professor of Economics in Nizam College. Vithal entered Nizam College in 1942 but left to join the Quit India Movement in Bombay. He shifted to Madras Christian College, graduated in 1949, and took the IAS exams. Vithal's cousin and Nizam College classmate went on a Nizam's scholarship to the University of Wisconsin from 1946 to 1951; later that cousin's son married Vithal's daughter (south Indians, like Muslims, often marry close relatives) and the young couple lived in Hyderabad.

The Vithals proudly considered themselves Hyderabadis. 'But that culture is no longer here,' he said, 'and we have yet to meet an Andhra who came here after 1956 who'll say he or she is a Hyderabadi.' Vithal stated that his own relatives from Andhra, whom he had not met, were coming and reclaiming him; his Andhra roots had come to Hyderabad and were taking over. He saw 'the erosion of my *mulki* self'. As a professor's son, Vithal had gotten a free education at Aliya and Nizam College: 'my classmates were from a high class, Muslims and others, but they never rubbed that in, we were simply there with them. It was quite a gracious culture, before.' Vithal's wife's cousin had been in the Indian Civil Service (ICS) in British India, so here again traditions of service linked Hyderabad State to India, the Nizam's Educational Department, the ICS, and the IAS collapsing into one family tradition.

Vithal and his wife saw their two sons both settling elsewhere, their elder son in Delhi and their younger son in the process of becoming a US citizen. None of the grandchildren were Hyderabadis, the Vithals said, even the ones from Delhi were typical Punjabis, conversant with Hindi and not Urdu. The Vithal son taking American citizenship called his father often, going through an identity crisis: 'Am I letting you down, Dad, here you are in India's Finance Commission and I'm settling here,' he asked. His father's response was that citizenship was a civil concept and being Indian was a cultural concept, so he could still be himself. Both father and son saw the son as Indian not Hyderabadi, and the son saw his father as Indian not Hyderabadi. This displacement of the Hyderabadi identity by an Indian one helped resituate and hold together the family tradition of service, but the parents were conscious of their loss.

The third Hindu family narrative comes from one of a whole new set of people, newcomers from the Andhra districts of the former Madras Presidency who moved into the city after 1956.

These relative newcomers now call themselves Hyderabadi—but not *mulki*; only a few of them or their children were socialized into the old *mulki* culture. Both Hindu and Muslim, these men and women had children and grandchildren abroad, some of whom have started websites grounding their new Hyderabadi identity in the capital city of Andhra Pradesh, while old Hyderabadis have relinquished the city as the focus of identity and have started websites based on their schools, Madras-i-Aliya, St. George's Public School, and others.

These elite newcomers to Hyderabad saw themselves as bringing Andhra culture to the city and improving or reforming the culture of Telangana. They too had children abroad, and in one interesting case, the family was conscious of a rupture in, a transitional identity of, one of its members. Retired in 1987, Justice P. Rama Rao came to Hyderabad from the Madras High Court in 1956, one of those whose arrival suddenly set back judges in Hyderabad State by jumping ahead of them in seniority. Justice Rao felt that the Telugu Desam government had 'claimed Hyderabad for the Andhras and induced people to give up the slang of Telangana, the Urdu in the Telugu, in favor of fluent, good Telugu'. He built two houses, first in an older neighborhood, Hyderguda, and then in what he termed a Hindu, South Indian new neighborhood in Banjara Hills. He and his wife had five children; four were settled in four different cities in the US. The eldest son, a doctor, was an 'old Hyderabadi', according to Rao. This son had attended Madras-i-Aliya (an English-medium school for the Indo–Muslim cultural elite), because Rama Rao, new to Hyderabad, had been influenced by G.N. Reddy, from Telangana and Registrar General at the time, to send his son to the same school as Reddy's son. This son therefore became an 'old Hyderabadi', went in 1977 to Chicago, an established center of the Hyderabadi diaspora, and was in partnership in Chicago with a Hyderabadi Kayasth doctor (very old Hyderabadi, the Kayasth caste members). This son might even be a member of the Hyderabad Association there, the Raos said.

Three other children of Justice Rao were settled in the US, but they remained within the dominant family narrative, that of successful newcomers to the city and part of a successful multi-sited family. The eldest daughter, also a doctor, went in 1980.

The second daughter was a lawyer in the US and the youngest son worked in the computer industry there. (The second son was refused a US visa, so he worked in Algeria, went to Paris for an MBA, then came home and became a real estate developer.) All those abroad were married within their Kamma caste before leaving home. Two said they wanted to stay abroad and two wanted to come back, but all the sisters of the Raos' sons-in-law and daughters-in-law were settled in the US. The grandchildren abroad were young, aged one to eleven, but all said they wanted to stay in the US. This was fine with the Raos, who had just visited the US for four months, spending one month with each child. 'We're happy here, they're happy there', they said. Note that they, like other satisfied parents, did have a son in Hyderabad.

The two transitions to the IAS above, of young Hyderabadi Hindus beginning their careers just before or after 1948 went well, and the transition of Justice Rao from Andhra to Hyderabad also went well, but transitions proved less easy for many Hyderabadi Muslims. Mehdi Ali, whose career suffered after 1948, started out in the Hyderabad Civil Service, the HCS, in 1941 and again the family tradition was of service. Two of his four brothers were also in the HCS, the only Hyderabad family with three sons in the HCS, he said. However, after 1948, his four brothers all lost their jobs; two were charged and briefly jailed by the Indian Army. Ali continued in government service, but whereas before 1948 he had opposed the growing influence of the militant Muslim Razakar movement and found his career blocked because of that, after 1948 he was not immediately taken into the IAS because of a suspected affinity with Pakistan. Ali did have relatives in Pakistan but has never visited there and wrote only one letter to someone there, a condolence letter.

Mehdi Ali's own HCS subordinates became his IAS bosses after 1948. His promotion to District Collector finally took place in 1949 because of Pandit Nehru's opposition to discrimination against Muslims in Hyderabad. After the 1956 advent of Andhra Pradesh, Ali served in Mysore and educated his children chiefly in Karnataka, and he was finally taken into the IAS only in 1972. Then, at the end of his career, Ali told a Governor of Karnataka with whom he worked closely of his setbacks, and that man secured his appointment to the IAS (but without appropriate seniority). Another injustice involved Ali's nephew, who, trying to follow the family tradition of government service, was temporarily barred by an Interview Board in India for correcting his date of birth on a form. The young man then went to Pakistan against his father's wishes and appeared before an Interview Board for the Pakistan Civil Service, where a senior member from Hyderabad reported that the youth's father had opposed the Razakars and got him rejected. Then the nephew was sent to the UK to do accountancy, but, failing the exam, became so depressed he had to be sent home. Since he had become a Pakistani citizen, it took three governors of Hyderabadi background (Padmaja Naidu of Bengal, Mehdi Nawaz Jung of Gujarat, and B. Ramakrishna Rao of Kerala) writing on his behalf to win him an indefinite stay in India, where he died.

Mehdi Ali lived alone in his house, a widower. Three of his four children were abroad, in Chicago, Toronto, and Saudi Arabia. When the son in Chicago got US citizenship, Mehdi Ali would get a green card and then sponsor his son in Saudi Arabia to the US, a faster way than brother sponsoring brother. His daughter in Hyderabad stopped daily to see him, and a granddaughter was arriving from Canada to study medicine in Hyderabad and be his companion. In this account, a service-oriented family fought to keep that identity in both India and Pakistan The family hopes are now placed in those abroad in Western sites and are no longer focused on government service. The family narrative includes members located in Hyderabad, the Middle East, and the West, drawing on them for elder care, career training, and career migrations for other family members in the several sites; degrees of separation are taken for granted and utilized.

Two other Hyderabadi Muslim families experienced dramatic changes as they moved from the past to the present and future, with family members straining to remain close despite distances. For one Hyderabadi Muslim family, post-1948 developments have meant not only separation by distance but by class, a dramatic case of upward mobility of a son abroad that has caused a predicament for his parents in Hyderabad. The parents owned the Muslim Sari Ghar, a residence-cum-workshop in a crowded locality near the Char Minar (the center of the old city of Hyderabad) where valuable old saris were polished (silver and gold embroidery) and renovated. This artisan family of Mohammed Muslim had many customers among Hyderabad's elite families, and the second son, Irshad Ahmed, was a very successful immigrant in the US. A biochemical engineer with a PhD from Cornell, he was settled in Washington DC (he had his own company with seven employees) and he wanted a bride from Hyderabad. His mother told me anxiously in Urdu (she and her husband did not speak or read English) that he wanted a literate, educated girl. She was giving out an English-language xeroxed biodata packet to her customers and seeking their assistance. The family talked of renting a house temporarily in a good locality in order to receive future in-laws in a better setting than the old city workshop, a strategy they were not sure would work. The parents now felt out of place in Hyderabad, unable to attain the bride their son deserved from there, and following him abroad was not an option for them. When I talked to the young man in Washington, he confirmed the social distance now separating him from his parents, whom he had brought to Washington for a visit. Not knowing English, they had not been happy, he said; Washington was unlike Chicago, where areas of dense Urdu-speaking settlement made parents like his feel comfortable. The selection of a bride who could bridge these degrees of separation was indeed daunting.

A final case of Muslim family resettlement also features challenges to the older generation resident in Hyderabad. Professor M.A. Muttalib, head of a family with a strong educational background in Hyderabad, saw himself as producing middle-class Muslim supporters of Indian democracy when he had five children (and his two like-minded brothers had five and six children respectively). A professor of Public Administration originally from Warangal district, Muttalib was a strong believer in the tolerance of Mughal and Hyderabadi culture. Muttalib and his wife were Hyderabadis. His wife did her high school, intermediate, MA and PhD (in Urdu literature), after her marriage at seventeen. When she went to Aligarh, properly chaperoned, for her degree, she did not touch beef, although many Muslims there ate it. In Hyderabad, middle class Muslims did not and do not eat beef out of respect for their Hindu friends, Muttalib asserted (I heard this from many others as well).

Professor Muttalib chose not to go to Pakistan after 1948, feeling he could serve better in India. However, most of the children in this extended family now live abroad and support democracy and cultural tolerance in the UK, the US, or Canada. Professor Muttalib's three sons are in the US, the eldest married to a Hyderabadi woman brought up there. Sponsored by this eldest son, the Muttalibs have become official immigrants to the US, as the younger unmarried sons could get visas faster by joining citizen parents. Muttalib's daughters, however, are married to Hyderabadi men who work in the Gulf (and one of them works in the Gulf herself), and these families plan to return to Hyderabad. Muttalib and his wife come to the US at least once a year for several months to keep their immigration status and to be with their American children and grandchildren. Muttalib dislikes these extended stays of non-activity, stranded in the suburbs and dependent on his sons, but his wife relishes time with her children and grandchildren.

The problem here is that the Muttalib sons abroad want the parents to settle with them in the US, while the daughters expect to remain in Hyderabad and want the parents there. Professor Muttalib feels useless in the US, but he sees the need (after 9/11) for a moderate Muslim presence in the US as well as India now. The family narrative strives to incorporate allegiance to two countries and three work locations, the sons and daughter-in-laws in the US, the daughters and sons-in-law temporarily in the Middle East, and the professor's own still-valued work site, Hyderabad.

Finally, two Anglo–Indian families who eventually left Hyderabad for Australia in the 1990s experienced protracted and painful separations from relatives and from Hyderabad. Both families finally shifted entirely out of their homeland after maintaining diasporic networks for decades after 1948. Anglo–Indians played important roles in Hyderabad State. The Anglo–Indian teachers employed by the city's elite schools and the nobility were important educators in old Hyderabad, and many other Anglo–Indians served at all levels of the military and railway establishments.

Established in India in the late eighteenth century and longtime Hyderabadis, members of one leading Anglo-Indian family were all leaving, as the sons and other young relatives of J.W. and Marjory Edwards settled in Australia and elsewhere abroad. Many Edwardses were teachers, in Madras-i-Aliya, St. George's, and as private tutors in leading families. J.W. and Marjory ran the respected Golden Rose School across from the Methodist Church. She was headmistress of St. George's Preparatory School and Educational Advisor to the Golden Rose School, set up by the Anglican Domiciled European Community of Chaderghat. The Edwards had relatives in London, Marjory's uncle Dr. Dennis Gay, but their relatives also included the Luschwitzes, Alex Norton, Ivan Oliver, and others who migrated to Australia in the 1950s. The Edwards had tried Australia then too, but Marjory and J.W. were rejected because of the 'white Australia' policy; they were accepted in 1967 but did not go then.

The Edwards's sons left in the 1970s, part of a professional migration to Australia. As J.W. said, 'educated and capable people don't get rewarded for their work anymore; we were a cosmopolitan lot, but the spirit is gone'. The parents finally followed their sons, in 1977, but, unhappy in Australia, they returned to Hyderabad after three months. I encountered Lyn Edwards, the adult son of J.W. and Marjory Edwards, in Hyderabad in 1991 when he was visiting his parents from Australia, and his person and comments reflected his new context, Australia. This confident, athletic man was dressed in unusual attire for Hyderabad, bright Bermuda shorts, short-sleeved knit shirt, and rubber thongs. Lyn split a Kingfisher beer with me and talked about his Hyderabadi mates in Sydney, particularly those on the Deccan Blues cricket team. He described one of the first events he attended in Australia: 'It was a 21st birthday party, given by my teammate, Killer Khan, for his daughter. The party had disco and everything. When I entered, I said, 'what the hell's all this', and Dr. Khan said, 'well, that's the way here'. . . Australia's changed a lot since the old White Australia days, now it's 'spot the Aussie' contests'. Their sons were confident immigrants (but not educators) in Australia, yet despite their feelings of loss and abandonment the parents were reluctant to leave Hyderabad. Kerry Edwards, the younger son whose move to Australia allowed him to play cricket with his older brother, finally brought his father over to Australia in 1995, after their mother's death.

Another older Anglo Indian couple, Charles and Blossom Corfield, finally moved to Melbourne in 1993 after three decades of trying to migrate to Australia. Charles, an officer in the British and then the Indian Army, had been held captive by the Japanese during World War II. His wife came from a respected Hyderabadi Anglo–Indian family: Blossom's mother had taught in the Court of Wards (for minor children of members of the nobility and jagirdars) and knew all the old elite families. Herself an alumnus of the elite Mahbubiyah Girls School and Nizam College, Blossom named numerous classmates in the UK, the US, Pakistan, and Australia. Her Urdu was excellent, and she cooked *bagara baigan* (eggplant in a thick tamarind sauce) and other specialties of Hyderabad extremely well.

The Corfields were Hyderabadis, but, after 1948, Hyderabad had felt less and less like home. Over the years, the Corfields had seen their six children scatter around the world, three settling in Australia and three taking Irish or British citizenship. The Corfields had gotten papers to migrate in 1962 but his parents were in their eighties and could not be left in India; they tried again after his father's death, in 1965, but the children were very small and they were engaged in a protracted court case. They sent their children on ahead, their daughter marrying an Indian Australian in 1985. Then Charles's cousin and his wife, Henry and Joyce Corfield of Sydney, Australia, visited them in Hyderabad and urged them to migrate. The Corfield children and grandchildren in Australia, like other Catholics from India, including those of Goanese, Tamil, and Telugu ancestry, were marrying partners of Italian, Greek, Sri Lankan, and Australian backgrounds whom they met through church, cricket, or dance clubs; like younger Hyderabadis of all religious backgrounds in Australia, they were becoming Australian.

Without continuity in educational or occupational lines in Australia, the Corfield family narrative highlighted certain conspicuous symbols of their status in Hyderabad. The Corfield family residence back in Secunderabad had been named Tiger Hall by the last Nizam because of its numerous decorative tiger skins—one relative had shot thirty-two tigers (Corfield 1993: 163). Tiger Hall was up for sale in 1993 since all of the children had emigrated, but the sale and the importation of those tiger skins to Australia posed problems. Yet the Corfields were determined to bring them to Australia, symbols of their homeland and their ties to the former nobility there. And like so many Hyderabadis of all backgrounds abroad, Blossom Corfield cooked *bagara baigan* and other Hyderabadi specialties for me in 1993.

The eight family networks and narratives above must be considered in the context of changes in Hyderabad to reinforce the argument that it was those left in Hyderabad who faced the greater ruptures, the greater need to devise family narratives to hold together their now multi-sited lives. Having their families stretched across national boundaries produced stress among family members in Hyderabad. I have not written here about the great rupture produced when part of a family moved to Pakistan, when one site, Hyderabad or Pakistan, was almost always deliberately erased from the divided family narratives (see Leonard 2007). But people's stories otherwise strove to straddle the several sites where relatives were settled and to provide themes of continuity from the past.

Parents left in Hyderabad were the ones who faced the challenge of creating such narratives, of providing the themes that connected the networks across time and place. Parents with one or more sons still in Hyderabad saw the family life as most continuous, as daughters abroad could always be visited but a son needed to be there for support in old age. The parents with sons settled abroad and daughters married to men working in the Gulf faced difficult decisions, torn between going to reside with their sons (the more culturally acceptable option) or staying alone in Hyderabad near their daughters; they tried to reconcile competing themes, competing sites, for their narratives. Gender differences surfaced in the narratives, reflecting different patterns of visiting abroad, as mothers could and did stay longer with their children while fathers could not stay long or preferred to be back in Hyderabad.

Stories had to account for delayed or reluctant migrations, as parents who wanted to join their children abroad could be held up by the immigration laws of the new site or by litigation or property settlements in Hyderabad. Sometimes 'property settlement' was a euphemism, as they really were waiting for an elderly parent or relative to die so that inheritances could be settled. Property in Hyderabad was thought to be a magnet pulling the emigrants back, and family after family mentioned ancestral property or investment in new property as performing this function. But properties, especially homes, had altered in form and function because of the diaspora. Gracious, old-fashioned residences, large enough for joint family living, were pulled down and new flats constructed, with the parents in one flat and another one or two flats left vacant for the children's holiday visits. Aging couples with no children or servants left to assist them were moving to apartments in multi-storey buildings, only to find that they could not properly receive their visitors or see them out as the old etiquette demanded.

Language changes in Hyderabad and abroad led to disruptions of family traditions. People bemoaned the fact that their own children and especially their grandchildren could no longer speak Urdu (or Telugu or Marathi or Kannada), much less read and write it. In Hyderabad itself, knowledge of Urdu was declining, and of course the change dated from the Police Action and the replacement of Urdu with Hindi and English in the schools. In a Muslim family noted for educational achievements, Khadija Mehdi had to choose Urdu or Sanskrit for her son's second Public School language during her husband's absence, and she chose Urdu. Her husband returned and disapproved: 'The children now have to learn Hindi, so Sanskrit would have been better.' Even among working class families in the old city, where Urdu remained the home and street language, Urdu was declining. Those who went to the Middle East were opting for English-medium schools for their children, whether they were the Indian Embassy schools in the Gulf or the private schools in Hyderabad newly accessible to them. Major shifts in linguistic competence opened up new vistas but also erased entire worlds of poetry, jokes, and performance traditions.

Daily life in Hyderabad involved changes in eating and dining habits as those left in Hyderabad accommodated those abroad. New foods were being introduced directly by family members from abroad. (In 1981, before this was common, my daughter and I were startled to be served 'vegetarian burritos' in a traditional Gujarati banking family's home by a daughter-in-law visiting from California.) Dinner times were shifted to accommodate TV programs from abroad that could be discussed with relatives settled there. Certain days and times were reserved for taking overseas phone calls: People declined invitations or arrived late because Dolly was calling from Canada, Syed from Melbourne, or Shanta from London at a preset time.

Despite the many changes, the older generations clung to the old friendships, the crosscutting networks that anchored them in Hyderabad city and state. People called upon each other or phoned each other (across countries) on the holidays still mutually observed by Muslims, Hindus, Anglo–Indians, Parsis, and Sikhs—Id, Diwali, New Year's Day, and the birthdays of family members. One heard stories of orthodox Muslim women bringing whiskey to Hindu friends who appreciated it, and Muslims calling Hindu friends in the wee hours of the morning, saying they had to get up and come for a wedding ritual that could not be performed without them. Hindus were loyal to their Muslim servants in the old city during times of communal riots and curfews, braving the police to take them food and water. Such stories made little sense to the children of Hyderabadi immigrants in Pakistan or elsewhere and will probably be forgotten. The children's own memories, being constituted in new settings abroad as they entered schools, made friends, and met others in their neighborhoods and workplaces, were orienting them to quite different worlds. Their narratives, their family and life histories, will be anchored in the new sites.

REFERENCES

Ahmed, Irshad. Interview with author, 19 November 1995, Washington, D.C.

Ali, Mehdi, Interview with author 5 and 26 October 1993, Hyderabad.

Bilgrami, Miriam, and Khadija Mehdi, Interview with author, 21 October 1991, Hyderabad

Corfield, Charles and Blossom, with son Joe and daughter Christine Wates, Interview with author, 14 November 1993, Melbourne.

Corfield, Justin J. (1993). *The Corfields: A History of the Corfields from 1180 to the Present Day*, Australia: Corfield & Company, VIC.

Edwards, J.W., and Lyn, Interview with author, 20 October 1991, Hyderabad.

Leonard, Karen Isaksen (2007). *Locating Home: India's Hyderabadis Abroad* (Palo Alto: Stanford University Press; Oxford University Press, 2008).

Muslim, Mr. and Mrs. Mohammed, with Lalitha Gir, Interview with author, 25 October 1991, Hyderabad.

Muttalib, M.A., Interview with author, 14 October 1991, Hyderabad.

Raman, B.N., Interview with author, 26 September 1991, Hyderabad.

Rao, Justice and Mrs. P. Rama, Interview with author, 7 November 1991, Hyderabad.

Umapathi, Pushpa, Interview with author, 25 September 1991, Hyderabad.

Vatuk, Sylvia (1990), 'The Cultural Construction of Shared Identity: A South Indian Family History', *Social Analysis* 28 (1990).

—— (2004), '"Hamara Daur-i Hayat:" An Indian Muslim Woman Writes Her Life', pp. 144–74, in David Arnold and Stuart Blackburn (eds.), *Telling Lives in India: Biography, Autobiography, and Life History* (Delhi: Permanent Black).

Vithal, Mr. and Mrs. B.P.R., Interview with author, 18 October 1993, Hyderabad.

7

The Place(s) of Transgressive Sexuality in South Asia: From Ritual to Popular Culture

PNINA WERBNER

Sexuality outside marriage, public or uncontrolled sexuality, is regarded in South Asia among Hindus and Muslims alike as dangerous and threatening to the social order. One prevalent folk idea, as Vatuk reports (1985: 143), is that women endanger male virility because of their 'lustful nature', surplus of blood and (dangerous, hot) sexual desire. The question is: by adopting uncritically this male perspective on female sexuality, are we not disregarding women's views of *male* sexuality? Is there not, perhaps, a counter-belief among women that (hot) male sexuality is equally dangerous for women?

To answer this question, the present paper considers critically a series of studies which respond to debates in the scholarly literature about cultural constructions of gender and sexuality in South Asia. I begin with two studies which, I argue, start from diametrically opposed questions, and use somewhat different ethnographic materials to prove their case. Gloria Raheja and Ann Gold in *Listen to the Heron's Words* focus on women's sexually explicit folk songs in Rajasthan and Uttar Pradesh (Raheja and Gold 1994). My own study of the Pakistani *mehndi* pre-wedding ritual and other ritual celebrations, based on fieldwork in Manchester conducted in the decade between 1975 and 1985, while encompassing folk songs, analyses their framing and embeddedness in a wider cosmological set of assumptions that includes the treatment of the bride and groom with magical substances, ritual clowning and masquerading, joking as well as singing at *mehndi* rites (Werbner, 1986 and 1990/2002: Chapter 9). The settings are also different: village India and Manchester, England, but many of the assumptions and performative genres are shared in common. At the time of my fieldwork Manchester had a relatively affluent Pakistani population of some 15,000, the majority Punjabis and north Indians, many originating from East Punjab.

Raheja and Gold, in the introductory chapter of their joint book, explain that their study of sexually explicit folk songs and the women who sing them is intended to challenge the widely held colonial and scholarly construction of the Indian 'Woman' as 'a silent shadow . . . veiled and mute', accepting her subordination to her in-laws, submissive, chaste, sexually repressed, passive and unquestioningly obedient' (1994: 3-4). Against the Subaltern Studies historians' view that the subaltern cannot 'speak' (Spivak 1988), they suggest that a shift from 'historical archive to ethnographic inquiry', and particularly the focus on women's songs, enables us 'to grasp the hegemonic discourse on kinship and gender, on the one hand, and women's subjectivity and agency, on the other' (Raheja and Gold 1994: 14). That agency, the songs highlight, was not merely, they propose, affirmative of the social order, but questioned and subverted it.

Recent Subaltern Studies historians have argued that gendered constructions of Indian women as defenceless in the face of male abuse were used by British colonial administrators and missionaries to authorise their role in India as defenders of women, vulnerable and coerced by their own society. The 1829 British prohibition of *sati,* widow immolation, which afforded women a protective mantle, legitimised—so the argument of the new historians goes—their continued colonial presence in India. Against that, however, Mani (1989) has shown that the debate on whether to prohibit *sati* was located discursively in a colonial discussion of 'correct' Brahmanical traditions; it did not focus in the first instance on the barbarism of *sati* and hence the need to protect defenceless women's human rights or, more broadly, on Christian ethical principles (1989: 94–5, 116). Instead, the debate on sati was part of a wider colonial attempt to codify personal law, based on traditional texts. The more pragmatic question for the colonial authorities was whether *sati* could be 'safely prohibited through legislation' without provoking 'indigenous outrage' because of its 'traditional' authorisation in scripture, or whether it was to be understood merely as an economic strategy deployed by families aiming to rid themselves of the expensive encumberance of widows (1989: 92), and thus unlikely to inflame religious passions.

In a contradictory discourse which stressed women's unbridled agency, Christian missionaries and colonial administrators were outraged by the apparently loose morals of Indian women. Banerjee (1989) records the horror of the missionaries and colonial officials at the 'indecent' public performances of women (p. 149). The growing puritanism of the Bengali elite at the end of the nineteenth century was influenced by Victorian values. Paradoxically, as Raheja and Gold report, Indian nationalists too, while resisting British colonialism, also tended to disapprove of Indian women's sexually explicit folk culture (see also Kelly 1991 on Fiji). Like the missionaries, they tried to suppress any overt expressions of female sexuality (Banerjee 1989). Gandhi's asceticism and sexual abstinence set the tone: 'Gandhian politics gave celibacy a new charge', John and Nair suggest (1986: 16), while at the same time, paradoxically, sexual 'repudiation demanded that sexual desire be talked about endlessly'. Gandhi became the 'eunuch for the nation'. Violence was, in Gandhian cosmology, an 'ingredient of male desire' while the ideal woman became the 'chaste wife' or celibate widow (ibid.: 17). Indian women, for Gandhi, were the true nationalists, with their silent courage and capacity to endure suffering. Ideally for the nationalists they were supposed to be both civilized, in a Western sense, while being guardians and preservers of tradition. To add to this, Raheja and Gold propose that despite the subaltern studies historians' critique, they too fail to include women's voices in their rewriting of colonial history. Alongside them, Western feminists have tended to construct women in India and the global South more generally purely as victims, without capacity to act independently. Such Eurocentric constructions have collectively continued to underline the superiority of the West.

Raheja and Gold's aim, then, is to recover the indigenous voices of local Indian women. At the same time, their intention is to highlight the fact that Indian women do not speak with a single voice. On the contrary, their voices reveal 'multiple perspectives, shifting purposes and reflexive or ironic commentaries' (pp. 9, 14–15), as Mohanty too has argued (1991: 55). The theoretical framework they deploy draws on James Scott's notion of hidden transcripts, disguised modes of resistance and counter-hegemonic discourses, which disrupt dominant ideological constructions of gender (Scott 1985, 1990). Scott, it will be recalled, argues that all dominant, hegemonic discourses have their limits. Subordinates see through the claims of superiors even when they dare not challenge them openly.

According to Raheja and Gold, village women do not simply accept cultural constructions of themselves imposed by male relatives. They certainly do not embrace self-abasement. Nor are they silent or mute. Instead, they have their own alternative visions of the world. They compose their own mythologies. These are expressed mainly through the medium of folk songs and tales. The songs challenge patriarchy and male ideas about female sexuality even if, ultimately, they do not have the power to overturn the dominant social order. Indeed, Raheja and Gold report that village women sing their sexually explicit songs openly, within earshot of men. What is not fully taken into account by the two authors, however, and this is the nub of my criticism, is that such songs are sung on prescribed ritual occasions and that the risqué jokes, sexual barbs and mock challenges they articulate are customary expressions of sexual or gendered conflict on *framed* occasions; that the songs, obscene joking, mocking and masquerading are, in other words, licensed, substantively marked as 'hot', and are thus also *ontologically transformative*. To the extent that the songs move beyond their prescribed ritual moments and come to be secularized as 'folk' or performative traditions, they lose this substantive-transformative-ontological capacity, but acquire the capacity for public protest and subversion and thus, perhaps, a place in history.

The customary limits of such counter-resistive expressions in Raheja and Gold's ethnography are underlined by the fact that the same women who deploy these subversive discourses continue to defend and uphold dominant discourses and the social order in other, everyday contexts. This implies, I suggest, against Raheja and Gold's disclaimer (1994: 24), that Indian women's songs of sexuality sung on ritual occasions can indeed be interpreted as 'rituals of rebellions' in Gluckman's terms (1963)—not in terms of their cathartic function, but in the way they transform the ontological condition of participants ritually through the enactment of conflict. Such transformative rituals of rebellion, which usually aim to renew or awaken the fertility of persons or the community, are rituals of *revitalization*. They deploy conflict productively and reproductively to mark, juxtapose, oppose and ultimately unite opposites. This is evident, for example, in McKim Marriott's account of Holi as a ritual of annual revitalization and 'love' which fails to overturn otherwise oppressive hierarchies of gender and caste (Marriott, 1966). As Gluckman argued, such rituals of rebellion challenge figures of authority such as men or chiefs, and express endemic, irresolvable conflicts in the society without threatening the social order or leading to a revolutionary consciousness (although for Gluckman, the possibility of incipient rebellion, if not revolution if the chief was unjust, *was* contained in these rituals). In this respect there is clearly a difference between Indian women who sing sexually explicit songs that mock men specifically on ritual occasions, usually associated with fertility and reproduction, and Indian or Pakistani feminists who challenge traditional laws that discriminate against women and demand from the state that they be reformed or abolished. The feminists deny that men should have more rights than women. They demand a total revolution of the traditional social order. Not so popular folk songs.

Raheja and Gold gloss over the key fact that rituals of rebellion are expressions of everyday conflicts that do not lead to radical social rupture or change. They are 'framed' events in Goffman's terms, performed in especially set-apart spaces, and are often, paradoxically, rituals convened to affirm cosmic fertility and to renew the social order. So too, the women studied by Raheja and Gold sing sexually transgressive songs which challenge men and openly refer to copulation on specific festivals or rituals of fertility and reproduction, such as Holi. Although they sometimes sing these songs on other occasions, just for fun, this is usually done in private, with only women around. At the same time, since such rituals express conflicts in everyday life, it seems fair to assume, as Raheja and Gold propose, that they do create subjective reflexivity and consciousness of an alternative social order. Equally persuasive is the fact that while being integral to some ritual moments, obscene singing and joking can also be performed 'out of frame', on the sidelines of events, obliquely subverting a central official message (Goffman 1974: Chapter 7). A major strength of the authors' analysis is their argument that the songs women sing are not merely 'texts' to be interpreted but positioned performances enacted from particular locations (1994: 147–8; Raheja 1995: 50). In this respect the authors arguably succeed in creating a bridge between postcolonial and subaltern studies and anthropological ethnographic analysis.

Listen to the Heron's Words certainly shows that women valorize sexuality in their folk songs and use sexual insults on ritual occasions. But the book's aim is to go further and argue against split representations of women in South Asia which image them as divided into two types. In popular Hindu mythologies women's sexuality is often depicted as dangerous and bad, while motherhood is constructed as fertile, good and nurturing. Split representations of women, common in South Asia, draw a contrast between a fertile but chaste nurturing mother, imaged as a cow, and an erotic but barren bad mother, imaged as a mare (O'Flaherty 1980). Against this, Raheja and Gold propose that Indian women are not split between the ideal and the real. They actually have a unitary sense of identity, one which encompasses both sex and motherhood. It could be argued, however, that because the authors start their analysis by rejecting the image of the chaste Indian women, in the final analysis they end by privileging women's sexually outrageous bawdiness, which stands in stark contrast to their public chastity and obedience. In effect, then, Raheja and Gold ultimately retain the opposition between discourses of sexuality and chastity.

A key reason, in my view, why Raheja and Gold can only reproduce a new version of such female split images arises from their exclusive focus on textual or discursive material at the expense of the silent language of symbolic, material and bodily substances. To take a contrastive example: in my work on *mehndi* rituals among Punjabi Muslims (Werbner 1986; 1990/2002: chapter 9), I attempt to probe the integration of sexual obscenities, joking, singing and masquerade in the cosmological and symbolic logic underlying such split representations, in order to demonstrate that they are part of a single unified idea about the cosmos.

My starting point for the ritual analysis is an indigenous cultural dilemma: how, in real life, can one achieve fertility without sexuality? The answer to this question is pitched first and foremost against the alternative indigenous folk construction of women in South Asia (and, indeed, in many Muslim societies where women are defined as potential sources of *fitna,* disorder) cited at the outset of this paper, one which highlights not their essence as sexually repressed victims but as sexually wild, hot and dangerously promiscuous, closer to nature than to culture and thus in need of domestication and control. Linked to this is the indigenous view that men legitimately control the public sphere, that is, the public domain of culture. By contrast, women are necessarily restricted to the domestic domain—being essentially close to nature as a result of their association with body fluids—menstruation, child bearing, cooking and child socialization. Being natural, women are barred from the public domain of culture. According to scholarly work drawing on this set of indigenous oppositions, the wedding ritual aims to control women's wild sexuality and establish male dominance over the bride (see, for example, Selwyn 1979).

Against this interpretation, my analysis starts from the fact that for South Asians, human sexuality is desired. In marriage, it is good and fertile. Uncontrolled, outside marriage, it is regarded as disorderly, hot and threatening to the social order. This view creates a paradox, a *cultural dilemma*, at the transitional moment of marriage. Pakistanis keep young virgins in *purdah*, protected from any contact with marriageable young men. Hence the moment of marriage is the moment of total exposure to what was previously strictly taboo, namely sex. The virginal bride is, I argue, *too cultural,* not natural enough. Her natural desires and sexual instincts have been kept under cultural lock and key. They have to be released and her exposure to a total stranger must be effected culturally *before* the marriage is consummated.

My interpretation draws on north Indian ideas about nature and fertility. Pakistanis believe that fertility in nature is a combination of heat and cold—of sun and rain—that is, it is always a balanced mixture (see Beck 1969). So too human fertility must combine and balance these features of hot and cold. Unlike humans, animals in nature can be sexuality uncontrolled and still reproduce, but in human society such uncontrolled sexuality is regarded as extremely dangerous—it is too hot and therefore, rather than bringing fertility, it is believed that it causes infertility. Heat is also associated with pollution, hence sex has to be cooled and purified. In the wedding *mehndi* the women who manage the ritual seek to juxtapose the heat of sex with coolness in order to make the bride and bridegroom's sex safe and fertile. The operation of symbolic substances goes towards achieving this combination of hot and cold substances for the sake of human fertility. Paralleling and reinforcing this symbolic manipulation are sexually explicit songs and androgynous masquerading (or cross-dressing) which are 'hot', much like the ritual substances. This makes evident why a singular focus only on the songs is inadequate. They have to be grasped in the broader context of the juxtapositions and processual ontological transformations effected through the ritual.

To understand north Indian wedding rituals, including wedding songs and insults, it is thus essential to recognize differentiations across the life course: 'Indian women' do not form a single category, as Raheja and Gold too argue, but without seeing the full implications of their argument. It is certain categories of women—young virgins—who are expected to be totally chaste and non-sexual, mute and submissive. Kept in seclusion, purdah, it is, above all, the sexuality and fertility of virgins and young brides that must be managed ritually, and it is they who must be protected from the hot sexuality of the opposite sex, of the male bridegroom. Wedding songs are part of an elaborate ritual process which also uses food and other magical substances, as well as transgressive joking, erotic dancing and clowning in the women's quarters, to effect a *transformation* in the condition of both the bride or bridegroom. Both boy and girl have to be made into sexual, and potentially fertile, human beings.

We see this in the *mehndi*, the henna mixture which is smeared on the bride and bridegroom. The *mehndi* is an anomalous, self-contradictory substance, and as such it is a ritual transformer. The henna is a green leaf which is mixed with water and lemon and in that wet stage it is said to be extremely cold. Its touch to the skin is very cold. But when it dries on the skin and is washed off a few hours later, it turns red, dark red. Red is a hot colour associated with blood and hence also with life and with the blood of childbirth. This is an iconic feature of redness - it stands for blood and all the ambiguities of life and death associated with blood. But in its quality as heat the *mehndi* substance is a symbolic shifter; it shifts the bride from cold to heat. This is underlined by the fact that her hennaed hands are passed over a hot oven after which she is not allowed to wash. The heat produced is, however, not a polluting and dangerous heat because it is a heat framed in coldness.

The same logic applies to the obscene joking and ritual clowning and masquerading that occur during the *mehndi* ritual. The young girls, friends of the bride often dress up as male figures adorned with beards and attired in ridiculous looking old clothes. Such clowns are prone to making sexy and obscene gestures and remarks. They are clearly regarded as very hot, figures of disorder which appear suddenly and just as suddenly vanish. The clown performs in front of the bride who sits in the corner, sad and crying, while her friends decorate her hands and feet with beautiful henna designs. The vulgarity of the performance is greeted by all the women, except the bride, with gales of laughter.

But older women too engage in sexual repartee, indicating, as Sylvia Vatuk has argued, that older, sexually experienced women do not become less sexual with age. On the contrary, 'the widely reported belief in South Asia [is] that sexual intercourse with an older woman is far more dangerous for a man' (Vatuk 1985: 144). There is no ritual marking of the menopause and the key distinction is between the virgin (*kanya*), the married woman whose husband is living, and the widow (ibid.: 145). An example of joking involving older women during the wedding is the following dialogue, in which the 'clown', a young woman dressed up as a disgusting old man, attacked the bride's mother:

Old man: 'Give me your daughter!'
Mother: 'You can take me'.
Old man: 'You're too old!
Mother: 'Look at you, you're old too'!

On another occasion, the bride's older sister commented on the inexperience of the groom, having successfully pulled off his shoe: 'I can manage a lot stronger than this one [i.e. the groom]. He was only born yesterday'![1]

Let us remind ourselves of the central dilemma implicit in the wedding ritual. Pakistanis want their daughters to be sexually active and fertile, and to enter into a successful, happy marriage. But sex is hot and dangerous. Moreover, male sex is particularly hot and dangerous. On the other hand, for men the blood of menstruation is polluting, hot and dangerous. So when they consummate their marriage, the bride and groom are effectively endangering each another. They need to be purified and made cold. *But they also need to be heated up*. Both these aims have to be achieved simultaneously.

My argument—that just as women are conventionally regarded as dangerous by men so too are men regarded as dangerous by women—draws support from Laura Ring's analysis of out-of-control 'hot' 'anger' among Sindhis and Punjabis in Pakistan. In her ethnography of a Karachi apartment building Ring found a prevalent attitude among women that 'Male anger is seen as immune to discipline or reform. Because of its boundless destructive potential, this anger is to be tactically avoided as much as possible—and failing that, it must be endured' (Ring 2006: 110). From women's perspective, male anger is intimately associated with blood and the physical 'transgression of limits—in particular, the breaching of bodily boundaries' (ibid.). Yet they socialize their sons in ways that encourage this expression of anger which is associated also with masculinity and ordering capacities.

Even in Manchester, the rites before and during the wedding retain their force so long as Pakistani Punjabis continue to keep young virgins in purdah and to believe that disordered sexuality is dangerous. But the ritual does more than change the physical or ontological constitution of the person. It is also reflexive and indexical in very specific ways even beyond gender. For example, in Manchester the transgressive joking during the *mehndi* comments on the current condition of the ethnic community in Britain. Jokey gifts highlight the general promiscuity and easy availability of sex in British society. The gifts thus also create a sense of boundary between the immigrant-settler community, which is much stricter with its young girls, and the rest of the society.

Second, the ritual clown is used by the girls and the women more generally to challenge certain Pakistani customs such as arranged marriages. The clown is a combination of male and female, young and old, an androgynous figure, a transvestite. Performatively, 'he' is used to comment on relations between men and women, young and old. Here the particular congregation attending the wedding rites and the particular issues bothering them are crucial. In some weddings there may be an attack through the clown on the older generation's arrangement of a marriage between a young girl and an older man, a union considered disgusting by most young girls. In other weddings, the antagonism between the sexes is highlighted. Women mock men. Yet not all the women participate in the joking. In particular the bride remains silent, 'ashamed' and weeping because she is leaving home. She enjoys the joking while pretending not to look. It is the rest of the women who celebrate sexuality.

The specificities of the verbal play are thus highly indexical and embedded in symbolic practices which are customary and draw on cosmogonic ideas about human and natural fertility in very specific ways. Because the sexuality of men and women is mutually dangerous, the bride and bridegroom are treated in complementary ways. Both are smeared with henna to make them hot on a background of coolness. In addition, the boy has milk poured over his head and is given milk to drink. The girl is fed with nuts which symbolise semen. The young girls and women stuff the boy's mouth with *mithai* (South Asian sweets). The transition in the wedding for the groom is from being nurtured by his mother to being nurtured by his wife—who also nurtures him sexually. There is in the ritual thus a play on ideas of nurture and sexuality. The boy has to be separated from his mother so that he can receive both the sexual services and the nurturing services of his future wife.

The *mehndi* ritual also underlines the fact that women control the domestic domain. In their hazing of the bridegroom, they are making clear to him that in this domain his wife will be dominant and he will have to submit to her authority. The ritual clown invades the domestic domain and threatens to disrupt it. The women take the power of nature-as-fertility that the clown represents, just as they take the natural substance of the *mehndi*, and then they cast the ritual clown out. The bride and bridegroom are left in a condition of cool heat, safe sexuality, which is associated with fertility.

To sum up, then: like Raheja and Gold's analysis of sexually transgressive songs in *Listen to the Heron's Words*, my analysis of the wedding ritual in *The Migration Process* denies the tendency in the scholarly literature on South Asia to stress split constructions of women as being either totally chaste or totally promiscuous. Both works recognise the power and agency of women in their own right, and their control over their bodies and sexuality. But I interpret this control as embedded in complex ideas about the cosmos, nature and regeneration, which are based on the notion of balance, the juxtaposition of opposites. For married women, among Muslims, there is no contradiction between sex, fertility and happiness, as long as these occur within marriage.

Ultimately, however, my point is also that women manoeuvre within real limits. Folk traditions do not make women revolutionaries even if they make them perpetual subversives of male pretensions of control. In the women's view, men's sexuality is dangerous, especially for innocent young women. So too, through domestic rituals women set limits to male arbitrary domination. They assert their dominance in the domestic sphere and over their husbands in it.

FROM RITUAL TO SECULAR POPULAR CULTURE

The singing, dancing, joking and masquerade in the *mehndi* rituals I observed, although drawing on a customary archive, was relatively spontaneous, a dramatic production staged by the bride givers, bride receivers, and their friends. But in Pakistan as in the rest of South Asia, certain social categories or professional castes perform more formalized, explicitly sexual dramatic roles during life-cycle rituals. Among these the *khusra* (elsewhere known also as *hijra*), cross-dressing effeminate males, sometimes castrated or hermaphrodites, who usually live in a group with other *khusre,* play 'an impure but a very auspicious role' paralleling that of the ritual clown (Pfeffer 1995: 31). Their main role is to perform at weddings and at the birth of a son. Pfeffer comments that ironically, 'emasculated dancers without sex or gender guarantee virility of Punjabi men and fertility of women and lineages'. Theirs is a 'regenerative power' (1995: 34), but they also have the power to curse if not remunerated. He interprets their performance as a 'sacrifice'; the *khusre* lacking sex, are 'sex givers' (p. 35), but it seems to me more plausible to argue that the unstable mixture of male and female which the *khusra* dramatises and embodies is the source of 'her' auspiciousness and fertility.

Hijre or *khusre* are not the only social category to perform auspicious dances in front of respectable elite audiences during religious festivals. Writing about urban Calcutta in the nineteenth century, Banerjee reports that a range of women sung of adultery and love, ridiculed male hypocrisy, irresponsibility and cowardice, and dealt with love affairs in a 'ribald' manner which was 'condemned as obscene by the educated Bengali gentry and finally banished from "respectable" society by the end of the century' (1989: 137). The *kheur* songs sung by women were often openly erotic, playful and bawdy; they expressed 'hearty unashamed appetite' (139). Banerjee interprets these ritual performances in political terms—as a 'challenge' to orthodoxy, an 'oblique criticism' of Brahmanical purist conventions (139), affording women a 'dissenting space', a 'symbolic solace' or 'revenge' (140). Such 'ritualistic displays', Banerjee suggests, 'could widen the behavioural options for women' or 'encourage disobedience' of the 'lower orders' (141). One is reminded of the transgressive behaviour of the woman saint-renouncer, Mira Bai: her association with male ascetics, her singing and dancing, and her merging at death with the (male) stone image of Krishna, draped in her sari, may be the mystical source of her fertility (Harlan 2001). Clearly, however, whatever auspicious ontological transformations the women's singing effected, as *ritual* performances its specific contextualised, framed effect within rituals or religious festivals, is glossed over in the feminist subaltern literature in favour of an ideological stress on women's resistance. Such transgressive women form part of an Indian feminist narrative of decline from a golden age which John and Nair (1998: 11–12) identify as nostalgia for a time when courtesans and other women performers led socially autonomous lives.

Banerjee's interpretation is linked perhaps also to an important transition that occurred in nineteenth century Calcutta: the *secularisation* of ritual and religious poertry as these were increasingly deployed in dramatic and theatrical performances before audiences (142). In 1891 there were 17,023 actresses, singers, dancers and their accompanists in Calcutta (132). Women formed troupes and parodied religious poems. They invoked the lifestyles of prostitutes and other secular themes. Working women composed 'doggerels' grounded in their daily experiences rather than 'social problems', such as *sati* (145–6). They drew on folk humour, bawdy quips and profanities (146). Although these 'obscene', 'licentious and immoral' performances were banned by over-zealous, puritanical Indian elites at the turn of the twentieth century, they resurfaced in a new form in Indian cinema, a point I return to below.

In Manchester, the move from the inner sanctum of women's *mehndi* rituals to more public events has been evident in the fund-raising performances of a women's group in Manchester, *Al Masoom*. During *chand rat*, the 'night of the moon' on the last day before Id, the organization held parties in Manchester to celebrate the end of the Ramzan fasting period. During these parties, the ritual singing of romantic love songs and erotic dancing signalled the imminent return to everyday sexuality and nurture. The ritual moment was clearly defined—a movement from sexual abstinence towards renewed fertility and growth.

In Pakistán *chand rat* is a street festival in which girls and women paint their hands with *mehndi* and buy each other bangles and jewellery. Jewellery bazaars stay open well after midnight. Here, for example, is a blog from Karachi:

> One of the highlights of *Ramazan* in Karachi is *Chand Raat*—the entire city doesn't seem to go to sleep until 6 AM, and there's this mad shopping frenzy in the air, combined with this city-wide spirit to

just aimlessly stroll the streets and take in the sights and sounds. What are your *Chand Raat* rituals—do you do the same thing every year, or has the excitement worn off as you got older? (http://karachi.metblogs.com/2005/10/31/chand-raat/)

Another blog describes the sexual undertones of the festival, echoing the *mehndi*:

> *Mehendi* [*sic*] sites are numerous and usually crowded to the brim with girls having their hands painted, on this night it also appears as if the bachelor guys ensure that families cannot have a respectful walk around. I wish I could wrap these guys up and ship them to *gawadar* for one night, as I feel they have no moral values, and tend to be a far bigger nuisance value destroying the spirit of the event. (http://karachi.metblogs.com/2005/11/04/chand-raat-celebration/)

In one sense the particular parties held by *Al Masoom* in Manchester were simply an organizational strategy for generating female solidarity by drawing on familiar popular cultural resources, variations on customary rituals such as the *mehndi*, transposed into a new context of voluntary activism. Nevertheless, seen against the background of the attempt by the women's association to assert its right to fund raise for philanthropic causes and assume its rightful place along with men on ceremonial occasions attended by Pakistani and local British dignitaries, and in public meetings held in Manchester (Werbner 2002: Chapter 10), the sexually explicit dancing and singing in the privacy of all-women celebrations took on new connotations. In particular, it revealed the ambivalence experienced by north Indian women who are public activists in their approach to a male-dominated world. The songs sung celebrated men not as enemies but as lovers. They invoked romantic love as well as sexuality, even if they did so in order to empower women as a solidary, exclusive, gendered community of committed activists. The secret and closed nature of the dancing and singing in the *chand rat* parties expressed this ambivalence. In their public actions, the women were willing to enter into open confrontation with men and to criticise them publicly. Yet in the privacy of the women's quarters the significance of the hidden transcripts sung customarily on ritual occasions was reversed: rather than being forms of counter-hegemonic resistance, they revealed the continuous valorization of sexual desire and a nostalgic yearning for romantic love.

Paradoxically, perhaps, the more that modern, contemporary Pakistani *mehndis* come to be opened up to young men as well as women, the more prettified and romanticized they become. In the few such 'mixed' *mehndis* I know of (one I attended in Pakistan, others I watched on video), there was a marked absence of sexually explicit episodes of joking and masquerade by the girls and women present. This is evident also in Indian movies 'for the family', marked by a lack of 'vulgarity', a mere hint at backstage eroticism, with the 'bawdy folk tradition of women's songs' 'sanitised' for mixed audiences (Uberoi 2006: 148; John and Nair 1998: 30–1).

In a further move towards secularizing the sexual themes of the *mehndi,* Al Masoom put on a series of amateur dramatic performances for women only, as part of its fund-raising events. These routinely included a fashion show, dancing, poetry and Koran reading. Most of the plays, written by the charismatic leader and her daughter, included *mehndi* staged performances in which the women sang, danced and dressed up as men. The plays' social messages parodied men and satirised them along with other stock figures of fun: the over-authoritative mother-in-law, hypocritical religious clerics, greedy men and awkward diasporic male visitors from England to Pakistan (the shows were held in Manchester).

CONTEMPORARY SEXUAL PURITANISM IN INDIA AND PAKISTAN

Nineteenth-century missionaries, colonial officials and elite reformists combined forces to clamp down on overt expressions of female sexuality by professional performers, even when their performances took place in the seclusion of the women's quarters (Banerjee 1989; John and Nair 1998), but they did not succeed in banishing these performances entirely, as Raheja and Gold's book and the work of other anthropologists has illustrated. Ordinary women continue to perform these songs, dances and masquerade during the rites preceding weddings and other religious festivals. So too, expressions of erotic sensuality have been incorporated, albeit in sanitized forms, into the expanding Indian cinema. By the late twentieth century protests by sex workers and movements for alternate sexualities became increasingly overt and public in India (John and Nair 1998: 33–6).

Countering such growing contemporary public exposures of sexual transgression and desire, however, has been a new wave of Hindu nationalists and (some) feminists. Even Marxists, who have allowed women greater public visibility, impose on them a strict moral code (ibid.: 32–3). Women's movements in India have fought against sexual violence and victimization, but unlike the rural Rajasthani, Punjabi and north Indian women described by anthropologists, only recently have they 'opened up spaces for talking about female desire' (ibid.: 9).

A more concerted attack on female sexuality has come from the BJP's anti-obscenity drive, demanding increased censorship of film and media images (Fernandes 2001: 158). Fernandes reports that the Hindutva 'platform was concentrated on the supposed contamination of the purity of Indian culture, embodied in the potential threat to the purity of women's sexuality'. The BJP-dominated Maharashtra state prohibited dancing women and waitresses employed in Mumbai's clubs and bars from working after 8.30 in the evening, which led, in turn, to mass protests by the women whose livelihoods were threatened (ibid.: 158–9). But the BJP moralist discourse of 'protection' was not restricted to them: it was also taken up by the press and media (160). So too, Lambert discusses the difficulty encountered by public HIV-Aids educators in India attempting to discuss sexual intimacy explicitly outside highly prescribed contexts (Lambert 2001: 61).

Not only in India itself but in far flung parts of the Indian diaspora, controversies have arisen over public expressions of female sexuality, as in the condemnations in Trinidad of 'chutney-soca' in the 1980s and 1990s. This popular genre, drawing on pre-wedding ritual and birth rite songs 'full of humour and sexual explicitness', was performed by east Indian women accompanied by young male drummers in front of audiences of up to 10,000 people (Niranjana 1998: 126–7).

In a parallel move, Islamists in Pakistan and throughout the Muslim world have condemned instrumental music and singing, particularly women's voices, as well as acting, masquerading and any other overt expressions of sexuality—even in women-only gatherings. In Pakistan, manifestations of sexual transgression are regarded not only as infringing strict Koranic injunctions on female sexuality, but as 'Hindu' backsliding. The attempt by Islamists to suppress such 'Hindu' expressions may be violent: when Sindhi (Muslim) medical students in Karachi celebrated their examination results by throwing paint on one another in an echo of Holi celebrations, they were attacked by Islamist students as Hindu, and this was followed by riots in the city (Ring 2006: 94–5).

As I have elaborated elsewhere (Werbner 1996, 2002), such attacks by Muslim puritanical ('fundamentalist') movements have rendered the space of fun highly contested for Pakistanis. Outside the mosque, a sensual Punjabi aesthetics of music, dance and verbal licence has been defined by the Islamists as unIslamic and sinful, and particularly so with regard to the conduct of women, their sexuality and their right to be visible in public. This is often stressed in relation to veiling. What is less often theorised is the equally doctrinaire redefinition of instrumental music, dance and masquerade (and hence also of ritual celebrations, Hindi films and musical concerts) as sinful, though the rise of the Taliban in Afghanistan and more recently in the North West Frontier Province of Pakistan has highlighted this tendency in both the Pakistani national and international media and press. Their moral crusade has included the banning of music, films and videos, of posters, billboards and hoardings bearing pictures of women models or film stars, and even of kite flying. Burqa-clad stick-wielding young women Islamist students at the Lal Masjid (Red Mosque) in Islamabad, capital of Pakistan, incinerated 'sinful' videos and CDs confiscated from local shops in public bonfires. Such iconoclastic zealotry indicates the extremes to which this puritanical movement is willing to go to ban any signs of women, femininity or sexuality—even in the private domain. Its stated aim is to restrict bodily expressions of emotion and desire. Today it is not only Hindus who are targeted but, by analogy, the permissive West.

Hence Chapter 6 of a Deobandi text on etiquette for women

depicts the sinful pleasures associated with customary celebrations:

> Everyone knows what sin and evil the dancing of harlots [professional singers and dancers in India who were regarded as prostitutes] entails. All the men look at unrelated women. That is adultery of the eyes. They hear the sound of the women singing and talking. That is adultery of the ears. They talk with these women. That is adultery of the tongue. . . . If dancing is this evil, just think how sinful the people must be who arrange for dances. . . . Moreover, the musicians play various instruments. . . that too is sin. Hazrat Apostle of God. . . . declared: "My Provider ordered me to destroy these instruments".'
> (Metcalf 1990: 95)

Women, the guardians of (allegedly Hinduised) 'sinful custom' (as against purified Islamic law) are particularly prone to sin:

> Now, as for the dancing arranged for the women [in exclusive female celebrations], you should consider it equally illegitimate, whether there are drums and other instruments or not. Books forbid the performance of monkeys—isn't it much worse to have people dance? Moreover, the men of the house sometimes catch a glimpse of the dancing, with all the evils described above as a result. Sometimes the [women] dancers sing, and their voices reach the men outside. The men who hear women sing are committing a sin, as are the women responsible for the singing. (ibid.: 95)

Masquerade too is prohibited: 'Some women put a man's hat on the head of the dancer. It is sin for a woman to look or act like a man. . . In short, all the dancing and music that goes on today is a sin' (ibid.: 95).

Along with singing, dancing and masquerade, ostentatious dress and jewelry are sinful ('the noble *hadis* forbids jingling jewellery, because Satan is present in every sound' (ibid.: 109).

Just as the English Puritans attacked the permissive excesses of Elizabethan England, so too 'fun' in the form of music, dance and customary celebration has been delegitimised and marginalised by Muslim reform movements. Their scripturalist zeal is not limited to South Asia. Patrick Gaffney describes how in Upper Egypt, a student musical comedy performance was interrupted: '[B]earded militants entered forcibly and took over the stage, expelling the actors. They declared that the production was not in keeping with Islam and they demanded that it be cancelled completely. In its place, they announced that they would conduct an Islam programme' (Gaffney 1994: 100).

In similar vein the Islamists prevented the establishment of a cafe on campus because it would encourage 'idleness and mixing of the sexes' (ibid.: 103). In revolutionary Iran, too, the sinfulness of dancing, music and especially the cinemas were, Beeman tells us, 'singled out for harsh attacks from the mosque and religious schools', and were defined as instruments of Satan, the great tempter (Beeman 1983: 196, 210). Hammoudi reports attacks by Islamists in Morocco on the Berber masquerade ritual of Bilmawn, celebrated after the Great Id. Bilmawn is an androgynous figure. On his back hang a phallus and testicles, on his chest a large, single breast. He is accompanied by several ritual masqueraders representing Jews, with their leader being the rabbi (Hammoudi 1993: 58; see also Werbner 2001). The masqueraders are allowed almost unlimited license. They swear and attack onlookers, enact sexual copulation in public, in front of women, enter the women's homes while the men of the house are absent, demand or steal food while scattering ash from the sacrificial fire at the mosque, in a ritual of fertility and purification. Objecting to the ritual as *bida,* unlawful innovation, the Islamists say that '. . . these are customs from before . . . these are the *jahiliya* (ignorance). . . . The people are Muslim, and all of a sudden they call themselves Jews and rabbis! It is not possible. And then, someone who imitates a people afterwards belongs to that people!' (1993: 66).

One could multiply further examples from the contemporary Muslim world. In her recent ethnography of the pietist movement in Egypt, Sabah Mahmood (2005) shows that women embrace voluntarily the normative asceticism of a strict normative Islam. In Britain there has been a marked increase in the number of women adopting the full face veil (*niqab*)—an indication that Islamic Puritanism has not yet had its day and that women's wedding popular culture continues to be under siege, with men attempting, often through the agency of women, to control even the inner spaces where *mehndis* are celebrated in transgressive licence with song, dance, risqué joking and masquerade.

CONCLUSION

The public and private celebration of love, sexuality and fertility by women in South Asia, and in the overseas South Asian diaspora, this paper has shown, has encountered sustained and repeated opposition by a wide range of conservative modernist movements, from Christian missionaries, colonial administrators and Indian nationalists in the nineteenth and twentieth centuries, to Hindutva nationalists, Islamists and even Indian Marxists at the turn of the twenty-first century. The value of anthropological work on north Indian women's expressive sexuality, as performed in rituals, folk singing and other forms of popular culture, has been to show that, despite this sustained puritanical attack, ordinary South Asian women of all ages continue to assert their right to express sexual desire, to mock men and explore their sexuality through different aesthetic media of song, dance and masquerade. Such expressions of popular culture need, however, to be contexualised, this paper has argued, in a wider cosmology of fertility and auspiciousness that imbues ritually transformative substances, and which frames the clowning, masquerading and joking that occur as episodes within such life course *rites de passage*. The explicit expressions of sexuality during ritual effect an ontological transformation, endowing persons at moments of transition with desired auspiciousness, fertility and reproductive capacity.

NOTES

* This paper was first presented to the Pakistan Workshop in 1999. I would like to thank the participants for their comments. I am also grateful to Karen Leonard for her immensely helpful suggestions.

1. These dialogues are taken from Werbner (1990/2002: Chapter 9). Joking at weddings varies from one place to another but is widely prevalent (see, for example, Fruzetti 1982: 14, 80–1; Kolenda 1990; Yagi 2008; Banerjee 1989: 159). Yaki reports on wedding rituals in Utter Pradesh that during the nine days of the ceremony, women sing gālī (insult or abuse songs) which are divided into two types: one type insults the bridegroom and his relatives while the other has a sexual meaning (Yaki 2008: 40).

REFERENCES

Banerjee, Sumanta (1989), 'Marginalization of Women's Popular Culture in Nineteenth Century Bengal', in Kukum Sangari and Sudesh Vaid (eds), *Recasting Women: Essays in Colonial History,* New Delhi: Kali for Women, pp. 127–79.

Beck, Brenda E.F. (1969), 'Colour and Heat in South Asian Ritual', *Man (N.S.)* 4: 553–72.

Beeman, William, O. (1983), 'Images of the Great Satan: Representations of the United States in the Iranian Revolution', in Nikki R. Keddie (ed.) *Religion and Politics in Iran,* New Haven: Yale University Press.

Goffman, Erving (1974), *Frame Analysis: An Essay on the Organization of Experience,* Boston: Northeastern University.

Fernandes, Leela (2001), 'Rethinking Globalization: Gender and Nation in India', in Marianne deKoven (ed.), *Feminist Locations,* New Brunswick: Rutgers University Press, pp. 147–67.

Fruzetti, Lina M. (1982), *The Gift of a Virgin: Women, Marriage, and Ritual in a Bengali Society,* New Delhi: Oxford University Press.

Gaffney, Patrick D. (1994), *The Prophet's Pulpit*, Berkeley: University of California Press.

Gluckman, Max (1963), 'Rituals of Rebellion in South-East Africa', in *Order and Rebellion in Tribal Africa,* London: Cohen and West.

Hammoudi, Abdellah (1993) [1988], *The Victim and its Masks*, trans. by Paula Wissig, Chicago: the University of Chicago Press.

Harlan, Lindsey (1995), 'Abandoning Shame: Mira and the Margins of Marriage', in Lindsey Harlan and Paul B. Courtright (eds) *From the Margins of Hindu Marriage,* Oxford: Oxford University Press, pp. 204–27.

John, Mary E. and Janaki Nair (1998), 'Introduction: A Question of Silence? The Sexual Economies of Modern India', in Mary E. John and Janaki Nair (eds), *A Question of Silence? The Sexual Economies of Modern India,* New Delhi: Kali for Women, pp. 1–51.

Kelly, John D. (1991), *A Politics of Virtue: Hinduism, Sexuality, and Countercolonial Discourse in Fiji,* Chicago: The University of Chicago Press.

Kolenda, Pauline (1990), 'Untouchable Chuhras Through Their Humour: "Equalizing" Marital Kin Through Teasing, Pretence and Farce', in Owen M. Lynch (ed.), *Divine Passions: The Social Construction of Emotion in India,* New Delhi: Oxford University Press, pp. 116–53.

Lambert, Helen (2001), 'Not Talking about Sex in India: Indirection and Communication of Bodily Intent', in Joy Hendry and C.W. Watson (eds), *An Anthropology of Indirect Communication,* London: Routledge, pp. 51–67.

Mahmood, Sabah (2005), *Politics of Piety: the Islamic Revival and the Feminist Subject,* Princeton: Princeton University Press.

Mani, Lata (1989), 'Contentious Traditions: The Debate on Sati in Colonial India', in Sangari and Vaid (eds), pp. 88–126.

Marriott, McKim (1966), 'The Feast of Love', in Milton Singer (ed.), *Krishna: Myths, Rites, and Attitudes,* Chicago: The University of Chicago Press, pp. 200–12.

Metcalf, Barbara Daly (1990), *Perfecting Women: Maulana Ashraf 'Ali Thanawi's Bihishti Zewar,* Berkeley: University of California Press.

Mohanty, Chandra T. (1991), 'Under Western Eyes: Feminist Scholarship and Colonial Discourses', in Chandra T. Mohanty, Ann Russo and Lourdes Torres (eds), *Third World Women and the Politics of Feminism,* Bloomington: Indiana University Press, pp. 51–80.

O'Flaherty, Wendy Doniger (1980), *Women, Androgynes, and Other Mythical Beasts,* Chicago: University of Chicago Press.

Pfeffer, Georg (1995), 'Manliness in the Punjab: Male Sexuality and the Khusra', *Sociologus* 45, 1: 26–39.

Raheja, Gloria Goodwin (1995), 'Crying when she's born, and crying when she goes away': Marriage and the Idiom of the Gift in Pahansu Song Performance', in Harlan and Courtright (eds), pp. 19–59.

Raheja, Gloria Goodwin and Ann Grodzins Gold (1994), *Listen to the Heron's Words: Reimagining Gender and Kinship in North India,* Berkeley: University of California Press.

Ring, Laura A. (2006), *Zenana: Everyday Peace in a Karachi Apartment Building,* Bloomington: Indiana University Press.

Scott, James C. (1985), *Weapons of the Weak: Everyday Forms of Peasant Resistance,* New Haven: Yale University Press.

—— (1990), *Domination and the Arts of Resistance: Hidden Transcripts,* New Haven: Yale University Press.

Selwyn, Tom (1979), 'Images of Reproduction: An Analysis of Hindu Marriage Ceremony', *Man (N.S.)* 14: 684–98.

Spivak, Gayatri Chakravorty (1988), *In Other Worlds: Essays in Cultural Politics,* London: Routledge.

Uberoi, Patricia (2006), *Freedom and Destiny: Gender, Family, and Popular Culture in India,* New Delhi: Oxford University Press.

Vatuk, Sylvia (1985), 'South Asian Cultural Conceptions of Sexuality', in Judith K. Brown and Virginia Kerns (eds), *In Her Prime: A New View of Middle Aged Women,* Massachusetts: Bergin & Garvey Publishers, pp. 137–54.

Werbner, Pnina (1986), 'The Virgin and the Clown: Ritual Elaboration in Pakistani Weddings', *Man* (N.S.) 21, pp. 227–50.

—— (1996), 'Fun Spaces: on Identity and Social Empowerment among British Pakistanis', *Theory, Culture and Society*, 13, 4, pp. 53–80.

—— (2001), 'The Limits of Cultural Hybridity: On Ritual Monsters, Poetic Licence, and Contested Postcolonial Purifications', *JRAI (incorporating Man)*, vol. 7, no. 1: 133–52.

—— (1990/2002), *The Migration Process: Capital, Gifts and Offerings among British Pakistanis*, Oxford: Berg Publishers.

—— (2002), *Imagined Diasporas among Manchester Muslims: The Public Performance of* Pakistani Transnational Identity Politics. World Anthropology Series. Oxford: James Currey Publishers and Santa Fe: New School of American Research.

Yagi, Yuko (2008), 'Women, Abuse Songs and Erotic Dances: Marriage Ceremonies in North India', in Yoshitaka Terada (ed.), *Music and Society in South Asia: Perspectives from Japan,* Osaka: National Museum of Ethnology, pp. 35–47.

8

Healing Madness through Ritual Trials

HELENE BASU

Sylvia Vatuk's work is so rich and multifaceted that one finds inspirations for developing new ideas in all kinds of directions. Her insistence that anthropologists should listen to the people and understand their worldview has always been encouraging for someone situated at the periphery of global anthropology. I want to start by referring to Sylvia Vatuk's recent interest in historical and contemporary legal cases relating to family law in India (Vatuk 1996, 2008). This makes an interesting contrast to my interest in ritual institutions in India which thrive on the distrust of governmental institutions and the legal system.

My fieldwork in Gujarat has led me to such a ritual institution that constitutes a different realm of administering justice. However, it would probably not be considered legitimate by modern public prosecutors and judges. In western India, this realm is circumscribed by Hindu temples and Muslim shrines conceived of as alternative 'moral courts'. At such courts, human and non-human offenders are tried through rituals for specific misdemeanors creating trouble in people's mind, body and behavior. This is the case, for example, at the Balaji temple in Rajasthan known for healing madness. As Pakaslahti noted, the temple was referred to as a 'royal court' (*darbar*) (Pakaslahti 1998: 136ff). Appearing before the court were the spirits of the dead (*bhutpret*) who had taken possession of a patient. Before beginning with a cure at the temple, patients had to 'file a petition' in the form of an offering to the gods. When the patient was admitted, the spirits made their 'appearance in court', and 'their case was heard' in the ritual trance performed by the patient. A similar conceptual frame of court trials is used at the Muslim shrine of Bava Gor in Gujarat which provides the focus of my paper.[1]

Sites such as the shrines of Bava Gor and Balaji vividly disclose the persistence of practices based on the association of madness with possession and sorcery in contemporary India. This is not to say that temples and shrines are manifestations of an unchanging 'tradition' opposed to 'Indian modernity'. They are 'turbulent centers'—to borrow a term from Kapferer (1997)—contradicting modernization theories of the 1960s. Contrary to these theories, beliefs in witches, harmful spirits and destructive people doing black magic have not disappeared with an increase in industrialization and modern forms of urbanization. Neither could globalization wipe out what appears as superstition from the rational perspective of the modern. Spirits and anti-social practices of sorcery are part of people's perceptions and experiences of everyday life in postcolonial Gujarat. To become mad means to have been hit by an attack of sorcery or by an intrusive spirit. The crisis draws attention to the fact that to survive against odds and adversities in modern India is not very different from fighting off demanding spirits or the destructive intentions of others. This, at least, is the view of those who go to shrines where madness is treated. Such places are sites where the pressures arising from Indian modernity are tackled from below. Bava Gor is a subaltern Muslim *dargah* (shrine) closely connected to the history of former African slaves and seamen, laborers and domestic servants (Basu 2008a). The trials performed there are embedded in an ethos of the poor and aim at empowering the weak and the vulnerable through the control of sorcery. Although the clientele at Bava Gor refracts categories of class, caste, ethnicity and religion to some extent, the shrine is still deeply embedded in the social life worlds of the laboring classes. While modern elites, both secular and religious, dismiss such institutions as 'backward traditions', it is significant that ritual centers treating madness continue to be of great relevance to people's lives in the here and now.

Until recently, not many anthropologists have studied madness in India or elsewhere in South Asia. Those who did found that sorcery—along with spirit possession—is a widely recognized source of madness (Bhattacharya 1986); Skultans 1987; Wilce 2004; Basu 2008b ; Pfleiderer 1981, 1994). According to Gujaratis, spirit possession and sorcery are conceived of as specific types of 'illnesses of the mind' (*magaj ni bimari*). This class of distress distinguishes 'illness of the spirits of the dead' (*bhutpret ni bimari*) from 'illness of the dirty techniques' (*maili viddhya ni bimari*) according to its source. Spirits are non-human agents inhabiting ambiguous cosmological spaces. They may extend into the world through regenerative or destructive effects, they may purify or pollute. Sorcery, by contrast, is deemed to be practised by human beings intending to harm and destroy other human beings by using techniques of black magic (*jadu*). Both illnesses become manifest in similar symptoms of possession trance. Possession is bad, but even worse are human attacks of sorcery. In the following, I shall examine what these illnesses do to the individuals affected by them and how 'healing' is conflated with bringing human and non-human beings, who act 'immorally', to trial.

In medical anthropology, possession refers to culturally constituted symbolic articulations of mental distress that are translatable into a psychopathological vocabulary such as 'depression' or 'psychosis' (Halliburton 2005). Possession is considered an 'idiom' for expressing distress and mental illness (Nichter 1982). Questions of healing provide the focus of this kind of research (Kleinman 1980). Significant studies have been carried out by psychiatrists in India who took culture into account and applied anthropological methods of research; they found that religious healing may indeed have positive effects even upon psychiatric disorders such as schizophrenia and psychosis (Pakaslahti 1998; Raguram et al. 2002). In their accounts, narratives of sorcery and spirit possession give voice to cultural expressions of deeper, underlying forms of psychological distress and pathologies. While such clinical insights are of great importance, as an anthropologist my focus is on the links between sorcery and madness in terms of social practice.

Studies exploring ritual healing in South Asia have demonstrated regional variations of a seemingly typical pattern grounded in dyadic healer-patient-relationships that often accords to a 'shamanistic model': Healers are chosen mediums of the gods who go into a trance on behalf of patients to communicate with and take control over spirits and other non-human agents responsible for the affliction (e.g. Kapferer 1991; Sax 2004). While trance is significant in the type of healing practiced at the shrine of Bava Gor too, healers are not involved. The guardians of the shrine do not define their ritual roles as healers but as a kind of alternative policemen who execute the authority of the saints against human sorcery and spirit possession. The agents deemed to cause madness are brought to trial at the court of Bava Gor. Healing is understood in terms of liberating the victims of harmful agents from ill-disposed outside forces. Guardians of the shrine organize the context of the ritual trials but they do not intervene in the healing process itself. Until recently, this pattern rested on two complementary types of ritual trials performed at the shrine. One type identified human culprits violating social and moral norms by committing acts of theft, adultery or black magic through an ordeal, the other disclosed the identity of damaging presences of spirits and sorcery spells afflicting madness through trance.

In contrast to madness the study of sorcery has a long and controversial history in anthropology.[2] Anthropologists are especially critical of modern representations of sorcery as irrational beliefs and actions (Kapferer 2003). Contemporary theoretical approaches treat sorcery as a special type of social action that follows its own rationality in explaining personal misfortune, or, more generally, imponderable events and social crises arising from the uncertainties of life. It is based on the belief that emotions of one person can damage another. Sorcery implies knowledge of how a person's intention to do harm can have effects in the world through specific techniques of manipulation. This kind of knowledge gives power over people to those who command it. Practices of sorcery are embedded in cosmologies and their inherent dangers embodied by 'matter out of place'. They build upon ambiguous relationships between human and non-human persons and violate moral standards of sociality. Accusations of sorcery may accompany or incite social conflicts. As Kapferer pointed out, sorcery is about how people 'make and break their social life-worlds' (Kapferer 1997: 2).

The common classification of sorcery with other anti-social acts (theft, adultery) situates the moral court of Bava Gor at the interface of healing, social control and justice. Social attitudes towards madness and ways of handling mental trouble are intrinsically connected to cultural values, social experiences and emotions associated with sorcery. Madness is not located in individual failures but in conflicting social relationships and realities. Madness and sorcery are marked by ambiguities and converge in the fear they both provoke (Wilce 2004; Kapferer 1997). Kapferer described sorcery shrines in Sri Lanka as places where people are empowered by destroying life, health or family life by cursing and sending spells of sorcery. 'Healing' is brought about by the same means here which people assume to have shattered their own lives. A different model prevails in Gujarat. Here, Muslim saints possess regenerative and destructive powers enclosed in the model of the court. Through their dual powers the saints heal madness and restore sanity; they identify and punish wrong-doers and administer divine justice. This local model resonates with the literal meaning of the term *dargah* referring both to a royal and a saintly 'court' (Metcalf and Joint Committee on South Asia 1984: 8). The double-face of the historical Sufi court combining political and divine power is transcended in the image of Bava Gor as a counter court—a court that empowers the poor and the abject to surmount their troubles. In contrast to the sorcery shrines described by Kapferer, the *dargah* is a place where ambiguity is eliminated but not celebrated. This will become more apparent when exploring the meanings of the shrine from the perspective of those who seek remedies there.

THE MORAL COURT OF BAVA GOR IN GUJARAT

The shrine (*dargah*) of Bava Gor lies at the edge of what is called the 'Golden Corridor' of Gujarat: the belt connecting the industrial and commercial metropolitan cities of Ahmedabad, Vadodara and Surat with Mumbai. After independence, Gujarat emerged as one of the leading industrializing states of the Indian Union. Trade and commerce have a long history here and the region is dotted with hosts of urban centers. Agriculture is highly commercialized too. Capitalism is flourishing and since the liberalization policies in the early 1990s the economy in Gujarat is booming. The state attracts migrant workers from more 'backward' regions such as Orissa, UP or from Tribal Areas in Maharashtra; conversely, large numbers of Gujaratis have migrated to Great Britain, the US, Canada and the United Arabian Emirates in the more recent past. Investments by Non-Resident-Indians further fuel economic development. However, class, caste, ethnicity and religion have remained significant factors circumscribing chances of participating in and benefiting from these developments. While more jobs are available to people of the lower classes, competition has intensified and the gap separating the rich and the poor has widened. Moreover, the unleashing of the economy was accompanied by the spectacular success of the Hindu religious nationalist movement (Hindutva) in Gujarat. Paralleling this development amongst the Hindu majority (*c.* 80 per cent), Islamic revival movements gained ground amongst the Muslim minority (*c.* 12 per cent). The latter is internally as highly diversified in terms of social identity (kinship associations), sect and class as the Hindu majority. The BJP has dominated state politics in Gujarat since the late 1990s. Under the rule of the BJP, Muslim business people complain of harassment, while Muslims seeking a job hardly find regular employment even if they are educated and qualified. In the 1980s, 1990s and 2002 Gujarat was centre-stage for violent communal conflicts that killed hundreds and thousands of Muslims and Hindus. As a result, most of the formerly mixed neighborhoods in the many urban centers dissolved into homogenous Hindu or Muslim localities.

Bava Gor is a site resisting this trend. The shrine attracts supplicants from Hindu, Muslim, Adivasi and even Parsi communities. They come from villages, dilapidated urban neighborhoods or from one of the rapidly growing modern housing colonies in the cities. The shrine is situated on top of a range of hills in a forest area where the majority of the population are Adivasis (Scheduled Tribes). The *dargah* is referred to as the 'shrine in the wilderness' (*jungli dargah*). It is inhabited by Bava Gor, his sister Mai Mishra and their brother Bava Habash who are collectively known as 'masters of the spirits' (*jinnat na sarkar*). The peripheral spatial location is matched by the marginal social status of the people who own the shrine. They belong to the small

Muslim community of African origins (*c.* 20,000–30,000) known as Sidi whose houses are spread all over the poorer locations in urban (and a few rural) Gujarati environments. From their perspective, Bava Gor is a central shrine of saintly ancestors embodying the history and social identity of their community in Gujarat (Basu 2004).

One group of Sidi families lives in the village below the shrine and manages its ritual affairs on behalf of their own community as well as on behalf of pilgrims and supplicants. They are the guardians of the moral court (*mujavar*). Here, I spent many months of fieldwork in the 1980s and again in 2004 and 2008. In the 1980s most people I met at the shrine found life was a tiring struggle. The fear of becoming further impoverished or even reduced to begging loomed large. People blamed the government for not keeping the promise given by Indira Gandhi to wipe out poverty. There was general agreement that the government would help the rich only, while the poor were left to fend for themselves. People did not trust the government and the politicians. Young men found it hopelessly difficult to get a job without paying a large bribe. The rich and the powerful were held to cheat and exploit the poor. In such a world, people without money and contacts to influential, powerful personalities had very little chance of getting ahead. Those who managed to arrive at a modest improvement of their situation often felt hampered and pulled back to misery by the envy of relatives and neighbors. In this social environment, Bava Gor and his co-saints stood on the side of those seeking justice who could neither trust the institutions of the state nor people close to them.

The court of Bava Gor came to life through Sidi people enacting ritual roles of the 'police officer' (*kotwal*), 'chief drummer' (*nagarchi*) and the 'deputy saint-judge' (*gaddivaras*). They set the stage for the ritual trials in which the saints reveal the truth. Divine justice was administered not only in cases of madness caused by sorcery or spirit possession but also of adultery and theft. The latter were managed by the 'police officer' in control of the ritual ordeal referred to as *bedi* (iron traps). Trucks used to arrive almost daily at the shrine carrying groups of people who brought a person accused of one of three crimes: practices of black magic (*jadu*), adultery or theft. They were referred to as *bedivale*. Some of the accused came voluntarily or had even themselves suggested to undergo the ordeal to prove that the accusation raised against them was unfounded; others had reluctantly agreed to succumb to the pressure of their challengers. To refuse to undergo the ordeal meant that one was afraid and therefore guilty. The groups of *bedivale* were received by the ritual 'police officer' leading them trough the ritual trial of the ordeal. The ritual began with a purifying bath of the accused. He was facing the police officer who fastened the iron trap around his ankles. He then repeated the words spoken by the police officer swearing a sacred oath of accepting the verdict of the saint as unconditionally true. While drums were beaten the accused was made to run with the iron traps around his ankles to the tomb of Bava Gor. If the rings opened on the way, he or she was innocent, if not, guilt was unequivocally established. If a person was found guilty in this way, punishment was left to the community. Often, however, the iron traps opened.

Already in the 1980s, Bava Gor was the last religious place where a ritual ordeal was still done in Gujarat. In the past, various forms of ordeals were widely practiced at both Muslim shrines and Hindu temples. After independence they had been abolished at most religious places that came under government control through the Religious Endowment Act of 1950. At Bava Gor, the ritual ordeal was given up after the death of the old police officer about four years ago. His son no longer performs *bedi* because quarrels result from it. If the verdict does not meet the expectations of accusers, he says, they start to fight. Today, ritual trials only take place against spirits and sorcerers accused of having caused madness.

Since the 1980s, the shrine has steadily expanded. Except *bedivale*, pilgrims and supplicants used to come only once a week, but nowadays every day at least ten to twenty people may be expected. Major days during the week are Thursday and Sunday, when more than a hundred people visit the *dargah*. They pay respect (*salami*) to the powerful saints Bava Gor, his sister Mai Mishra, and his brother Bava Habash and ask their blessings for all kinds of worldly matters such as marriage, children, jobs, visas to foreign countries, economic success and good health.

Over the years, new buildings have been added to accommodate those supplicants who stay for a longer time. There are ten rooms to let and two common halls where people can stay free of charge. These are used mainly by men and women suffering from mental troubles and by their caretakers. Their problems manifest in passionate emotions of rage, fear, sadness or hopelessness and are often accompanied by painful sensations in the body. People complain about pressure on chest, paralysis or stiffness of limbs, stomach pain, headaches and general physical weakness. People also suffer from difficulties in taking food, sleeplessness or extreme tiredness, incessant talking or complete dumbness. At the shrine, they are referred to as *hajrivale*. *Hajri* means 'presence' in Gujarati and denotes states of trance. *Hajrivale* are those whose mind-body-self and consciousness is occupied by an alien and destructive Other who causes their sufferings. This Other may be a spirit of the dead (*bhut*) or a *jinn* (Muslim spirit) seeking to satisfy its own desires. Or it may be a sorcery spell sent by a hostile person intending to harm or even destroy the victim. *Maili viddhyan*, the 'dirty methods', refer to techniques of sorcery that depend upon black magic (*jadu*) working with impure substances (cf. Basu 2008b). Sorcery specialists are believed to learn and teach their craft in the night of *kali chaudas*, the 'black fourteenth', which corresponds to the last night of the Hindu festival celebrating the goddess (Navratri). In this night, sorcery priests are said to gather naked at the cremation ground to disseminate knowledge about how to curse enemies and destroy them by spells of sorcery. Such destructive energies and actions of living people are imagined as disembodied as the spirits of the dead; through curses and spells a living person may take control over her or his victim's life. At Bava Gor, such actions are objectified and called 'things' (*vastu*). Things are impure and dangerous. They cause severe mental and social troubles. By torturing the person they have taken hold of and making her mad, 'things' create chaos in the social life worlds of their victims. Thus, *hajrivale* are people whose 'minds are out of tune' (*magaj barabar chalta nahi*), whose 'brains are finished off' (*magaj khalas*), who suffer from 'tensions in the mind' (*mansik*) or who are simply 'mad' (*pagal, gando*). In any case, the victims are controlled by the presence of Others inside their selves who cause them pain and defy the rules of sociality. *Hajrivale* come to the shrine to get rid of their mental troubles (*magaj ni taklif*) in ritual trials where the spirits of the dead and the living are summoned in trance.

In contrast to spirits and things posing ambiguous threats, the saints inspire trust. The 'masters of spirits' preside over a counter court balancing personal suffering, misfortune and pain that arise from strained and conflict-ridden social relationships in an uncertain world full of fraud and betrayal. Persons suffering from mental trouble (*magaj ni taklif*) and the people who take them to the shrine are called '*dukhvale*', people burdened with sorrows. They seek answers and solutions to worrying questions. Why is my wife acting so weird and not doing her work any more? Is she mad? Why has the medicine she got from the doctor and for which we spent so much money not helped her? Has someone put a sorcery spell over her? Or is it a spirit of the dead that tortures her? A *jinn*? Initially, supplicants harbour vague suspicions, doubts, and fears. One does not know how and why one's personal life has suddenly gone totally wrong. Ritual trials in which the saints reveal the truth in trances experienced by those in distress provide the means. Supplicants are first received at the court by the ritual police officer. He refers the complaints of the suffering to the 'saint judges'. In return for an initial 'court fee' consisting of Rs. 10, flowers, and incense sticks, the supplicants receive tokens of trust from the saints. These consist of a protective charm (a small black bundle containing a written verse from the Koran), blessings from a horse made of cloth and waived over the head of the afflicted and, finally, the medicines of Bava Gor to swallow: ash from a sacred fire and water left over from cleaning the tombs. After entry into the court, supplicants are given over to the care of the saints. The healing process unfolds in ritual trials in trance. The saints communicate with the afflicted and the afflicting agents. Supplicants need to find out from the saints who is causing their individual difficulties and sufferings and why. At the shrine, supplicants find unequivocal answers to these queries and their uncertainties are removed. By accusing a troubling agent through the trance of its victim, the saints are revealing the truth.

SORCERERS UNDER TRIAL

When I conducted fieldwork research at Bava Gor in March 2008, thirteen *hajrivale*, eight women and five men, were staying at the shrine seeking deliverance from mental troubles. Their days were structured by ritual time. At dawn and at dusk and after the *moulvi* had finished reminding people over loudspeakers to say the first and the fourth of their daily prayers (*namaj*), the saints held their *darbar* (court gathering). They summoned everybody to their graves for the burning of incense (*lobanbatti*). This is the time when the spirits of living sorcerers or those of the dead are challenged by the saints in ritual trials. While one 'court attendant' purified the tombs and their surroundings with burning incense, the drummer was beating a drum. These were moments of great intensity. Enticing the agents of trouble from their hidings, the saints heard and answered their cases in the trance of the afflicted. Trance, it should be noted here, is an ambiguous phenomena; it is both a symptom of possession and a method of healing.

During the hours between the morning and evening rites of burning incense, groups of afflicted used to gather around a fireplace near one of the graves. Oblivious of the heat, people spent hours here. I often joined them. There was little talk. Each one seemed engrossed in a bleak and sorrowful inner world. Occasionally, someone would turn into his or her 'thing', while another cried and a third one sat still and motionless. It was here that I met a man whom I shall call Ram.

Ram seemed an old man to me, although he was only thirty-five. His body was completely stiff and he never talked. Ram was taken care of by his wife, his wife's brother and the wife's brother's wife (*sali*). They were peasants coming from a village in a neighboring district. When I first met Ram early after his arrival, his feet were chained to a pillar in the hall where he was staying with his relatives. The relatives looked worried and harassed. His brother-in-law explained that Ram was 'doing a lot of *tofan*' (acting violently). He got into fits of uncontrolled rage. They therefore had to keep him fastened in chains for his own and others' protection. 'His mind has completely failed', added his sister-in-law. Although he never experienced trance, they were suspicious that Ram had become a victim of sorcery. While a psychiatrist might diagnose Ram as schizophrenic, his relatives looked to black magic. 'A lot of black magic (*jadu*) is going on in the area where we live', said his wife. Ram's relatives thought they knew who had harmed him when they arrived. For years, Ram had been involved in a dispute over the boundary between his and a neighbours' fields. Trying to solve this conflict, he went to a *bua* (priest of a goddess) and asked for help against the neighbour. The priest agreed but then cheated him by helping the neighbour instead of Ram. His relatives thought that the priest had put spells of sorcery that first attacked Ram's bullocks who died suddenly from poisonous fodder. Then Ram's mind was affected very badly. From a good and hard working man, his wife said, he had turned into a madman. Ram ran around the village shouting obscenities, threatened to beat people and collapsed into utter lifelessness. Over the last three years, Ram had turned on and off into a madman. In the beginning, the family had taken Ram to a mental hospital in the nearby city. He was given 'shots and shocks' (electroshock therapy) from which he returned more weakened then before, his limbs all loose and his mind empty. This created even more anxiety, as Ram's family feared that he might die in the mental hospital. His father-in-law said that Ram suffered from an illness of sorcery against which doctors had no remedy. He forbade the family to admit Ram ever again to a mental hospital. Then, a few weeks ago, Ram had once more elapsed into an episode of madness. It broke out when his wife had gone to her parents' home and he was alone in the house. This time, the family had brought the case before Bava Gor. They expected that the saints would confirm their suspicions of sorcery and make Ram normal again by liberating him from the spell sent by the priest.

Indeed, in the weeks to come, Ram's condition did improve. He was no longer taken to the toilet and fed like an infant by his wife. The chains disappeared and sometimes I met him walking around the *dargah* premises all by himself. Ram still did not talk much but occasionally he smiled and muttered a greeting. Life seemed to return to Ram and he became a person in control of himself again. However, Ram's improvement was accompanied by the rapid and unexpected deterioration of the mental health of his sister-in-law. She had been well before and had come to the shrine in order to help. In contrast to Ram, the *sali* now often experienced violent trances. She could not eat and vomited frequently. She screamed and cried in trance. Her husband had to look after her more than he had done with his brother-in-law. He was gripped with fear because, he said, he had seen death lurking in the shadow of his wife. Moreover, the family could not leave the shrine as it had expected. Worries about work to be done in the village and the children left with a brother added to their distress. It turned out that the saints had disclosed someone else in the course of the trial responsible for Ram's mental trouble. The suspicion they had harboured at the time of their arrival was only partly confirmed. It was true that black magic was involved; but it was not the priest acting on behalf of the neighbour who had attacked Ram by using sorcery. Now that Ram's *sali* (WBW) was affected, the situation had changed. The target of the enemy was not Ram alone but the whole family. In her trance the saints had disclosed an aunt of the *sali* to have cast a spell of sorcery. Processes of healing through ritual trials thus may take unexpected turns and are often open-ended (as is ethnographic research). At the time, I could not observe the further unfolding of the crisis because I had to return to Germany. Still, what could be gathered at this stage was that the blame had shifted from a distant neighbour to a closer relative. In the course of Ram's cure at the shrine the crises was re-centred as a conflict within the family.

Ritual trials often result in the identification of close family members as the cause of the problem. Another man, Suresh (Kanthibhai Painter), suffered from mental trouble caused by a sorcery spell from his mother. Suresh was in his early thirties and often sat with other afflicted people around the fire. In contrast to Ram, Suresh talked a lot about himself and his troubles which had started about three years ago. He said that his mother had used black magic (*jadu*) against him by serving him polluted food and potions. Hearing this, other people got upset. One asked incredulously 'How can his own mother have done such a thing!' Yes, she did, insisted Suresh, and he described his frequent and frenzied trances that led to his vomiting substances of rainbow colours. 'The things (*vastu*) my mother has fed me are coming out then', he said.

At the time of my fieldwork, Suresh stayed alone at the shrine for most of the week. He was married and lived with his wife and two young sons in one of the metropolitan cities about 80 km away. Until his problems started, he had worked in a textile company designing sari borders and earned good money. Suresh had met his wife in the company where she still worked in the canteen. His wife Nirmala and the sons came to visit him at weekends. On one such occasion, Nirmala told me the story of Suresh's illness and their troubles.

They were from different castes and had met in the company where they both worked. He had liked Nirmala and one day asked her to marry him. Nirmala's parents were dead and she had no brothers and sisters. She was alone in the world. She gladly accepted Suresh's proposal but his mother fiercely opposed their marriage. The mother was critical of Nirmala's irregular teeth and found her too plain. Ignoring his mothers' protest, Suresh got married to Nirmala. At around the same time, Suresh's father died. He had been a teacher in a primary school and owned a house. After the death, Suresh and his brothers sold the house and shared the price. The mother claimed a share of the money and quarrels ensued. Suresh accused his mother of having cheated him, while she apparently accused him of having kept money which was her due. Nevertheless, at first all went well after Suresh's and Nirmala's marriage. Suresh earned more than Rs. 7,000 a month. They took a loan and bought a house in a newly emerging colony at the edge of the city. Nirmala was pregnant. Trouble started soon after the birth of their first son. Suresh became moody and sad and often fell ill. He vomited frequently and felt physically weak and drained. On many days, he could not go for work and eventually lost his job. Then their first born son died after six months. Initially, Suresh went to one doctor after another and tried different kinds of medicine. He spent a lot of money but it did not help him. Then he went to another Muslim shrine near his city for more than a year. This too did not improve his condition. Finally, three months ago Suresh had come to the shrine of Bava Gor. Here the saints revealed in his trance that it was his mother who had sent sorcery spells destroying Suresh's health and his family. It was also disclosed that the mother was angry because Suresh had defied her wishes in regard to his marriage and she was envious of Suresh's money. Both Nirmala and Suresh were sure then that his mother had taken recourse to sorcery out of anger and revenge. The couple also believed that the death of their first son was caused by black magic employed by Suresh's mother. They felt socially harmed. All relationships to Suresh's family were broken, he was no longer on speaking terms with his brothers and their families nor with his mother. Suresh's problems were thought remarkable not only by other afflicted people but also by the Sidi guardians of the shrine (*mujavar*). Sometimes a *mujavar* would say 'It is Suresh's fault. Why did he not give his mother what she asked for? It would have been his duty. A son has to give the mother what she asks for'. Another would counter that a mother should not do black magic to her own son either. Both were seen as guilty.

Ram and his *sali*, Suresh and many other *hajrivale* had become victims of particularly severe forms of chaotic, defiant and destructive forces associated with physical and social death (madness). *Maili viddhya*, are said to be used by living persons harbouring passionate emotions of anger, envy or hatred against their fellow human beings. I have never met anybody admitting that he knew or even practiced methods of sorcery to harm somebody else. At the shrine, however, most people were convinced that such people actually do exist. Mental trouble produced by sorcery was considered worse than possession by impure or capricious spirits. People from the Sidi community who routinely deal with afflicted persons at the shrine report that living people are more dangerous than the dead. Sorcerers command a kind of knowledge unknown to most people. They escape control and order. Moreover, potentially destructive intentions of people are said to be like the air one is breathing. It may flow from anybody even without the person being aware of it. Harmful energies are invisible but always present and one can never be sure if a person harbours good or bad intentions toward oneself. One does not know if, as Sidi people say, someone's heart is white or black.

HEALING AND TRUTH

In the beginning, when people in distress arrive at the shrine, they do not know what has produced the difficulties they face in their lives. At the onset of a mental crisis people are unsure of what happened to them. Almost all the afflicted I encountered at the shrine had sought help initially at the clinic of a medical doctor. Only when medicine did not seem to do any good, suspicion arose that the source of trouble was to be found in 'something else'. At Bava Gor, this 'something else' invariably turned out to be black magic or possession.

Accusations of sorcery are made in a ritual space removed from the everyday social world of the afflicted. Bava Gor is a 'centre-out-there' produced by a special kind of pilgrimage. Here, pilgrims do not seek transcendent merits but relief from this-worldly pain. What may be called 'healing' at the shrine of Bava Gor is not centred upon the feelings and intentions of the afflicted individual but upon the destructive forces that have taken possession of a self. Healing merges with liberation from spirits and 'things' by punishing them. At the court of Bava Gor, spirits of sorcerers and the dead are 'caught' as a thief is caught. They must be brought under control to enable the self to lead a normal social life again, and the destructive agents must be punished. Both actions are performed by the saints in the trance of the affected persons. Performances of trials in trance unfold as processes in which the afflicted are liberated from destructive forces threatening to overwhelm him or her. Identification of a sorcery spell, accusations of sorcery, and actions of redress are all embodied by the afflicted in trance. While incense is burned, the truth of each case is gradually disclosed in individual ritual dramas.

The graves of the saints provide the stage. With the first sounds of the drum, those afflicted enter into a ritual trance manifested in poignant performances of speech and bodily movements. A sudden cacophony of screaming, shouting, crying, and pleading voices discloses the presence of the myriad spirits and 'things' that pester those afflicted. Women swirl their loose hair around their rotating upper bodies. Men's heads are jerking or beating hard on the floor. Actors in this kind of trance are said to feel pained and tormented with 'harsh words' (*dunvu*). Such performances of affliction and possession trances are not expressions of mental illness as has been occasionally suggested (cf. Kakar 1982: 75), but a method of healing. As the psychiatrist Pakaslahti rightly concluded, 'ritual trance cannot be reduced to psychopathology. It is basically a culturally approved procedure for treating psychosocial problems in a positive group environment. As a therapeutic method, it must be learned like any skill' (Pakaslahti 1998: 159). At Bava Gor, this method calls out the spirits and 'things' from their hiding places. The passionate utterances and violent movements of the afflicted in trance are those of the spirits arguing and resisting the saints' control and attempting to evade their punishments. The spirits of the dead and of living sorcerers use foul language, plead with the saints 'oh Bava, please don't catch me, please let me go' or try to trick them by making false conditional promises, 'if you get off me now I shall leave her . . . '. Bava Gor and his co-saints challenge the 'things' by forcing them to disclose their identities. Those accompanying a victim eagerly listen to the answers the spirits give to the saint, hoping to find out the identity of the afflicting spirit. Is it a spirit of the dead (*bhut*)? A Muslim *jinnat*, pure (*pak*) or impure (*napak*)? Is it a known human being who had cursed the patient? Had somebody performed black magic against one's daughter? As long as the relatives do not know the identity of the 'things', they anxiously ask them, 'who are you' and 'tell us your name!' The who, how and why of each particular mental crises is gradually revealed in repeated trance sessions over days, weeks or months. The trial and the negotiations with spirits and sorcerers may take an indefinite time, however, especially if, as is often the case, more than one act of black magic or several spirits are discovered burdening a patient.

When a person has attended the court of Bava Gor many times, his 'things' might finally give in and submit to the power of the saints. At one occasion, for example, Suresh's 'mother-thing' spoke in his trance while his wife was present: 'I am sorry, *bava*, please take my apologies. I will leave him. I have given pain to his wife, please forgive me. I have given pain to his sons, please forgive me.' This was a significant development because the spirit of the mother apologised and admitted to have done wrong. Redress is brought about when destructive agents plead for forgiveness (*mafi mangvu*) and promise to leave the troubled person. This confirms that the victim is right and the accused has committed a crime.

What Bava Gor and the other saints disclose in trance is unambiguously true. They define right and wrong and establish certainties. It is not a transcendental truth the saints embody but many kinds of this-worldly truths. Such truths are opposed to speaking lies (*jhut bolvanu*) which is considered a grave social offence. Nevertheless, lies, fraud, and betrayal are seen as common reasons for a host of difficulties people experience in their everyday social life. Against this, Bava Gor represents trust. What Bava Gor and his co-saints disclose to the victims of sorcery is true. In this way, true narratives of distress are constructed by the people listening to those in trance and making sense of it. Coherent stories evolve from multiple authors reading the bits and pieces disclosed in trance. An afflicted person awakening from his trance is told afterwards what he or she did and said. The caretakers of one person discuss their predicaments with other, similarly affected, people or with Sidi guardians of the shrine. Curing madness through trials in ritual trance is propelled by collective acts of interpretation. These are confirmed in the final act of the trial. Sorcery 'things' or spirits of the dead are detained by the ritual police officer who fixes a tip of hair of the victim with a big nail into a tree. They get expelled from the victim and are brought under the eternal control of the 'masters of spirits'. After this last act, the victim is freed from the hold destructive agents exercised over his or her mind (*magaj*) and sanity is restored.

Those who are identified in the process—such as the aunt of Ram's sister-in-law or Suresh's mother—are not involved in the production of narratives of distress and healing. They might not even be aware of the fact that they have been accused of sorcery. Such accusations are not told to somebody's face and no scapegoats are identified. Wrongdoers are challenged and punished by Bava Gor and his co-saints alone, not by the afflicted or those taking their side in family conflicts and ambiguous relationships. Neither do they curse them. Thus, in contrast to what Kapferer found in Sri Lanka, at the shrine of Bava Gor neither guardians of the shrine nor supplicants engage in cursing their enemies. Instead of revenge, people seek liberation from oppressive presences of others, that is, from the attacks launched by other human beings' destructive intentions. Again, as in the case of the afflicted, punishment is not exercised directly upon the accused but upon the 'spirits' of the spells, those emotional experiences (envy, hatred) of the enemy that effect troubles in the live of his/her victims. Redress is achieved by pleadings for forgiveness and punishment consists in the symbolic imprisonment of spirits and sorcery 'things'. Justice is administered for the person who had become a victim of destructive, anti-social forces and who is now restored to strength and sanity.

Liberation from madness

The liberation from madness afflicted by sorcery or spirits is a process through which an afflicted person may gain new insights into the circumstances of her life. It allows for reflexivity and personal transformations. After a cure at Bava Gor, people often decide to change their personal lives and invent new identities for themselves. This was the lesson Mumtaz learned from her troubles and her cure.

Mumtaz was between 40 and 45 years old. She had come about three weeks earlier from a harbour town at the coast of Saurashtra where she lived in a Sidi neighbourhood. The former fishing village lay close to a rapidly industrialising city. Mumtaz was to go home soon when I met her. She had received the 'order' (*hukm*) of the saint to come when she was emotionally troubled and now she had been given 'permission' to leave. Her troubles had started some months ago. She always felt very sad. First she stopped talking to people, then she stopped going for work. She became *shamshun*, completely dumb and withdrawn, I learned from her two sisters-in-law who accompanied her. Her family was worried. Mumtaz refused to eat and she could not sleep. She often experienced trance seizures and some unknown presence in her demanded chocolates and fruits, expensive items for the family budget. She was married and had four sons. The husband rarely worked and, Mumtaz complained, he used to spend a lot of money on gambling and was generally irresponsible. The family depended mostly on what Mumtaz earned from working as a maid in a Rajput household. For Rs. 100 a month she cleaned the dishes and washed the clothes. At the shrine, the saints had revealed the reasons for her troubles. Mumtaz had become host to an impure spirit of the dead (*bhut*) that had taken possession of her body-mind while she was at work. The spirit had attacked her while she had washed sheets of her employer soiled with menstrual blood. After three weeks at the shrine, the spirit had been caught and imprisoned by the saints. Her condition improved and her husband came to fetch her. I asked if she would go back to work for her employer? No, Mumtaz said. She would stop working altogether. Then she pointed to her husband and said: 'Now he will work. He will stop gambling and work instead.' The husband looked embarrassed and agreed. What would she do instead of working as a maid? She would do *seva*, ritual service for Mai Mishra, the female saint. Mumtaz aspired to a new ritual identity for herself.

CONCLUSION

Translating fieldwork experiences into textual evidence carries the risk of constructing one's own model instead of that created by the society studied. This is the issue Nabokov raised against Kapferer's account—which is greatly inspired by phenomenology—of sorcery practices in Sri Lanka. Nabokov challenged Kapferer on the basis that it was in fact he who saw sorcery practices as empowerment of the lower classes (Nabokov 2000). She, by contrast, emphasised the destructive effects of sorcery on a personal level of experience; in her account from Tamil Nadu, she demonstrated the damaging effects sorcery has upon the personal life of the people with whom she worked.

The fieldwork situation of madness and sorcery described suggests that both approaches have value. Sorcery surely is an 'idiom of the political' as much as madness is an 'idiom of personal distress'. But perhaps fieldworkers carry also the biases of the people whose practices they study into their texts. My attempts to comprehend the meanings of madness at Bava Gor have been biased by the people who are affected by it. They may be mentally troubled people, spouses and other family members, or the people who offer them a stage for curing themselves, the guardians of the shrine. What makes people go to the shrine in the first place is the personal experience of misfortune and disaster, madness being one of the gravest. Social death is emerging from madness afflicted by sorcery, by people harbouring dangerous emotions such as envy, greed or hatred. This is what people fear most: the deadly passions of another human being. These are aroused more in times of political violence and uncertain changes, but they always involve closely related people with whom one spends much of one's life. Viewing sorcery as a significant aspect of madness thus discloses a broad dimension of sociality concerned with negatively evaluated social relationships and their practical interactions (the 'poison in the gift').

Kapferer considers sorcery shrines to be 'sites of class struggle' where the destructive intentions of the poor and abject become means of resisting the exercise of power of the ruling classes (Kapferer 1997: 255). The evidence gathered at the Muslim shrine of Bava Gor does not support such a view. Both the ritual ordeal (*bedi*) and the trials performed in trance (*hajri*) confirm suspicions or reveal them as unfounded. The saints enforce gendered norms and rules of the dominant social order. Although they are saints of the poor, they do not defy the normative morality of the society; they are no revolutionaries. In all classes, theft, adultery and sorcery are considered anti-social actions. The saints are guardians of social morality by bringing those forces under their control that threaten to destroy life and all that is considered morally good. The *bedi* ordeal featured potential wrongdoers, while *hajri* ritual trials feature the victims of sorcerers and possessing spirits. Thus, ambiguities are removed and truth is established at a counter-court in a political world that is experienced by many people as distant, hostile, and threatening.

However, suspicion that someone is suffering from mental trouble caused by either spirits or by acts of black magic performed by ill-disposed people grows only after various other kinds of medical treatments have been tried in vain. This kind of reasoning follows a logic of expulsion typical for the diagnostics of sorcery. When those afflicted with madness through black magic seek help at the moral court of Bava Gor, they do not merely hope to find a cure from illness but they also expect redress or punishment of the wrongdoer. Thus, by considering a moral court exclusively in terms of healing, as a 'faith healing center' as it is called in the parlance of medical pluralism, the dimension that conflates curing madness with ritual procedures countering the effects of sorcery would be lost.

The situation at the court of Bava Gor also differs from the one described by Pakaslahti at the Balaji temple. Healing of mental illness was achieved, according to Pakaslahti, by a re-integration of the afflicted into the family. Social relationships were healed and restored in accordance with cosmological moral models. In this process of re-establishing normative values in the cure, the involvement of family members played a major role (Pakaslahti 1998). The cure at Bava Gor, by contrast, completes the open disruption of social relationships that had been disturbed before. Following the logic of sorcery, accusations made in trance mark a separation from at least some members of the family. If and how these separations are realised in practice, when those healed from their affliction return home, are questions for further research. Here, the practices of Bava Gor open a window to how people living in the 'unorganised sector' of contemporary Gujarat tackle madness as an effect of troubled social relationships.

NOTES

1. Research material presented here was made possible by a generous grant of Fritz-Thyssen-Stiftung.
2. For a useful summary of anthropological approaches to witchcraft and sorcery, see Stewart and Strathern 2004.

REFERENCES

Basu, Helene. 'Ritual Communication: The Case of the Sidi in Gujarat', in *Lived Islam in South Asia: Adaptation, Accomodation and Conflict*, ed. Imtiaz Ahmad and Helmut Reifeld, Delhi: Social Science Press, 2004: 233–53.

—— 'Music and the Formation of Sidi Identity in Western India', *History Workshop Journal*, 65 (2008a): 161–78.

—— 'Schmutzige Methoden: Geisteskrank durch Besessenheit und Schwarze Magie in Gujarat/Indien', in *Un/Reinheit Im Kulturvergleich*, ed. Martin Voehler and Angelika Malinar, München: Fink Verlag, 2008b.

Bhattacharya, Deborah. *Pagalami: Ethnopsychiatric Knowledge in*

Bengal, Syracuse: Foreign and Comparative Studies/South Asian Series, No. 11, 1986.

Halliburton, M. 'Just Some Spirits': The Erosion of Spirit Possession and the Rise of "Tension" in South India', *Medical Anthropology* 24: 111–44 (2005).

Kapferer, Bruce. *A Celebration of Demons: Exorcism and the Aesthetics of Healing in Sri Lanka*, 2nd edn. Providence, R.I., USA, Washington, DC, USA: Berg; Smithsonian Institution Press, 1991.

—— *The Feast of the Sorcerer : Practices of Consciousness and Power*, Chicago: University of Chicago Press, 1997.

—— *Beyond Rationalism: Rethinking Magic, Witchcraft, and Sorcery*. Pbk. edn. New York: Berghahn Books, 2003.

Kleinman, Arthur. *Patients and Healers in the Context of Culture*, Berkeley: University of California Press, 1980.

Metcalf, Barbara Daly and Joint Committee on South Asia. *Moral Conduct and Authority: The Place of Adab in South Asian Islam*, Berkeley: University of California Press, 1984.

Nabokov, I. 'Deadly Power: A Funeral to Counter Sorcery in South India'. *American Ethnologist* 27.1 (2000): 147–68.

Nichter, M. 'Idioms of Distress'. *Culture, Medicine and Psychiatry* 5 (1982): 379–408.

Pakaslahti, A. 'Family-Centred Treatment of Mental Health Problems at the Balaji Temple in Rajasthan', in *Changing Kinship Patterns of Family and Kinship in South Asia*, ed. A. Tenhunen, S. Parpola, Vol. 84. Helsinki: Studio Orientalia, 1998: 129–66.

Pfleiderer, B. *Die Besessenen Frauen Von Mira Datar Dargah. Heilen Und Trance in Indien*. Frankfurt/M: Campus, 1994.

Pfleiderer, B. 'Mira Datar Dargah: The Psychiatry of a Muslim Shrine', in *Ritual and Religion among Muslims in India*, ed. Imtiaz Ahmad, New Delhi: Manohar, 1981: 195–234.

Raguram, R. et al. 'Traditional Community Resources for Mental Health: A Report of Temple Healing from India', BMJ 325 (2002): 38–40.

Sax, William. 'Healing Rituals: A Critical Performative Approach', *Anthropology & Medicine* 11.3 (2004): 293–306.

Skultans, V. 'Trance and the Management of Illness among Maharashtrian Families', *Anthropology Today* 3.1 (1987): 2–4.

Stewart, Pamela J. and Andrew Strathern. *Witchcraft, Sorcery, Rumors and Gossip*, New Departures in Anthropology, Cambridge: Cambridge University Press, 2004.

Vatuk, Sylvia. 'Identity and Difference for Equality and Inequality in

South Asian Muslim Society'. *Caste Today*, ed. Chris Fuller, New Delhi: Oxford University Press, 1996: 227–62.

—— 'Divorce at the Wife's Initiative in Muslim Personal Law: What Are the Options and What Are the Implications for Women's Welfare?', in *Redefining Family Law in India: Essays in Honour of B. Sivaramayya*, ed. A. Parashar and Dhanda, London: Routledge, 2008: 200–35.

Wilce, Jim. 'Madness, Fear and Control in Bangladesh: Clashing Bodies of Power/Knoweldge', *Medical Anthropology Quarterly* 18.3 (2004): 357–75.

9

Courage and Authority in the Next Generation: Shifts in Gender Expectations and Performance in a Hyderabadi Sufi Healing Tradition

JOYCE BURKHALTER FLUECKIGER

In the fall of 2007, I returned to the Sufi healing site in Hyderabad where I had worked intermittently with a Muslim female religious healer, Amma, from 1990 until her death in 2001 and about whom I have written in *In Amma's Healing Room: Gender and Vernacular Islam in South India* (2006). As a female spiritual healer who met the "public"[1] (meaning, here, men and women, Muslims and non-Muslims) and charged money for her services, Amma sat in what is traditionally in South Asian Sufi traditions a male ritual role of *pir* or *sheikh* (see Eaton 1984; Ewing, 1997; 1984). At the height of her practice in the 1990s, Amma regularly met 50-60 patients a day, who came for healing and counsel regarding 'trouble in the house' (*pareshani*), infertility, marital problems, childhood fevers, failing businesses, missing children, possession by *jinn* or *shaytans*, negative influences of evil eye, and chronic pain or illness. Amma used to say that she was a "doctor" for problems caused by *shaytani* (evil forces; literally, the devil), and that illness caused by *shaytani* could only be cured through spiritual practice, not by allopathic medicine. But she was equally firm that illnesses and troubles not caused by such negative spiritual forces were beyond her domain of authority; she specifically named heart disease, typhoid, polio, and cancer.

I returned to Amma's healing room to observe what had happened to the healing practice after her death in 2001: who had ultimately taken up the mantle of spiritual and healing authority? Had traditional gender roles shifted in her family and community after Amma had cracked open their boundaries? How had the healing practice and Amma's immediate family changed with the death of a charismatic matriarch who defied traditional gender roles? Finally, what difference had Amma's unusual gendered work made in the lives of the women among whom she lived?

AMMA AS BOTH EXCEPTIONAL AND MODEL OF POTENTIALITY

Amma never saw herself as ordinary woman. When I first met her in 1989 and over the intervening years until her death in 2001, Amma often told personal narratives in her healing rhetoric that set her apart from other women, narratives that implied she was chosen by God, that she had unique spiritual gifts, fortitude, and discipline that enabled her to fill the role of ritual healer traditionally held by male *pirs* (see Flueckiger 2006). She introduced herself to my husband when he came to her healing room the first time with a description of her birth: 'I was born during a big storm [*tufan*]; they often told me about the big storm during which I was born. Ever since then, I've continued to be a big *tufan*, and I deal with the *tufans* of others [her patients].' She took pride in her love of learning and work ethic, saying she was 'born to work. I'm strong because of my habit of working hard. It's not my habit to sit lazily in one place.' On another occasion she attributed this discipline and love of learning as having come from God himself, 'Like you [speaking to me in my role as researcher], I have the desire to learn everything. It's a desire from God. I also got it from humans, from the pious ones [*buzurgan*; pious ancestors] around me.' She told of being identified as a young girl in school by her Hindu teacher as being someone who was unique and who would become famous. She reported being engaged in 'Allah's *bhakti* [devotion]' ever since she was a small girl; she had had visions of 'written words across the sky', which she equated with the *kalma* (Muslim declaration of faith). Finally, after her marriage, she went without her husband's knowledge to a *pir* (Sufi master and teacher) to learn from him and became a disciple. She went to this *pir*'s own *pir* to learn the healing practice. Before taking up the role of public healer, Amma sat *chilla* (ascetic meditation) for forty days, during which time she said she became like a skeleton and would spit out the food Abba tried to feed her.

Amma saw few of these characteristics requisite of a successful spiritual healer in other women. She thought they lacked the spiritual acumen, courage (*himmat*), strength, and patience needed to confront the evil forces that disrupted the physical, social, and psychological bodies of the patients who came to her healing room. And it was true that among the Muslim women I met in Hyderabad who engaged in some level of religious healing, Amma *was* unique in the public nature of her practice. I met many female householders who blew *dua* (personal prayers and supplications) on family members. I met only a few who treated non-family members: one woman interpreted dreams of clients who spent the night at the *dargah* (grave shrine of a saint) at which her husband was the caretaker; while another interpreted the shriveling patterns of drying lemons that she had given her clients to keep in their homes for a week. Amma distinguished herself from these women in that she wrote amulets (writing being associated with male practice) and that she met both Hindu and Muslim patients. When Amma heard I had visited these other women, she dismissed their power, saying, 'But what do they *give* [i.e., amulets]? They don't give anything; they're in it just for the money.'

I once asked Amma if she was teaching her healing practice to her (then mid-thirties) daughter-in-law or her daughters. Amma was surprised I could even imagine such a thing, exclaiming, 'No, they don't have the heart [*dil*] for it. If a possessed patient came in front of my daughter-in-law, she would faint from fear. She has no strength/courage [*himmat*]'. Amma frequently said, 'There are only two castes [*jati*] in the world: men and women,' but in the context of her role as healer, she placed herself on the male side of that presumably non-negotiable boundary. She more than once asserted her unique authority by saying, 'I have the form [*nakal*] of a woman, but the heart [*dil*] of a man.'

Amma's husband, Abba, had met and become a disciple of his *pir* after Amma had admitted to him that she had become a disciple of that same *pir*. She went to a second *pir* to learn the specifics of the healing practice based on 'opening the mystery of numbers' (*abjad ka phal kholna*), in which the healer diagnoses and writes prescriptions dependent upon numerical calculations based on a patient's name and that of his/her mother (each "Arabi" letter being associated with a particular number). Abba used to tell me that Amma was able to practice healing with the "public" only because he had given his permission. I realize now, more than when Abba and Amma were living, that there *were* unique circumstances that gave space for Amma's unusual practice—primarily her mutually supportive relationship with Abba, his own ritual authority as a *pir*, and his lack of literacy in the Arabic script. The latter was perhaps the most important incentive for Abba to give his 'permission' (*ijazat*) to Amma to learn and publicly practice the healing tradition dependent on the Arabic script. (He was proud of his minimal literacy in English letters, which he said he learned while serving in the British army; this service, he said, had prevented him from learning Arabic/Urdu script.) However, Abba was equally dependent on Amma, although this was never stated openly, in that most of his disciples came to him through Amma's healing practice. Between them, they creatively shared the teaching and healing roles of a *pir*.

While Amma viewed herself as an exceptional woman—who was 'like a man', as she said—other women in her community and family often said any woman *could* engage in this practice as long as she fulfilled the prerequisites of being literate in Arabic script (in which the amulets are written) and was married to a *pir* (which would give her authority to practice in public). However, they could not name another woman who had fulfilled them. They had observed Amma in her everyday roles outside the healing room—wife, mother, and friend—and thought that if it was possible for her to garner such authority and spiritual healing power, other 'ordinary' women, too, could do so.

While Amma was still living, early on in my fieldwork in the 1990s, her daughter-in-law Lateefa told me that she did not practice this kind of healing (*ilaj*) only because she was still too young (implying people would not listen/defer to her, that she needed more experience to be given necessary authority), not because, as Amma had asserted, of her gender or that she did not have the courage for it. After all, Lateefa had watched and lived with Amma for over 15 years before Amma died; she never excluded herself from the possibilities/potential of female action in the public sphere that she had witnessed. I concluded my discussion of gender roles in Amma's healing practice in my book, *In Amma's Healing Room*, with the speculation that while Amma did not directly challenge patriarchal traditions that limited public healing to men, 'for the women listening to [and watching the enactment of] Amma's story, its telling extends the boundaries of gender and that her very presence in a public ritual role embodies an alternative gender ideology' (2006: 167).

After Abba's death in 1998, his succession in spiritual authority and lineage became an issue of bitter dispute. While Abba was living, his mantle of authority had protected and authorized Amma's practice. However, in the Sufi tradition in which Abba had been initiated, the line of succession technically is male only. His son Khalid had inherited this spiritual authority (*khilafat*) from Abba when he was only in his twenties, and four other male disciples had also been given *khilafat* before Abba died. Upon Abba's death, Amma was sidelined for a little over a year, neglected by many of her and Abba's disciples as they renegotiated their position with Khalid and the other male disciples who had been given *khilafat*. Khalid moved out of their home to the other side of town, where he practiced healing in his home when he came back from his workday at the university post office. Many local patients followed another of Amma's key disciples, Mustang, to his domestic healing room in the neighborhood adjacent to Amma's healing room. Before Amma died in 2001, the rift had been healed, Khalid and his family had moved back in with her, and most disciples had returned to some kind of relationship with Amma. But Amma's spirit and health were broken, and she never renewed her lively practice before she died two years later.

GENDERED AUTHORITY IN THE NEXT GENERATION

When I returned to Hyderabad in 2003, Amma's daughter-in-law Lateefa rather shyly admitted to me, as we were eating lunch one day in her living quarters and the healing room was locked, that she had begun to sit at Amma's healing table when her husband and son were at work and school during the day, but that the number of patients was only a shadow of the 50–60 patients who used to wait in long lines to see Amma. In 2005 and 2007, when I again visited briefly, Lateefa was more often in the healing room writing amulets during the day than she had been in 2003, but the daytime clientele was still small. Most patients waited to come to the healing room when they knew Khalid and their twenty-year-old son Akbar would be at home in the evenings and on Sunday. Lateefa helped write and fold amulets then when the lines got long. When the men were not there, I noticed that Lateefa spent more time talking with women about their personal problems and advising them than she did writing amulets. Because of the lesser number of patients, she had more time than Amma had had to talk about and advise regarding dowry, marriages, infertility, and disputed family property.

Amma often used legal terminology to describe her practice, for example equating the written amulets she prescribed and distributed to the written judgments in a court of law:

> Allah gave power to the pen and paper. . . .*Taqat*—"power". He didn't give 'power' to the tongue. If someone gets angry, what happens? You take him and report him to the police, to the collector's office. Then they look at the petition. They don't listen to the word of tongue, only the written word. The 'judge' can send you to the gallows. And if he wants, he can bring you down from there with the stroke of a pen. . . . It's all in the pen, in the pen and paper. Only these two things.

I came to see Amma's healing room as an alternative or co-existing system to the formal court systems Sylvia Vatuk has analyzed (Vatuk 2008; 2006).

Interestingly, Lateefa does not use this legal language that equates her practice in the healing room with that of the courts. She does not see herself as a particularly exceptional woman and tells no stories of visions and dreams that 'called' her to the position of public healer, stories so common in Amma's healing rhetoric. Lateefa has gradually eased into the inherited position of *piranima* (wife of a *pir*) she now fills, and she serves as a kind of 'substitute' healer in the absence of her husband and son. She has learned what she knows through observation and has not been taught the tradition in any systematic way by a guru/*pir*, nor has she sat *chilla* (a 40-day meditative retreat) to garner particular spiritual insight or power. However, when her male kin are not there, she confidently deals with most patients and engages in lively conversations about the details of their cases.

Still, there seems to be some limit to Lateefa's authority. One revealing episode reflects back to Amma's comment that Lateefa did not have the courage to deal with possession. Returning from Abba's ninth death anniversary celebration (*sandal*) at the *dargah* that has developed over his and Amma's graves, we found a 15-year old girl lying in the courtyard moaning and writhing, with her older sister and brother worriedly looking on. Lateefa walked right past her with barely a glance. Surprised, I asked if she wasn't going to do something, or if she *could* do something. She simply answered that they would wait for 'Sahib' (Khalid) to return. But her 23-year-old son Akbar came home before his father and immediately went into action, beginning the treatment with the same words and intonation Amma had used with possessed patients, 'Tell me your name! Tell me your name!' as he hit a stick on the healing table to get the attention of the possessing *jinn* or *shaytan*/devil. Eventually the possessed girl spoke the name of the *shaytan*, and Akbar wrote some amulets for her family to burn and for the patient to drink. He prayed *dua* over the patient and told her relatives to return the next Sunday when his father would be present.

Lateefa is still considered a younger, middle-aged woman, not yet forty; she is still menstruating and raising teenagers at home. Amma herself did not begin meeting the "public" until after the birth of the youngest of her 13 children, after which she told me she and Abba did not 'live as husband and wife'. Until Amma reached menopause, she complained, she had had to 'sit out' for a week every month, and she was thankful to God when she finally reached menopause (see Vatuk 1992 for a discussion of sexuality and the middle-aged woman in India). Lateefa denies she does not have courage to deal with 'big cases', but she told me that there is no need for her to do so since there is someone else (her husband or son) to take them on. Lateefa may gain more authority when she becomes postmenopausal and has a daughter-in-law of her own to take over the household tasks that now occupy a good part of her day. When I asked if she was interested in filling a larger role in the healing practice (*ilaj*), she smiled and nodded affirmatively, even as she verbally deferred to Amma: 'For Amma's daughter-in-law [*bahu*], son and grandson to continue her practice helps to make known Amma's name.'

Another young woman who could have potentially inherited Amma's practice (although not at the same site, since she is married and lives across town) is her youngest daughter, Rehma. She is married to her parallel cousin from both sides: the son of Amma's sister and Abba's brother. Abba's brother is also a *pir* and has given his *khilafat* to his only son, Rehma's husband. Both Rehma's father-in-law and husband practice the Islamic medical system of Unani (primarily dispensing herbs) and also write amulets (*taviz*) in the Sufi tradition in which Amma was trained. Rehma's husband told me many years ago, when Amma was still living, that he would not permit his wife to meet the "public" in the way that Amma did, that it was not proper for a woman to meet men like that. Even then and continuing to the present, however, Rehma meets women every now and then, in the living quarters of their house rather than in the healing room, and writes *taviz* for them when they do not want to share their problems with a man. She confidently answered my recent enquiry into whether or not she still wrote *taviz*: 'Why wouldn't I? I grew up sitting at Amma's knee, didn't I?'

Rehma not only writes *taviz* (albeit for women only) and interprets the sway of prayer beads held over a patient, but she also informally teaches women in her community, much as the way in which Amma used to teach in her healing room. During Abba's death anniversary celebration in 2007, I heard Rehma on several occasions give teachings to the women gathered around her, as we waited for a ritual to begin or for meals to be served, when a topic such as dowry or veiling or other women's issues came up. About dowry, she began: 'The Quran doesn't actually teach that we should practice dowry. We just think that. But actually, Islam is very "easy". It's only people who make it "heavy", carrying it like a "heavy basket".'

While neither Amma's daughter nor daughter-in-law sit in the same kind of public ritual role or with the full authority with which Amma sat—primarily because they are married to men who can fulfill both the teaching and healing responsibilities of a *pir* in ways that Abba could not—both women carry a confidence that assumes their ability and even right to heal and teach. They are active partners to their husbands in decision-making, planning for and staging the ritual events for which their husbands are publicly responsible (such as monthly *sama* ritual assemblies during which *qavvali* is performed, and annual death anniversary rituals of Abba and other ancestral *pirs*). They also participate in the healing practice: Lateefa when her husband is at work, and Rehma when women want to talk to a woman rather than a male healer.

DISPERSION OF AUTHORITY IN THE SECOND GENERATION

Spiritual authority in the second generation is no longer as concentrated as it was with Amma and Abba. Of course, were one to have worked with Amma's *pir* and *his* family and disciples in the next generation, a similar observation of dispersed authority may well have been drawn. However, Amma rarely talked about other disciples of her *pir*, and the only ones I met were her brothers-in-law. She took pride in the fact that she was the only woman to whom her own *pir* had given authority to heal and that she had had a closer relationship with him than other female disciples.

Abba gave his *khilafat* to five disciples, including his son Khalid, and each of them has a *chilla* (domestic shrine) at his home and practices at least some minimal level of healing through dispensing *taviz* (the *taviz* are now xeroxed from a master copy obtained through Khalid, rather than being handwritten as they were by Amma). One of Amma's closest disciples and a convert from Hinduism, Mustang, has a lively, lucrative healing practice in his home and a large Hindu clientele from the immediate neighborhood. He is the only *khilafa* disciple who practices healing full time, earning enough to enable him to give up his carpentry business altogether. His wife is not involved at any level in Mustang's healing practice. Being a convert from Hinduism herself, she is not well-versed in the intricacies of many Islamic practices such as *namaz* (daily prayer), nor does she read or write Urdu or Arabic.

The healing tradition practiced in the second generation is still in transition, and there will surely be further shifts and negotiations of authority and roles in the coming years as various actors grow older and move from one life stage to another. Khalid is still working as a university employee, although he suffered an aneurysm in spring 2007, leaving him with a weakened left arm and leg. In the fall of 2007, he had just returned to work at the university and spent several hours each week going to physical therapy or visiting doctors. At this time, Khalid rarely sat at the healing table for more than a half hour at a time, and he seemed more than willing for his eldest son Akbar to sit in his stead. When the two sat together at the table, Khalid periodically disagreed with how Akbar had treated a returning patient, but Akbar did not always defer, continuing with his own treatment plan. Akbar remembered many details of patients' stories and previous visits in ways that Khalid did not. An interesting innovation in the practice in this next generation is that they now have a notebook in which they write down patients' names and diagnoses, as well as when they have been told to return to the healing room.

Rather than in the healing room, Khalid's primary energy is now focused on the maintenance of the *dargah* and setting up a trust fund. The goal of the trust, officially named 'The Welfare Society of Dargah Hazrath Peer Shah Hussain Alam Quadri' (the full name of his deceased father, Abba), is to ensure the *dargah*'s viability after Khalid's own death and to generate funds to educate girls and marry young women who cannot afford dowries. Khalid is also the president of the local mosque and supervises the *madrasa* of about 50 male students located in the neighborhood mosque. These are institutional administrative responsibilities that Amma and Abba did not have.

Along with Amma's daughter Rehma (who does not live on site), her grandson Akbar is the person whose personality, interests, and mannerisms are closest to Amma's. In the fall of 2007 Akbar was only in his early twenties and employed at a Muslim college as office staff; he was awaiting the results of his final exams for an MA in English and hoped to continue for an MPhil and become a teacher. One afternoon, I observed him writing amulets and prescribing rituals to a 17-year-old woman who had just had a miscarriage. He spoke confidently to the patient's mother and was also at ease and smiling in his conversation with the young woman, with an open, direct manner that would not have been appropriate for a young man with a non-related young woman in any other context. I later asked him if patients sometimes thought he was too young to be sitting at the healing table dealing with such intimate, 'heavy' matters. He smiled, 'I'm only here by the grace of Dadaji [paternal grandmother]. If they notice my age when they walk in, they soon forget it.'

When I commented on Akbar's open, *jamali* (easy-going, charismatic) manner, intonations, and even entire phrases in healing rhetoric that were uncanningly like Amma's, he answered, 'It's necessary to sit with *sukun* [peacefully]—like she did—and to listen carefully; only then people will talk from their hearts.' His father Khalid, like Abba before him, had little of this patience and love (they were characterized as *jalali*, fierce and angry), traits that patients used to say were unique to Amma and that was why they came to her instead of other male healers. Amma herself used to say that Khalid was like an 'express' train, rather than a passenger train, asking patients their names, their mother's names, and one, two—roaring ahead full speed—he was done, whereas she took time to listen to patients.

Akbar is still developing his personal and spiritual skills. He recalled the day he was sitting with Amma at the healing table when he was in about seventh grade and began copying on his own sheet of paper what she was writing. She was thrilled when she saw what he was doing and, he says, she began to take an active interest in teaching him how to calculate diagnoses and write amulets as prescriptions. He has not yet sat *chilla* (meditative retreat), although he hopes to do in the future to garner more spiritual discipline and power. He also realizes that he will need to be married before he receives his father's *khilafat* and himself become a *pir* who can practice healing independently of his father's authority.

In fall 2007 Khalid and Lateefa were looking for a bride for Akbar and expected him to get married sometime in the next year. He himself was ambivalent about marriage, telling me that it only caused problems. But he realized that as an oldest son, in particular, there was no choice. I commented to his parents that I hoped they would find a smart, articulate young woman who would 'match' Akbar's qualities. They were not so sure. They said they wanted a young woman who will stay home and not want to go out to work, as is proper for a *pir*'s *bahu* (daughter-in-law) and a future *pir's* wife, somehow overlooking the model Amma and Lateefa had lived out. As for educating his own daughters, Khalid says his responsibility is to educate them (the eldest wants to be an IT engineer or a doctor), and whether or not they work outside the house is the responsibility of their in-laws.

With the dispersion of authority in the next generation after Amma and Abba's deaths also comes its specialization or compartmentalization: healing and teaching authority and practice no longer seem to be as intimately woven together as they were in the healing room during Amma and Abba's time. Amma often interspersed her healing rhetoric with teaching, and when Abba used to sit in the healing room minding a small dry goods store, he, too, often gave teachings. Both healing successes and teachings in the healing room recruited most of Abba's new disciples and were reason for existing disciples to come daily to sit in the presence of Amma and Abba in the healing room. When I mentioned these differences to Khalid, he responded, 'Why waste time teaching here when they [patients] don't want to hear. I teach now on Monday nights for an hour, to the disciples who want to hear. Like, why are we on this earth? How should we live? We do *zikr* [ritual recitation of God's names]: *Allah-hu*. We call it *halka* [light weight] *zikr*.' I asked about the participation of women in these evening events, and Khalid confirmed that they do not attend. I asked, 'Then how do they learn?' To which he answered, 'Their husbands tell them', as if this was no problem at all.

In the years since Amma's death, I have not been in Hyderabad regularly to see how many, if any, new disciples Abba's *khilafas* are initiating. I do not know how or how many have been recruited and their gender distribution. But with little teaching taking place in the healing room, I would speculate that fewer disciples are drawn directly from Khalid's patient clientele than in the days of Amma and Abba's cooperative healing/teaching and that perhaps fewer disciples altogether are being recruited.

SHIFTING FOCUS BETWEEN DOMESTIC HEALING ROOM AND PUBLIC *DARGAH*

The biggest shift in the healing tradition between generations is, of course, the absence of the charismatic figure of Amma—and the concurrent development of the *dargah*, the grave shrine for her and Abba. The *dargah* was built on family property on what was then the outskirts of Hyderabad, near Falaknuma Palace, clear on the opposite side of the city from Amma's healing room on the Osmania University campus. (The 'auto' ride takes well over an hour between the two sites.) The foundation of the *dargah* was built in 1998 as a cement slab, with Abba's small raised grave covered with a *chadar* (embroidered cloth spread). It was built in the middle of a large tract of undeveloped land covered with Hyderabadi boulders and thorn bushes, with open vistas looking out on Falaknuma Palace, which sits above on a rocky hill. By Abba's second death anniversary, a small railing had been built around Abba's grave. When family relations were still tense over succession after Abba's death, Amma used to worry that when she died, her grave would be put down on ground level, beneath Abba's, in the flood plain that was often muddy. But, she said, if that happened, she would 'get right up out of her grave' in protest. However, when Amma died in 2001, the cement platform was expanded, and her grave was built along side of Abba's. Amma's name, Rukhiya, was added to the name plate of the *dargah*, and a small metal dome was built above the graves. By 2002, a full metal, green-painted lattice-work enclosure (*jali*) had been added around the two graves; a few houses had been built on the muddy road that now led to the development, and a mosque had been constructed right next to what was by now called a *dargah* (rather than simply a *mazar*/grave, as it had been the first years after Abba's death).[2]

I did not even recognize the *dargah* when I returned to Hyderabad in 2005. It was now a four-walled enclosed room with marble-like tile flooring and a large cement enclosed dome painted light green. Amma and Abba's graves had been raised about four feet and electric chandeliers hung above them. In the summer of 2007, Amma's disciple Mustang added a fancy 'silver' enclosure around the graves. The open *jungli* expanse around the *dargah* is now totally filled in by new houses, shops, and several mosques.

When I spoke to Khalid in 2005 of my forthcoming book about Amma, he was most concerned that I provide updated pictures of this new *dargah* (it was too late). He wanted to make sure that readers knew he was fulfilling his responsibilities for its upkeep and that it was thriving. In these conversations, Khalid never mentioned nor did he seem to take pride in the fact that he was also sustaining the healing practice. The center of the tradition from his perspective, at least performatively, had shifted from the domestic healing room and courtyard to the public *dargah* and its associated rituals of weekly visits on Thursday nights, monthly *samas*, and Abba's annual death anniversary celebrations (*sandal*). Fancy invitations to the *sandal* are sent to politicians and disciples, and announcements of the *sandal* are printed in Hyderabad's Urdu newspapers. Celebrations begin with elaborate processions (for which police permission must be obtained) from the healing room down the main road for a few miles, after which disciples get into buses and cars. They get out of the vehicles and again form a procession when they get close to the *dargah*. Flags are carried aloft by riders of several camels and horses, Khalid and other senior disciples carry a big tray of sandal paste, and the procession is led by professional musicians. At the *dargah*, Abba and Amma's graves are anointed with the sandal paste and covered with new embroidered cloths and piles of fresh flower petals, after which several hundred guests and disciples are fed at a nearby "function hall". The *sandal* celebrations end with an all-night *qavvali* performance in the *dargah* itself.

As interesting as the shifts from healing room to *dargah* in site and architecture are the shifts these have caused in ritual. Monthly *samas/qavvali* are now held inside the *dargah* rather than in the domestic courtyard of the healing room. The mere fact of the *dargah*'s distance from where most disciples live results in fewer women attending the *sama* (due both to time and transportation constraints). So, too, at Abba's annual death anniversary celebration (which I observed most recently in 2007), many fewer women than men attended, even though Khalid had rented buses for both female and male disciples and guests were invited to spend the night at the nearby 'function hall', where curtains had been hung to provide gender-segregated space.

These days, at the *sama*, the men and *qavvals* (musicians) sit on Abba's side of the *dargah* and women on Amma's side. At the first *sama* I attended in the *dargah* in 2005, a bedspread serving as a curtain to demarcate gendered space (*purdah*) had been hung between Amma's grave and the wall, behind which women sat. But for the 2007 *sandal*, they had not planned ahead and when the *sama* began, a quick effort to hang the bedspread failed when the thin wire holding it up broke. Khalid sent word to the women that they should sit in the courtyard of a disciple's home across the street and listen over loudspeaker. I, however, was called into the *dargah* to take pictures. Rehma (Amma's daughter) and a few elder women came with me and, rather poignantly, used Amma's grave itself as the *purdah* between them and the male disciples sitting on the other side.

On this occasion, Lateefa and most of the female disciples and relatives sat at a distance outside the *dargah* itself, a distance Amma herself would never have tolerated. I remembered Amma's manipulation of the *purdah* in the domestic courtyard during one *sama* when Abba was still alive. The male disciples were making very sure it hung all the way to the floor, and she kept pulling it up a few inches. Finally she berated them, 'Do you think we don't want to see?!' Sitting behind this rather loose *purdah*, women took off their *burqas*; it was domestic space. The male disciples would join the women behind the *purdah* during the late night tea break in the middle of the *sama*. This seemingly defied the necessity for gender segregation, and when I asked Amma about it, she smiled before acknowledging that I had made a good observation. But now at the site of the *dargah*, nearby "function hall", and the road in between the two, female disciples and relatives think much more consciously about how they are going to observe *purdah* and propriety in these public spaces. The women keep their *burqas* (black 'veiling'cloaks) on as they walk between *dargah* and "function hall" and for the duration of the *sama*.

REVISITING "COURAGE" IN THE NEXT GENERATION

Members of the next generation who have taken up positions of authority after the deaths of Abba and Amma have not had to actively create their positions of authority in the ways Amma did. Khalid, Akbar, and Lateefa have all inherited their positions. Were Lateefa to be the primary healer, as Amma was, she might have had to create a performative verbal repertoire, including personal narratives of exception and narratives of successful healing, to create and sustain authority for her public ritual role. But, at least at the present time, she defers to her husband and son as the primary actors in the healing room. She substitutes for them when they are absent and she assists when they are sitting at the healing table. However, Lateefa, Amma's daughter Rehma, and Lateefa's two teenage daughters have all internalized the *potential* for expanded gender roles that they saw Amma fill. They, other women in the neighborhood, and female disciples experienced Amma as a woman like themselves, not as the exceptional woman—'like a man'—that Amma emphasized in her healing rhetoric. Lateefa sustains Amma's qualities in the healing room that drew many patients there instead of other sites where male healers presided, and that is primarily her patience and 'ability to listen'. It remains to be seen whether Lateefa will grow further into a role of public authority after she reaches menopause and her son gets married and brings into the family a young daughter-in-law. She seems to be marking her time, waiting until age itself confers additional authority. Further, Amma's healing authority has been diffused in the next generation, among her son, daughter-in-law, grandson, and several disciples. In 2007, the most active site of healing was not in Amma's healing room, but rather in that of Mustang (Abba's and Amma's disciple), whose clientele was drawn from his primarily Hindu neighborhood.

Amma's and Abba's relationship was truly symbiotic. They shared in and depended on each other for the two roles of a *pir*, teacher and healer. The healing room was the primary site of teaching, where both Amma and Abba participated in teaching disciples and new patients. The healing room and its courtyard was the primary site of daily (healing), monthly (*sama*), and annual ritual (Gyarwin Sharif, the *sandal* of the founding *pir* of the Qadri Sufi lineage, Sheikh Abdul Qadir Jilani). Now, with the establishment of the *dargah*, ritual activity has been divided between two sites, with the *dargah* becoming the dominant site for the *sama* as well as Gyarwin Sharif and Abba's *sandal*. As noted, Khalid's focus has become the *dargah* and the public face that it presents to the community, rather than the healing room. Concomitant with this shift is Khalid's opinion that teaching at the healing table is 'wasted' in front of those who are not interested, and he has shifted the site of his primary teachings to Monday evenings, for male disciples only. And so we see shifts in the next generation of increased institutionalization, fragmentation of ritual roles and sites, and a reassertion of traditional gender roles. But, Lateefa and Rehma both hold onto self-perceptions of courage, knowledge, and potential that may manifest further as they grow older.

FIELDWORK ACROSS GENERATIONS

I close with a few observations about the fieldwork implications of working with Amma's single extended family for nearly 20 years and of becoming part of that family into the next generation. In the fall of 2007, I was the age that Amma was when I first met her in 1989. Many of her grandchildren were born after our first meeting, and I have watched the youngest of her children become teenagers, get married and have children of their own.

Most significantly, working with a single family over time and across generations has raised for me the dangers of freezing ethnographic data and research on the printed page and has pushed me to think of ways to leave room on the printed page for continuing dynamism. But there are other implications for long-term fieldwork across generations. When Amma was alive, I spent most of my time sitting with her and had few extended conversations with other family members and disciples outside of her presence. I am of the same generation now as those who are left in the second generation; we were, in relationship to Amma, siblings and of equal 'age authority'. On the one hand, this permits an easy give-and-take discussion of everyday, personal and family matters, including the specifics of my life in the US, in which Amma did not always show the same interest.

But our conversations and interactions are also constrained by this generational equality. Neither Khalid nor Lateefa see it as their role to 'teach' me about the healing practice or the 'correct way to live' as Amma and Abba did. They assume I know these things from my many years of working with Amma. It seemed difficult for Khalid to give me blessings, placing his hand on my head, unless sitting at the healing table in a specific ritual context that required it. And it was equally difficult for me to touch his feet upon arrival from and departure to the US, as would be a ritually appropriate gesture by a disciple to a *pir* or elder, and as I had done to Amma and Abba. Khalid is much more brother than *pir* to me, and his wife is in a relationship with me that warrants embrace alone rather than embrace and feet-touching. Khalid drove me to the airport when I left Hyderabad in the fall of 2007 and I asked him for *dua*, as I would have from Amma and Abba. He awkwardly said we did not need to do that (*koi zaruri nahin hai*). His seeming embarrassment could, of course, have been because it was a public context, at curbside drop off, but I also suspect it was embarrassment of performing an authoritative ritual act outside of a ritual context to someone whom he considered his sister.

Finally, interacting with the second and third generations, I do not hear the personal narratives that recount how they became who they are, the kinds of personal narratives that I and other new disciples and patients used to hear from Amma. If I were to enter the healing room now as a new fieldworker, perhaps I would hear these stories and narratives about Amma herself, her uniqueness, and the authority she transmitted to the next generation. But Khalid and Lateefa and other disciples do no tell me these kinds of stories unless I elicit them, because I have lived so much of that history with them and am myself now a part of their story.

NOTES

1. Words in double quotations are English words used in Urdu conversations.
2. The distinction between *dargah* and *mazar* may be only local, as I have seen the two words used interchangeably in other written scholarship on Islam in South Asia.

REFERENCES

Eaton, Richard (1984), 'The Political and Religious Authority of the Shrine of Baba Farid', in *Moral Conduct and Authority: The Place of Adab in South Asian Islam*, ed. Barbara D. Metcalf, Berkeley: University of California Press, 333–56.

Ewing, Katherine (1984), 'The Sufi as Saint, Curer, and Exorcist in Modern Pakistan', *Contributions to Asian Studies*, 18: 106–13.

—— (1997). *Arguing Sainthood: Modernity, Psychoanalysis, and Islam*, Durham: Duke University Press.

Flueckiger, Joyce Burkhalter (2006), *In Amma's Healing Room: Gender and Vernacular Islam in South India*, Bloomington: Indiana University Press.

Vatuk, Sylvia (2008), 'Divorce at the Wife's Initiative in Muslim Personal Law: What are the Options and What are Their Implications for Women's Welfare?', in *Redefining Family Law in India*, ed. Archana Parashar and Amita Dhanda, Londan and New Delhi: Routledge, pp. 200–35.

—— (2006), 'Domestic Violence and Marital Breakdown in India: A View from the Family Courts', in *Culture Power and Agency: Gender in Indian Ethnography*, ed. Lina Fruzzetti and Sirpa Tenhunen, Calcutta: Stree, pp. 204–26.

—— (1992), 'Sexuality and the Middle-Aged Woman in South Asia', in *In Her Prime: New Views of Middle-Aged Women*, 2nd rev. edn., ed. V. Kerns and J.K. Brown, Urbana: University of Illinois Press, pp. 155–70.

10

'A Splendid Thing for the Empire': Some Reflections on Ethnography and Entextualization in Colonial India

GLORIA GOODWIN RAHEJA

INTRODUCTION: BODIES AND SPEECH IN COLONIAL ETHNOGRAPHY

> 'If at every university there were a thoroughly good anthropological school it would be a splendid thing for the Empire.'
>
> R.C. TEMPLE, *Anthropology as a Practical Science*, 1914.

What theoretical language is most useful for explicating the relationship between colonialism on the one hand and anthropology, ethnography, folklore and the colonial production of knowledge of India on the other in the latter half of the nineteenth-century, and what exactly are the uses to which British administrators put the massive ethnographic knowledge that was produced alongside and within official documents and reports? How is the production of colonial ethnographic knowledge about 'custom' related to issues of power, discipline, and the manufacturing of an illusion of consent to colonial rule? (Raheja 1996, 1999a) What kinds of hierarchies of credibility (Stoler 1992) were established vis-à-vis competing native sources of colonial knowledge? Which accounts of 'tradition' and of 'custom' and of compliance to colonial rule were given credence as various kinds of ethnographic categories and administrative procedures were constructed? And what kinds of homogeneity or heterogeneity existed among the ethnographic practices of colonial scholars and administrators?

The production of colonial knowledge in the form of ethnography, folklore and language study in nineteenth-century India has of course been the focus of an enormous body of scholarly inquiry that builds upon Bernard S. Cohn's pioneering work on the complex relationship between colonial power and colonial knowledge (Cohn 1985, 1987, 1996). In her 1999 paper, 'Shurreef, Herklots, Crooke, and the *Qanoon-e-Islam:* Constructing an Ethnography of The Moosulmans of India', Sylvia Vatuk put forth a particularly striking analysis of the ways in which Madras Presidency native Ja'far Sharif's 1832 'auto-ethnographic' text *Qanoon-e-Islam* was transformed as it moved from his pen to the pen of the editor Gerhard Herklots and finally to the hands of William Crooke who published a new edition of the work in 1921. The Herklots and Crooke editions of the book are quite different, and Vatuk is thus able to make a compelling argument not only about the power-ridden dialogism at play as colonial ethnography was constructed from the words of those subject to British rule but also about the heterogeneity of the perspectives held by various European scholars and administrators on the Indian landscape, and about the ways in which changing historical currents, crises and contingencies shaped the ways in which the text was presented to British readers, including the many colonial administrators who consulted it. In short, Vatuk's paper is about the entextualization of the speech of the colonized. In this paper, I will be drawing upon my own published and on-going research on the relationship between the politics of colonial disciplinary procedures on the one hand and entextualizing practices on the other, to begin to construct a sort of catalog of the various modes of entextualization that occurred in nineteenth century India, especially with regard to colonial understandings of criminality and revolt and their connection to 'custom'. This is a vast topic and so the present paper contains merely a few reflections on some of the ways we might begin to conceive of it in relation to the production of ethnographic knowledge in colonial India.

Let us first review some of the ways in which the speech of the colonized has been understood in previous writing on colonial ethnography in India, the ways in which historians and anthropologists have so far attempted to grasp the connection between ethnography and empire that Temple claimed to discern so clearly in 1914. Nicholas Dirks has suggested that the development of a colonial sociology of India involved a shift from an orientalist reliance on texts to a focus on the Indian body, which could be calibrated by anthropometry and other scientific techniques, 'the body that had been in precolonial times subjected by tradition, now the body as caste that could be measured by science, significantly always a body that could be described without any reference to mind, will, or agency' (Dirks 1992: 70). Similarly, Pels argues that the earlier 'Orientalist articulation of knowledge on foundational *texts* gave way to the ethnological articulation of knowledge on *bodies*' by the latter part of the nineteenth century (Pels 1999: 83). And Christopher Pinney has written that one of the most powerful impulses at this time was the desire to establish order, which for colonial India meant an orderly arrangement of supposedly caste-based physical characteristics, which could be produced through an array of scientific techniques such as anthropometry, photography, and fingerprinting. He sees in much colonial photography and visual art attempts to establish 'a framework for the inspection of bodies of Indians by an imperial power', the surface of the body serving as the object of theoretical concern (Pinney 1990: 254). Pinney goes on to suggest that nineteenth-century anthropological investigation in India 'relied on evidence which in semiotic terms is called 'indexical'—physical traces of the object under study, like the rings that cold glasses leave on tables' (1990: 258).

This way of characterizing the colonial ethnographic enterprise as centered on the surveillance of Indian bodies may seem very persuasive, because we can see for ourselves the massive colonial displays of physical caste 'types' in documents like Watson and Kaye's *The People of India*, and we can peruse the hundreds of pages of statistics concerning supposedly caste-based patterns in anthropometric measurement in H.H. Risley's *Tribes and Castes of Bengal*. Bodies do appear, at first glance, to be the overriding preoccupation in the ethnography of colonial India in the late nineteenth century. As evidence of this, Pinney quotes from a talk entitled 'The Study of Anthropology in India', given by Denzil C.J. Ibbetson in 1890, in which Ibbetson suggests that physical measurements are 'the most valuable of all, because most trustworthy'.

> No one who has not made the attempt can well realise how difficult it is to secure a full and accurate statement of custom on any given point by verbal enquiry from Orientals and still more, from semi-savages. . . . Cranial measurements, on the other hand, are probably almost absolutely free from the personal equation of the observer.
> (Ibbetson 1890: 121, quoted in Pinney 1990: 258)

Pinney interprets this as a testimony to the obsession with indexical evidence and the preoccupation with the surveillance and measurement of Indian bodies in the late nineteenth century. I read Ibbetson's remark rather differently. Anthropometry is not much in evidence in Ibbetson's own ethnographic writing, which is in fact almost entirely concerned with evidence obtained 'through verbal enquiry'. Thus his remark might more plausibly be read as an indication of an anxiety or ambivalence about such colonial ethnographic enquiries, enquiries which do nonetheless loom very large in the administrative documents which he wrote and to which he contributed, particularly during his tenure as the Superintendent of Census Operations in the Punjab in 1881. This is not to deny that anthropometry and related modes of bodily inspection and of visual surveillance were fairly pervasive in nineteenth-century India; but I do want to question the rather simple notion that a later nineteenth century concern with bodies replaced an earlier concern with texts. David Arnold (2004) does remind us that an insistence on the physicality of race and on the differences between European and Indian bodies became the governing idea of the high imperial era, and the scrutiny and disciplining of Indian bodies—on famine relief works and in famine kitchens, in prisons (Arnold 1994), in state medicine (Arnold 1993), and in all the many investigations concerning racial theories of criminality or martiality—were obviously of great concern in colonial India. Yet the argument that there was a fundamental shift from texts to bodies in colonial ethnography seems to me to simplify a very complex relationship between Indian texts, whether written or spoken, and colonial discipline, and to obscure one of the most significant colonial uses of ethnographic knowledge. Orientalist preoccupations with Sanskrit and Persian texts certainly did give way to other modes of investigation, but these were much more complex than the inspection of Indian bodies. Indian words, not in Sanskrit texts but in folklore and everyday speech, did in fact come to be of major importance in colonial ethnography and colonial administrative documents, and they continued to be, throughout the period of colonial rule, critical to the project of justifying the colonial presence on the Indian landscape and manufacturing an illusion of Indian consent to colonial rule.

What then has been written of colonial reports on language and folklore in the nineteenth century? I will take two papers by Shahid Amin and Kirin Narayan as examples of these investigations.

In his editorial introduction to an edition of William Crooke's 1879 *A Glossary of North Indian Peasant Life*, Shahid Amin proposes to analyze Crooke's text as an instance of a broader colonial concern with native terms (Amin 1994: 36), and thus we may construe his remarks as suggestions about the character of colonial work on folklore and language more generally. Amin notes that there was a shift, about 1870, 'from description to cataloguing' and from 'reports' to the late nineteenth-century attempts at codification in the myriad 'handbooks', 'manuals' and 'glossaries' produced during the last decades of the nineteenth century (1994:37). While he notices the way in which these later documents represent the world of the Indian peasant as changeless and without history, what Amin sees as noteworthy about the handbooks and manuals and glossaries is the fact that they are 'almost bereft of native classification' (1994: 42). Whether Crooke is listing types of foods, cattle diseases, or agricultural implements, these are organized by English terms and categories: utensils are listed separately for Hindus and Muslims, there are 'garden crops' as opposed to 'field crops', and the listing of foodstuffs recognizes none of the myriad indigenous modes of classification, such as that of 'hot' *vs.* 'cold', foods eaten in times of plenty and those eaten in times of scarcity. 'In general', Amin writes, the format of Crooke's . . . glossaries raises the important issue of the metalanguage and translation as an act of power which defines the lexical world in metropolitan terms but allows the colony only the privilege of being the world of referents, lacking any powerful semiotic properties itself. This is how master vocabularies constitute themselves under colonial rule or in other situations of systematic domination. (Amin 1994: 48)

Amin's formulation is problematic in its assumption that a singular 'indigenous system of classification' could have been used to organize Crooke's lists of words, and that a critique of colonial ethnographic practice should focus on the erasure of such systems. Although I share with Amin an interest in colonial perceptions of Indian language I would argue that, to understand the relationship between colonialism and folklore, and colonialism and ethnographic investigation, we need to look not at the relationship between 'master vocabularies' and 'native classification', but at the erasure of linguistic and cultural pragmatics in colonial documents, the erasure of the situatedness of any speech that is inserted into colonial documents, and the erasure of the ethnographic occasion in which Indian speech is heard by the colonial administrator or ethnographer. The question we need to ask concerns not the structure of a native terminology, but the differential uses to which such terms and classifications are put as they are deployed in everyday conversations, how different principles of classification may come to have different salience for different speakers and in different circumstances, and the pragmatic aspects of the situation in which native terms are reported to colonial administrators or overheard by them.

Kirin Narayan (1993) has suggested that the distinguishing feature of colonial folklore lies in its insistence on a certain kind of 'authenticity' and on the collection and publication of texts in which no 'spurious additions' or references to contemporary events had been inserted. Folklore collectors, she points out, were interested in portraying a picture of unchanging traditions, emphasizing not only an exaggerated conservatism, but also, simultaneously, an exaggerated difference between the colonizer and the colonized. And she suggests that colonial administrators/folklorists ignored instances in which anti-colonial thematic elements were incorporated into storytelling performances and songs. Yet in many colonial folklore collections we do find songs and stories about contemporary events and relationships with the colonial power, such as those in William Crooke's collections entitled 'Songs of the Mutiny', 'Songs from Northern India Relating to the English', and 'Songs about the King of Oudh' published in *The Indian Antiquary* in 1911, in an historically situated song about colonial famine policy translated by George Grierson in *An Introduction to the Maithili Language of North Bihar, Containing a Grammar, Chrestomathy and Vocabulary* (1882), in songs about land revenue policies in J. Wilson's Sirsa settlement report (1884), in songs about the administration of Punjab irrigation works published in *The Indian Antiquary* by R.C. Temple and Flora Annie Steel (1882) that I will analyze below, and in a women's song about the 1911 imperial durbar in a collection of songs compiled by C.E. Luard (n.d.). In fact colonial administrators translated and published a plethora of folkloric narratives about the colonial encounter in the late nineteenth century. While the erasure of what Johannes Fabian (1983) would call coevalness was certainly characteristic of a great deal of colonial work on folklore, a reliance only on his ideas about the construction of difference may in fact occlude some critically important aspects of the colonial production of knowledge about India. A good deal of the folklore that colonial administrators compiled did indeed contain allusions to the coevalness of Indians and Britons on the colonial landscape. Why should the publication of this particular sort of 'folklore' have seemed necessary to the colonial construction of knowledge about India, and what in fact were the entextualizing strategies that were used to insert this speech into colonial administrative documents? Coevalness was recognized but it had to be managed in particular ways in order to be useful to the colonial project and it is on this management of often recalcitrant Indian speech that I focus upon in this paper.

Now, how shall we think about the question of an appropriate theoretical language with which to explicate the production of colonial ethnographic knowledge? Shall we focus on techniques of bodily surveillance and ways of classifying and ordering Indian bodies? Shall we think, with Amin, in terms of a set of alien categories and classifications being imposed upon and obscuring indigenous systems of classification? Shall we think, with Narayan, of the erasure of coevalness and representations of difference as the most significant aspect of colonial ethnography and folkloristics? There is no need, of course, to choose definitively among these alternatives, since all of them illuminate certain aspects of the relationship between ethnography and the colonial enterprise. It might be worthwhile, however, to try to find an interpretive language that will provide a more precise and nuanced understanding of why exactly 'folklore' and stretches of Indian speech came so often to be inserted into colonial administrative documents, a language that will enable us to understand the process through which these were extracted from the ethnographic occasion in which they were reported to the colonial ethnographer and recontextualized in administrative reports, handbooks, manuals, grammars, and glossaries. It is in terms of these processes, I suggest, that the most critical links between colonial discipline and colonial ethnography can be discerned.

Thus I am particularly interested in examining some of the occasions at which administrators and ethnographers encountered ordinary Indians most intimately and directly, spoke with them and addressed their questions to them: in the course of village inspections and inquiries such as those that took place on famine relief works and in famine poorhouses, in prisons, in judicial proceedings, in the course of revenue operations, in collaborations with 'native informants' and so forth. I am interested in the representations of Indian society that were constructed specifically at these sites of encounter, and which find their way into various kinds of reports and manuals, and as abstract and decontextualized ethnographic reports. I am also interested in the fact that Indians did not simply present their bodies or their fields for inspection and measurement; in these places, Indians also *spoke*. While it is certainly true that in many instances such speech goes unrecorded in the colonial archive because colonial administrators and ethnographers could not understand it or because they were uninterested in recording it, or because it may only have been produced surreptitiously out of earshot of any colonial authority, it is also true that the appropriation of

Indian speech occurred in a great many administrative documents, especially at those points where the illusion of consent to colonial rule was most in question. And frequently that speech was about the colonial encounter itself. And it is at those points that native proverbs, native songs, and native terms often erupt into the colonial ethnographic text. I am interested in those situations in which Indian speech became administratively useful, and in the ways in which it was excised from the situation of its utterance, decontextualized, and inserted into colonial reports, catalogues, and the like. (See for example Raheja 1996, 1999a, 1999b.) It is in that process that I think we can come to see what is in fact 'colonial' about the ethnographic activities of so many nineteenth-century administrators, and how it is that ethnography and the ethnographic reporting are connected to the exercise of colonial power, and deemed by men like R.C. Temple to be useful to the empire.

I suggest that we need to position our analyses at the intersection of three sets of ideas in order to understand these decontextualizing and entextualizing processes, and the relationship between ethnography and colonialism. We need to consider, first, that far from being certain of its claims to truth, colonial ethnography was often beset with a profound ambivalence and uncertainty about its ability to represent and comprehend Indian social realities and to describe and catalogue Indian bodies, as Sara Suleri has so eloquently argued (Suleri 1992). Secondly, we will need to consider Homi Bhabha's discussion of the colonial demand for authorizing narratives, narratives spoken by the colonized that would validate colonial knowledge and colonial policy precisely at those points at which the colonizers experience them as most fragile and most threatened (Bhabha 1994, especially 'Sly Civility'). Thus, colonial surveillance of Indian bodies had to be supplemented by a surveillance of speech, and by the entextualization of Indian speech at certain critical junctures, to provide an answer to that colonial demand to *tell us why we are here.* Thirdly, if such speech was always produced in a fraught encounter between a specific colonial ethnographer or administrator and a specific native man or woman at a particular place and time, then those specificities had to be erased if the speech was to be seen as an authorizing 'Indian' narrative, as a specimen of authentic and generalizable Indian speech, uncontaminated by the power relations of the colonial encounter itself. Thus, we need to consider the processes by which features of that specific interactional context, that specific 'ethnographic occasion', were cast into obscurity or distorted in the documents in which such speech was reported. In other words, in order to explicate the relationship between colonial power and colonial ethnographic knowledge, we may need to know why it is that colonial administrators found it useful to occlude the specific mediations of that knowledge and the relations of power in which those took place, in order to produce the illusion of consent to colonial rule.

We are just beginning to discern some of the ways in which, as Sara Suleri puts it, colonial ethnographers were uncertain about their own authority and ambivalent about the European production of knowledge about India. Although Pinney exhibits that excerpt from Ibbetson's speech as evidence of his certainty about colonial knowledge of Indian bodies and of the reliability of cranial measurements as ethnographic knowledge, actually those sentences only serve to underscore Ibbetson's sense of the unreliability of the other forms of colonial knowledge which he had to amass on a daily basis in his work as an administrator and census superintendent. The very diversity of Indian 'types' portrayed in texts like Watson and Kaye's *The People of India* was intended as 'an ethnographic manifesto of colonial legitimacy' (Suleri 1992: 104). We may recall here, however, Suleri's discussion of the way that commentary in that book and elsewhere 'hysterically insists on the static readability of physicality' (ibid.: 108) and thus betrays a radical colonial ambivalence about such colonial categories and a striking awareness of the fragility and inadequacy of colonial knowledge. Watson and Kaye's *The People of India*, she suggests, focuses on the supposed fixities of caste-based racial categories and bodily types 'as a means to stave off its hidden admission of cultural ignorance' (ibid.: 104). It is in fact an awareness of this inadequacy, this fragility, this ignorance that prompts the insertion of Indian speech into colonial texts at the same time as the triumph of scientific knowledge of Indian bodies was being uneasily declared. Folklore became the means by which Indian speech, often characterized as 'the true voice of the Indian people', was embedded into colonial texts to serve as authorizing narrative. And yet there were recalcitrant voices as well; these too are often found in nineteenth century ethnographic documents and administrative reports, where they too are pressed into service as authorizing narrative, as they are entextualized as the voices of the 'criminal castes' or as the speech of the superstitious and illiterate masses of Indian peasantry not yet able to discern the true nature of the colonial project.

That 'ethnographic occasions' (Pels and Salemink 1999) in colonial India were most often situated in disciplinary spaces such as famine relief kitchens, village fields in which revenue operations were being carried out, prisons and courtrooms, or involved primarily high caste assistants and informants, or interrogators and 'approvers', was hardly theorized by colonial ethnographers. Whatever 'customs' were enacted in these spaces were taken as unproblematic tokens of 'customs' enacted anywhere else. Whatever speech was produced in these varied disciplinary spaces could be taken as exhibiting the invariable 'mind of the people', although, as both Homi Bhabha and Partha Chatterjee have reminded us in different ways, assertions of 'tradition' and 'claims of conscience' in such colonial spaces might in fact have arisen from the 'yeast of modernity' (Bhabha 1994: 211). The possibility must be recognized that they might therefore be local responses to colonial power that 'opened to question some of the very procedures in the practice of modernity' (Chatterjee 1995: 5, 8). It seems evident to me, for example, that peasants had come to know, at least by the 1830s, that the surest way to forestall the progress of a colonial project was to raise the cry of religion or custom defiled (Raheja 1999b: 50–1).

Bauman and Briggs (1990) have called to our attention the ways in which oral narratives and other stretches of speech are transformed as they are decontextualized and excised from the situation in which they are produced, and entextualized as 'folklore' in various kinds of written accounts. They are interested in the operations that must be performed when such speech is removed from the interactional order and brought into national and international spheres (Bauman 1993). We need to ask what happens as this occurs, what are the means by which the specific interactional aspects of the original speech are erased from the ethnographic record in that process, and what the consequences of this erasure are. Extending Bauman's questions, I want to ask how colonial administrators and ethnographers perform this decontextualizing act as they ignore the fact that the Indian speech about 'tradition' that they record is in fact produced in colonial spaces and must be read, in some respects, in relation to modernity's yeast and to colonial power. We need to ask about the ways in which colonial ethnographers erased this fact, and about the uses to which the erasures are put in the project of demanding an authorizing narrative for colonial rule.

These are complex questions for the very reason that, as Vatuk so astutely pointed out, colonial ethnographic practice was marked by a high degree of heterogeneity and contradiction, and set within the context of sometimes rapidly changing political and disciplinary contexts. This paper can offer simply a set of reflections on the heterogeneity of modes of colonial entextualizing strategies, the beginnings of a catalog of them. I will reflect on some of the ways in which Indian speech (imagined speech, recollected speech, speech taken down in colonial disciplinary spaces, speech overheard, fictionalized speech, and so on) is set down and framed in a variety of colonial texts.

THE POLICING OF TRADITION: DISCURSIVE FORMATIONS AND REMEMBERING THE SPEECH OF A 'SUCKHEE'

I begin with one of the sites at which Indian speech was first entextualized in a colonial effort to illustrate 'the various customs and manners' of India, to police the boundaries of what could be deemed 'tradition', and to attempt to understand what they regarded as criminal behavior in relation to 'custom'. George Hadley's *Grammatical Remarks on the Practical and Vulgar Dialect of the Indostan Language Commonly Called Moors* was published in London in 1772, the year in which Warren Hastings wrote to the East India Company's Court of Directors that the Company's officers in eastern India 'have endeavoured to adopt our Regulations to the Manners and Understandings of the People, and the Exigencies of the Country, adhering as closely as we are able to their ancient uses and Institutions' (quoted in Cohn 1985: 289). The seventh and last edition of Hadley's work, entitled *A Compendious Grammar of the Current Corrupt Dialect of the Jargon of Hindostan* appeared in 1809. The book was designed to be used in teaching the language to functionaries of the East India Company. Like most other grammars and language texts of its day, it contained a section devoted to useful 'dialogues' that provide models for the manner in which Indians are to be addressed and commanded by the Company's officers, as well as an introduction to the 'Manners and Understandings' encountered amongst those Indians. These dialogues are arranged into two sections; the first is entitled 'Genuine and provincial practical dialogues, with notes descriptive of the various customs and manners of Bengal', and the second is 'Military dialogues, more particularly adapted to the use of officers, who are attached to the seapoy [*sic*] battalions'. Both sections provide Hindustani sentences and phrases that the sahib can use as he goes about the round of his ordinary daily affairs; the first section begins for example with a dialogue entitled 'to rise in the morning and ride out', and carries the sahib through the day with 'to speak to the groom', 'at breakfast', 'to ask to dinner', 'of a complaint and dispute', ending with a dialogue that enables him to procure the services of his native servant 'to retire and rest at night'.

Amidst these linguistic appurtenances to the orderly conduct of the Englishman's daily routine, the reader also encounters a dialogue, in this section, entitled 'Of a suckhee [sati, usually written as 'suttee' in colonial documents].' Hadley provides a note on this 'custom' at the beginning of the dialogue:

> There is nothing so repugnant to our manners and ideas, and the feelings of humanity in this strange ceremony, that we are not at all offended should our veracity be questioned, as it often has been when we have related it to persons totally unacquainted with the eastern world. But there is not a single circumstance in the following dialogue of which we have not been an eye-witness. It is an error to think these mistaken women compelled to burn; there is no compulsion in the first instance, though it is rather disgraceful for the wives of the Raujahs (Gentoo Princes) and nobility to survive their husbands. But if a widow enters her name with the Brahmin (which she must do within the twelve hours from her husband's death), there is no retracting, for the whole family would lose their cast [*sic*], (be rejected from their tribe), and they would throw her into the fire: nor is it confined alone to

(though more frequently among) the higher orders of life, as the widow alluded to in the dialogue was the widow of a shoe-maker.

Hadley thus attempts to persuade the reader of several things. First, the very placement of the dialogue about the 'suckhee' amidst the dialogues attendant upon the sahib's ordinary round of daily activities routinizes the occurrence of sati and conveys the impression that it is an extraordinarily widespread phenomenon, one which the English sahib might often encounter in the course of his daily routine. Second, the inclusion of the dialogue indicates that the sahib will be expected to speak and to hear Indian speech in such an encounter. Third, of all the speech that is produced in the seventy pages of Hadley's text devoted to 'dialogues', only in this one is there an assertion that the conversation is a remembered rather than imagined one; Hadley reassures the reader not only that he has been an 'eye-witness' to the events recounted here, but also that he has reproduced the speech of a particular woman, a Potter. Fourth, the sati's discourse with the sahib is the *only* instance in the dialogues in which an Indian woman speaks; the Hindu woman thus appears in Hadley's text as a *sati* and nothing else. And finally, the reader is informed that there is an important element of coercion in these events, in the sense that once a woman has determined on this course, her family is outcasted if she turns away from it; she burns, as she will tell the sahib, because her Brahmins tell her to.

The dialogue begins with a servant addressing our sahib in the morning.

> There is a suckhee to-day two miles out of town. Will master go to see it?
> What is a suckhee?
> A Gentoo widow burns herself with the corpse of her husband.
> It is wonderful. Come we will go to see it.

The dialogue continues then, as the sahib and his servant-informant reach the funeral pyre.

> What is that pit which is filled with faggots and straw?
> In the middle of that is the corpse.
> When the wood is burnt so that the corpse becomes visible (*comes in sight*), the widow jumps into the fire.

Who is that venerable old man who applies a long pole sometimes to the fire?

That is the widow's father.

Surprizing! Who are those two youths who strike the ground with their heads?

Those are the widow's two brothers.

Where is the widow, I chuse to hold (*speak*) discourse with her.

She is coming, Sir, in the midst of that crowd.

O! take care. Get aside, the grand master [the sahib] is coming to the lady.

O madam! Great grief affects (*to*) me on account of your sacrifice.

Why are you sorry? (*at heart*) I am very happy.

Do you think (*understand*) that God gave your life to you for the purpose to throw it away thus?

Sir, God gave me a husband; now he has taken him away from me; I shall see him again in Heaven.

How do you know? (*In what manner is there knowledge to you*)?

My Brahmin told (*to*) me so.

Don't you burn?

Certainly I must (*shall be to*) burn; my husband is dead, in this world what is there?

Another husband.

No Sir, I want not another; this is shameful discourse (*discourse of shame*).

If you repent, I will give you ten seapoys to take you to the Governor of Calcutta.

No, Sir. Behold, having taken this flower put in your bosom. While it shall stay there you shall certainly conquer in all battles.

Thanks madam; to you everlasting peace.

O God! pardon thy errors, Exalt (*increase*) thy station in Paradise. (A Persian couplet).

Why do these people bring the child and household stuff (*equipage*) to the lady; and why does she drive away the child and throw away the goods?

For this reason: to shew that all regard for the affairs of this world are at a conclusion (*finished*).

See, Sir, the faggots are half burned down; the corpse is visible (*comes in sight*).

Hearken! the drum beats (*plays*). The lady having made ablution, and changed her clothes, will come quickly.

What are these earthen pans which are tied to long poles?

In them is oil and grease; when the lady jumps into the fire, those people pour it on her body; then the smoke rises. They do this for the diminution of the lady's pain.

Indeed I am greatly affected for her (*my spirit burns*).

She is coming, and two Brahmins on each (*one on each side*).

Sir, do not touch her for this reason; you will ruin the whole affair, and she must (*will be*) to wash and change her clothes again.

Why do her eyes glisten thus?

She has eat opium and is almost mad. This is the Brahmin's contrivance.

See, Sir, now she jumps into the fire, and the drums and trumpets play (*for*) to overwhelm her cries.

This dialogue, constructed by Hadley for purposes of linguistic pedagogy as well as for ethnographic purposes, conforms precisely to the organization of British eye-witness accounts of *sati* that Lata Mani describes.

> Eyewitness descriptions of *sati* are generally organized around four moments: the narrator hastening to the spot on receiving information that a burning is about to occur; the monitoring of the widow's demeanor and the attempts to dissuade her; details of the practices that precede the burning; the setting alight of the pyre and the death of the widow. Most of the narrative is given over to a scrutiny of the widow. (Mani 1992: 396)

Thus in his dialogue intended to enable functionaries of the East India Company to acquaint themselves with the language of India, Hadley has in fact reproduced what had already become an established discursive formation in representations of the women's speech in the colonial archive. He claims to be reporting on the actual speech of a sati, but he is in fact setting forth for the reader the reverberations of a powerful and enduring discourse that had materialized in the very early years of the East India Company's presence on the subcontinent.

According to Mani, however, when the actual speech of women is recorded in the eyewitness accounts, it is possible to see that women speak not of scripture and their capitulation to 'tradition', but of the fear of disgracing her family, jeopardizing her son's future prospects, financial insecurity, and so forth (Mani 1992: 398–9). 'The testimonials of widows challenge the dominant representation of *sati* as a religiously inspired act of devotion to the deceased husband' (ibid.: 403). Actual women did not speak of scripture or of Brahmins when they were interrogated at the pyre; their subjectivity was, as Mani insists, far more heterogeneous than this. Yet blind conformity to scripture and 'traditions' is precisely the element of the widow's subjectivity that is dwelt upon by British commentators, and it is such blind submission to the dictates of 'tradition' that is stressed in Hadley's imagined dialogue.

In Hadley's supposedly remembered dialogue, there is an apparent assumption that women's speech echoes priestly male authority. As Hadley constructs his dialogue we are thus made to hear the voice of a woman who submits to the harsh dictates of 'tradition', the voice of an innocent victim of the 'priestcraft', who, as Hadley insists in a footnote, stand to profit from each performance of the sati rite. The speech of the sati is produced in this dialogue only to show the reader that it is the Brahmin who speaks for her. Women's speech is thus reduced to an echo of 'tradition' and of scripture. An answer to the colonial demand, *tell us why we are here,* the demand for authorization in the voice of the colonized, is thus conjured up in this illusory echo; the moral condemnation of a tradition that produces *sati* is one in need of the colonial civilizing mission, in need of the presence of the very sahib who is learning to speak the 'jargon of Hindustan' from Hadley's grammar. In this text it is through the entextualization of supposedly remembered Indian speech that an authorization for colonial rule is set forth. That the shape Hadley gives to the 'remembered speech' is one that was congruent with an already established colonial discursive formation prompts us to take note of the fact that the very words that are inserted into colonial texts as 'authentic' speech are often words that took shape in the world of the colonizers, not in the world of the colonized.

'IDOLATROUS VENERATION', 'POSSESSION OF THE LAND', AND THE ADJUDICATION OF CONFLICTING COLONIAL ENTEXTUALIZATIONS OF INDIAN SPEECH: GEORGE EVEREST IN GWALIOR[1]

In 1832 George Everest, the Surveyor-General of India and the Superintendent of the Great Trigonometrical Survey of India from 1830 to 1843, wrote to surveyors who were about to set out on a trigonometric expedition that year. Everest advised them to collect all manner of information, on the courses of rivers, the angles of elevation of any high peaks in the vicinity, the topography of the country and so forth. However, he also devoted a long and afterwards much-quoted paragraph to the kinds of information on the 'manners and language of the people' to be collected during the course of his survey operations:

> Are they Hindoos or Mahometans or what is their religion? Are they obliging or hostile to strangers? To what state of civilization have they attained? Their progress in agriculture, manufactures, etc. The weapons they use. The language they speak. Are they a truth-telling people or deceitful and prone to falsehood? . . . Are the people generally comfortable or oppressed? Are they wandering tribes or attached to their homes?'(Everest to Waugh and Renny, 5 November 1832. Board's Collections, 1833. F/4/1379, No. 55088, IOL.)

It is obvious that Everest's interests here are not in any sense purely 'ethnographic'. He situates an inquiry into whether the people encountered in the survey operations are 'obliging or hostile to strangers' (strangers who could only be the surveyors themselves) under the rubric of 'manners and language' and thus already envisions perhaps the problem of understanding confrontations of British surveyors and the Indian populace as a problem of understanding 'custom'. And given the very frequent opposition his surveyors encountered throughout India, he could hardly have been interested in 'the weapons they use' for purely scientific reasons. Indeed, although there is relatively little ethnographic description in the survey correspondence and technical reports, ethnographic narratives spill into the reports and cluster themselves almost entirely at the places where the progress of a survey has been halted or delayed by recalcitrant native opposition. Thus the disciplinary nature of the ethnography lies quite close to the surface in the Survey literature.

Accounting for the human opposition to the Survey is of paramount concern in these reports and correspondence. The literature of the Survey repeatedly evinces a concern with the problem of maintaining an illusion of consent to the Survey procedures, and an illusion of consent to colonial governance more generally. But, given the constant opposition they encountered and over which they obsess, their explanatory paradigms concerning native consent and the degree to which the mechanisms of the colonial state really were in consonance with the 'manners and understandings of the people' would seem to have been strained to the utmost. The solution to the problem, in the Survey literature, lay in a certain way that notions of 'tradition', whether described as 'superstition', 'religious prejudice', or a propensity towards 'idolatrous veneration' were written into their texts. (For a concise summary of the kinds of opposition faced by surveyors, see Edney 1997: 325–32 and Raheja 1999b: 35–6. Edney too notices, albeit in passing, that allusions to native 'superstitions' might sometimes serve to 'marginalize' local opposition to the Survey operations.)

This kind of indirect entextualization of Indian speech is often found in reports (and subsequent quotations from those reports) of the destruction of mark-stones and Survey stations whose preservation was deemed important to the continued usefulness of the survey measurements. Many of the numerous officially published survey reports and accounts devote considerable space to sections entitled, for example, 'The Measures Taken for the Protection of the Stations.' One such section in the *Account of the Operations of the Great Trigonometrical Survey of India* issued in 1879, written by J.T. Walker, who was then Surveyor General of India and Superintendent of the Survey, has this to say concerning the desired permanence of the survey stations:

> The stations of this Survey should be made to last as long as the world lasts, or at least they ought to be coeval with the present configuration of the surface of the country, perishing only with their standing points; for they have been fixed with much labor, much care, and much precision, and they should be preserved with equal solicitude. . . . If the present system [of protection] is perpetuated by future generations of officials, the duration of the stations should be coeval with that of the ground on which they stand, with the plains on which they are now the most conspicuous landmarks, and with the hills whose solitary summits they have rendered utilitarian, and brought into connection with the busy world below (Walker 1879: 72).

An 'illusion of permanence' indeed. But in inspections of the mark-stones, it was often found that 'deliberate mischief' had occurred, and the stations destroyed or the mark-stones carried off or defaced. Now, on the very first page of his chapter, Colonel Walker must account for this obvious absence of consent, as it were. He writes then as follows:

The natives of the region in which Colonel Everest was occupied, at the commencement of the modern period of the operations of the Survey, appear to have regarded the stations either with superstitious veneration, or with suspicion and dread.

To confirm his explanation, that stations and mark-stones are not removed for reasons involving any sort of political apprehension of their import, Colonel Walker quotes from a letter written on this subject by George Everest to the Government of India on 30 August 1836.

In some parts of the country, the platforms are regarded as objects of idolatrous veneration, and there are amongst the villagers persons who, I am told, make money by pointing out the centre and circle engraved on the stone, and descanting on its holiness and marvellous powers. In other parts of the country the most preposterous stories are propagated, regarding the incantations and ceremonies gone through in achieving this magic mark and laying it on the platform, such as that young pagan children—obtained by stealth if possible, or otherwise by purchase, at any price—are offered up as sacrifices, and that their skulls bear testimony to the fact.

I cite these absurd tales with the view of conveying the extreme state of barbarism into which these poor people are sunk, the mention of which, if there were no other consequences resulting, would be out of place in a public letter. It so happens that amongst those who entertain the latter notion, my harmless platforms and their central stones are looked on as the cause of every ill which afflicts the country, and, in the case of scarcity, the Rulers, taking advantage of this prepossession, proceed sometimes in the most reckless manner not only to pull the pile to pieces but in some cases to erase altogether the lower mark concealed underneath it,—a procedure which, as the mark is engraved on the solid rock in situ, cannot be effected without repeated blows of a sledge hammer. (pp. 73–4)

The writers of later official reports remark explicitly on and reiterate Everest's comment on the connection between the deliberate destruction of the survey markers and the 'barbarism' of the preposterously superstitious tales about them supposedly told by the rural populace. Notice that neither Walker nor any of the other producers of texts comment at all on Everest's remark about the role of the 'rulers' in the destruction; usually this detail is in fact entirely omitted in later official recountings of Everest's experiences with the 'superstitions' of the masses. And there are many such recountings. In his 1878 *Memoir on the Indian Surveys* for example, Clements Markham attempted to account for such destructive occurrences in 1862, when Walker, who had just been appointed Superintendent of the Great Trigonometrical Survey the year before, surveyed the eastern coast of India. To the 'superstition' theory, this time concerning 'spells' that the markers might cast over a district, he adds the notion that the destruction might be linked to Indian cupidity.

> Colonel Walker, mindful of the maxim that 'the ends of a base line should be guarded with religious veneration', gave much attention to measures for their preservation at Vizagapatam. In India such marks are viewed with cupidity not unmixed with fear. The natives have an idea that money is buried under these mysterious monuments created by the western strangers, while they feel a dread that they may cast a spell over the district. Hence they are exposed to a double danger, and those at Sironj were actually destroyed. At Vizagapatam substantial domes of cut stone masonry without openings were built over the marks at each end of the base line, and put in charge of the police. (Markham 1878: 62–3)

Survey reports are everywhere studded with such recountings. The 1882 *Account of the Operations of the Great Trigonometrical Survey* is typical in its report that, in the operations of the Amua Meridional Series in 1833–4, 'inconvenience was caused by the people of the country in digging up and carrying off the mark-stones, about which they appear to have entertained superstitious misgivings' (Walker 1882: v).

Why were his mark-stones destroyed in Gwalior, is what George Everest wants to know, and as he thinks and acts and writes his way through the practical problems and delays that the demolished stones occasion to his Survey work, a number of different plausible answers present themselves to him, which he writes of in letters to the Government of India and to the British resident at the Gwalior court. In his epistolary writings, Everest sets forth a politically complicated and sometimes contradictory scenario about what is happening to his mark stones and his survey parties. Of interest to me is the way that one of them is finally settled upon as true, the way that the epistolary complexity is whittled down to that single explanatory factor, the 'superstitious dread' of the people, in responses issued by the Government, in the published texts that Everest later produced, and in the many Survey documents that later recount these incidents.

Having already experienced problems in Gwalior in 1832, Everest was again preparing for survey work in that state in 1836. He wrote to Sutherland, the Political Agent in Gwalior, asking him to intercede on his behalf for protection from robbers, in the form of fifty of the Maharajah's horsemen, a supply of *purwanas* (written orders from the Court that he be accomodated in his operations), permission to open the gates of fortresses that would then be used as survey stations, and the guarantee of a supply of coolie labor. Sutherland replied that he could not assist him in the matter of the fortresses or the coolie labor (the latter on the grounds that the Durbar could not force people to take up employment with the Survey), but that Everest should be assured that all other aid would be afforded. Everest was unhappy with the reply, and insult having been added to injury, he learned somehow that he had been referred to by Sutherland, in a conversation with an Indian official, as 'one Major Everest engaged in measuring', which remark Everest considered an affront to his dignity, and he was indignant too that Sutherland had not, in a Persian letter, referred to him by his proper titles, 'the Surveyor General and Superintendent of the Great Trigonometrical Survey'.

He directed angry complaints about Sutherland to the Government, stating that Sutherland's opinion about the security that would be afforded him in Gwalior were 'inconsistent with all former experience, for the Gwalior local authorities have invariably thrown all manner of obstructions in the way of my operations'. When Everest at last arrived at the borders of Gwalior State, there was no escort and no provisions awaited him. He complained also that the headmen of villages had positively refused to supply him with provisions unless he produced a *purwana*, which he did not have. A bania merchant who had been supplying his party in this emergency suddenly refused to continue, 'for fear of offending the powers that be', according to Everest's account in a letter to the Secretary of the Government of India (Board of Control, Board's Collections, F/4/1654 No. 66137, 12 June 1837). Furthermore, Everest wrote that 'for want of proper attendants' he had been unable to procure coolie labor in the region. The Government responded by chastising Everest, conveying its 'disapprobation of the tone and tenor' that he had taken with Sutherland.

Everest was clearly having a difficult time. In the midst of all these troubles, he also sent, in 1837, a letter to the Government of India concerning the fact that survey markers at his principal and secondary stations in Gwalior had been 'dug up and destroyed in the same reckless manner' as on several previous occasions. Everest promised that he would investigate the matter further, so at that time he said that he would confine himself 'to remarking that there seems to be strong reason to conclude that the destruction has been effected by large parties of armed people connected either with the ruling powers at Gwalior or the subordinate authorities of that state'. But he also volunteered the opinion that 'in arbitrary and oppressive states like that of Gwalior . . . it cannot be expected that any person will volunteer information . . . implicating the rulers' (Board of Control, Board's Collections, IOL F/4/1821). Notice that in none of his letters did Everest hint that the destruction might have been caused by any 'superstitious dread' with which the populace might have regarded the survey platforms. And earlier, in 1830, in a book published in England and therefore not subject to the excessive scrutiny of his superiors, he had in a straightforward manner acknowledged that opposition to the Survey was frequently based on the realization that the mark-stones and signal flags of the Survey might be grounds for legitimate fear amongst the local populations: 'the natives were ready to view [the] signal flags with jealousy, as mere preliminaries to the possession of the land' (Everest 1830). It was Major Sutherland who first introduced this idea, in a letter he wrote to the Lieutenant Governor of the North Western Provinces, defending his own actions and those of the Gwalior Court. He says that he had already communicated to Everest what he thought to be the cause of the problem: that 'the people inhabiting the wild tract of country in the neighbourhood of Pahargurh took it into their heads that these new platforms were the cause of the failure of the periodical rains. They rose with arms in their hands and in such number as intimidated the police and accomplished the destruction of the platforms.' And if this is true, he adds of course, no responsibility would attach itself to either himself or the Durbar. The Durbar itself seemed to approve of this explanation, since shortly thereafter Sutherland sent a letter saying that he had the honor to report that the Durbar Wakeel had informed him that 'orders were issued to the Amils of the several districts, in which there are platforms, to afford such additional protections as might be necessary in this season of scarcity, in situations when the people were likely to attribute to them the failure of the rains'.

In 1839, Everest submitted a report on the progress of the survey to the Government. In reflecting on the difficulties he had encountered in Gwalior over the preceding years, he came to the conclusion that it was the Gwalior Court itself that had been the source of the trouble:

> As delays of this nature on the part of public functionaries cannot be too much deprecated, I deem it advisable to put that in question on record, in order that so serious a course of evil may be brought to the notice of those who are most interested in the progress of so costly a series of operations as that of the Great Trigonometric Survey of India; for though the natural difficulties attending the fulfillment of an undertaking of this sort, with an accuracy at all worth the trouble are under any circumstances exceedingly great, yet they are with few exceptions to be surmounted, and are generally speaking trifling, in comparison with those which are opposed to it by human perverseness in its various forms.
>
> There is perhaps hardly a country in the world in which Trigonometric operations might not be conducted, provided the human agents dominant in it could be brought to consent to give all the aid and support which the existing laws and usages empower them to afford, but if these are withheld, it is impossible for parties to subsist, and manifestly out of the question to occupy hill stations, for the space of time necessary to the completion of a series of observations, within any territory whatever.
>
> In the Gwalior territory for example, which is a conquered state,

ruled by a foreign power of Mahrattas, if the Government were to evince the slightest disinclination to further operations of this kind, every person in authority, from the highest officer to the lowest minion, would conceive himself bound to thwart those engaged in conducting them.

But it is not necessary that the Native Government should display any active opposition in such cases:—a lukewarm reception is quite sufficient to excite all those who draw their subsistence from the existing order of things to resist the intrusion of strangers, whom for many and obvious reasons they look on at all times with jealousy, but more especially when engaged in operations which they never fail to connect with projects of ultimate possession.

As to the mass of inhabitants themselves of states so constituted, they are a vanquished race, bestridden by a tribe of foreigners between whom and them mutual dislike and distrust exist. Their voice is of no weight; and if it were, men who have been so bowed down under a succession of ages of oppression are naturally victims of inertia and apathy; and beyond the means of securing existence for the passing hour, they have little care.

Nothing in short, but a decidedly manifested disposition of the reigning chieftain, and his ministers, suffices to restrain active opposition, and secure the requisite support in regard to supplies, protection, and other aid; and to convince people generally that this disposition does exist, there is no other method, but to place an accredited Officer of the Court in attendance on the Officer conducting the operations, furnishing him with written orders, with the power to address all local authorities, and with a sufficient escort to ensure attention to his calls, and deference to his station (Board of Control, Board's Collections, IOL F/4/1783).

In this very protracted correspondence concerning the lack of cooperation from the Gwalior Court and the demolished mark-stones and platforms, Everest had only once alluded to the possibility that 'superstitions' held by the populace were the cause of the destruction. It is there, in a letter sent to the Secretary of the Government of India Military Department, that we find our text on 'idolatrous veneration' and superstitious dread. But we notice also that Everest adds that rulers sometimes take advantage of this prepossession, and 'proceed in the most reckless manner' to pull the marks to pieces and efface the legends with hammer blows (Board of Control, Board's Collections, IOL

F/4/1654). In a letter written a few months later, Everest adds the detail that 'upon making minute enquiries among the villagers as to what prompted them to such wanton mischief, they frequently answered that "strangers came and desired them to do so"' (Board of Control, Board's Collections, IOL F/4/1654).

After all these letters of complaint, in which complex if not entirely momentous political issues were clearly at stake, and in which there were many and conflicting accounts as to what had been the cause of the destruction of the markers and platforms, a Military Letter from Bengal, dated 18 September 1839, was finally handed down, a letter that seemed to have constructed the definitive explanatory text and closed the matter for good, at least insofar as official epistolary communications were concerned. The Military Letter stated the following:

> The marginal numbers contain reports from the Surveyor General, regarding the demolition of several platforms at principal and secondary stations of the Great Trigonometric Survey in the Gwalior territory. It appeared in enquiry that the superstitious notion on the part of some of the inhabitants that the erection of those platforms was the cause of the failure of the periodical rains, induced them to rise, with arms in their hands, and in such numbers as to intimidate the police, and to accomplish the destruction of the platforms.
>
> The Gwalior Durbar expressed great concern on the occasion, and immediately gave instructions to the Amils of the several Districts, to afford these erections sufficient protection in times of scarcity, so as to obviate the occurrence of a similar proceeding on the part of the inhabitants.

Thus the final word was handed down, and one explanation was deemed to be the truth. The Military Letter contained not a single word about the obvious complexities of the matter, the local nets of power that connected Calcutta administrative offices, Sutherland, the Maharajah, the local officials, and the village people in hierarchies that must have been far too complex or far too risky for the Military Department to fathom. And so the theory of superstitious dread prevailed, in the official letter and in all the many places where that one paragraph of Everest's is quoted, shorn of its massive epistolary context. Sutherland is saved from official censure, the Maharajah is saved from having to account for the difficulties Everest encountered, and the Government itself is saved from having to choose between possibly alienating him with a rebuke, and dismissing Everest's complaints altogether. The idea of a uniform popular 'superstition' is very useful indeed, to everyone except, perhaps, Major Everest. Official reports for many years continued to quote Everest's one paragraph about superstition, with no remark on all the rest. And thus did the final official colonial explanation, the final entextualization of Indian speech regarding the destructions of the mark stones in Gwalior, involve only native 'superstition', despite the fact that in the original report this was only one conjecture among many.

SONGS OF THE PUNJAB: R.C. TEMPLE AND THE COLONIAL CRIMINALIZATION OF CRITICAL SPEECH

In 1882, R.C. Temple, who had served for many years in the Indian Army and was a cantonment magistrate in the Punjab when he carried out ethnographic inquiries there, commented upon and published in *The Indian Antiquary* two songs from the Punjab, collected by Flora Annie Steel, that concern food scarcities and the irrigation works that were built in the Punjab by the colonial government partly as insurance against famine. In the very different ways that Temple entextualized the two songs, the contrast between colonial attempts to contain and nullify the effect of critical speech, while conferring authority and authenticity on speech that appears to consent to colonial rule, is vividly drawn.

One of the songs Temple presents to the reader is a panegyric, praising the sahibs who built the canal and describing the enthusiasm of the villagers, who are made to say, collectively, 'The canal water has come and the thorns have become flowers'. Temple introduces the song by assuring us that the song was written 'by one of "the people"', and he does not further describe the origin or provenance of it, although he does observe that the song 'is written in very smooth verse, and the author shows his education by the frequent interlarding of Arabic and Persian words' (Temple 1882: 166). The signature line at the end of the text tells us though that 'Ghulam Ahmed asked me to tell the story of the canal, / So I have joined together some ten or twenty verses about it./I live in Firozpur and my name is Fattehu'd-din.' A footnote informs us that Ghulam Ahmed is a bookseller of Firozpur. We cannot from this information discern very much about the origin of this song or about Ghulam Ahmed's motives in commissioning it. But since the song begins with sixteen lines in praise of Major Grey, who was responsible for the construction of the Firozpur canals, I suspect that it may have been commissioned for performance in his presence. We can take note, however, that Temple does not describe the commission or describe the occasion on which the song was sung, nor does he characterize the author in any specific way: he is content to say that it was written by 'one of the people', and thus Ghulam Ahmed's speech is entextualized as if he spoke for 'the people', with no particularizing information at all.

The other song that Temple puts before the reader is very different, and Temple himself acknowledges the critique that it contains. In several quite perceptive notes to the song, he draws the reader's attention to the song's 'sarcasm in making the first fruits of the canal to be the profits of the watchmen and the contractor, and the presence of vegetables, etc., a secondary result': '*Where the canal goes there are the profits of the watchmen and the contractors./Also there are cucumbers, onions, and vegetables on the canal banks*'. Just after this verse, two more tell us that '*Where the canal goes there the people eat wheat and pulse/Where the Jats take the canal cuts there grow wheat and cotton*'. Temple observes that these verses too are sarcastic, since wheat and lentils are foods that are far beyond the reach of the poor and landless Sansis, and that only Jats, the relatively prosperous farmers of the Punjab, can engage in the remunerative planting of wheat and cotton, which were new cash crops at that time. A later verse describes the burden of the canal tax that must be paid to the government, and the lesser amount that must be paid at the village level for the use of the water: '*A rupee an acre to the Government and an anna to the Lambardar.*' The verse that follows describes the collection of cash fines from people who make a cut in the canal to draw water for their use without paying the tax: '*The Magistrate demands silver in payment of fines for cutting the canal./The Magistrate takes good silver for five feet of water.*' Here Temple notes that the fine inflicted in silver falls unequally on the rich and poor; both may draw water illegally from the canals but it is the poor who can ill afford the fines. And the next verse describes the punishment for this: those caught making cuts in the canal must, as Temple notes, 'use their own labour and the straw from their fields, which consequently have to be neglected while the work of repair goes on.' This order emanating from colonial policy is parodied in the song: '*Drive in the pegs! Give up your straw; and then your field will go to the bad.*'

This song is highly critical of the canal operations, on the grounds that the benefits fall to the government and to the high caste landholders, while the burdens fall most heavily upon the poor who may go hungry because of the fees and fines to be paid in cash. Though government policy stressed the importance of canal irrigation as insurance against famine, there is compelling evidence that it failed to provide such insurance, partly because as the Sansis tell us, cash crops were most frequently grown in canal tracts and the benefits fell largely to those who were prosperous enough to take advantage of them (Whitcombe 1972: 79–81). And thus there is in this song a profound sense of the inequality that the canals promote and of the several interconnected systems of power and intertwined hierarchies in which Sansis live their lives that was obvious even to Temple. His entextualization of this critical or at best ironic view of the benefits of canal irrigation is, however, far different from his entextualization of the panegyric. While the panegyric is described only as 'of the people', we are told that this song that takes up a critical stance is sung by the Sansis, which Temple tells us, in the very first sentence of the article, is one of the so-called 'criminal tribes' of the Punjab. Temple describes their wandering habits, tells us that they are 'great thieves', and relates the collection of the song to G.W. Leitner's publications concerning the supposedly distinctive languages of such 'criminal tribes'. He goes to great lengths to point out to the reader that this song of 'illiterate natives' is 'rough and homely in the extreme', its meter is rough and its rhythm uncertain, and that it 'exhibits in a most interesting manner the popular (illiterate) history and notions regarding the canals of Firozpur' (Temple 1882: 163–4). Thus the provenance of the song that is critical of the colonial state is set apart. Unlike other folklore specimens Temple comments upon, this particular song is not viewed as speech that reveals 'the mind of the people', but as the recalcitrant, marginalized, illiterate (and thus erroneous), coarse, and highly specific speech of a criminal caste. We are encouraged, by contrast, to imagine that the panegyric is the undifferentiated speech of the colonized, the 'voice of the people' that validates colonial claims to authority and truth. Temple thus deploys an entextualizing strategy aiming to authenticate Indian speech as 'of the people' when it is laudatory of colonial policy, but he deploys a criminalizing strategy when he comes upon recalcitrant speech that is critical of a colonial project and critical of the inequality it promotes. *Tell us why we are here?*

W.H. SLEEMAN AND CAPTAIN MEADOWS TAYLOR: CONTRASTING ENTEXTUALIZATIONS OF THE SPEECH OF THE THUGS AND THE HETEROGENEITY OF COLONIAL PERSPECTIVES[2]

During the course of his long term of service with the East India Company from 1809 to 1856, W.H. Sleeman became best known for two projects to which he returned time and again. He wanted to capture and prosecute Thugs and he wanted to collect the speech of the colonized. It is of course no accident that the two projects overlapped quite a bit, but even when not pursuing Thugs Sleeman constantly found himself speaking with Indians he met on his journeys and writing down what they had to say. In 1849–50, while serving as Resident of Lucknow, he made a long tour through the kingdom of Oudh in order to 'see the state of the country and the condition of the people' (Sleeman 1858: 1). During the course of the journey, he wrote frequently to H.M. Elliott and often spoke of his conversations with the Indian peasants he encountered along his route. On March 1850, he wrote to Elliott and described his ethnographic methods, as it were:

> Every facility has been afforded us by the Durbar for seeing the Country and communicating with the people; and I have done my best to profit from the opportunity. I have traveled on an elephant in order to see as much as possible of the surface of the Country over which I

have passed, and I have communed freely with the people of all classes during these three months. I have been marching with as few halts as are usually made by a Regiment marching to its destination in the periodical relief; and I have, I believe, within this time learnt more of the feelings, opinions, and requirements of the people, and of the real working of the system of administration pursued in Oude, than I would have learned in a long life spent at the Capital (Sleeman 1849–50).

Sleeman took note of those conversations in the diary he kept during his travels, published in 1858 as *A Journey Through the Kingdom of Oude*. Throughout this work we read his comments on those ethnographic occasions: 'In the evening I had a long talk with the people of the village, who had assembled around our tents' (Sleeman 1858: 35). Conversation after conversation appears also in his *Rambles and Recollections of an Indian Official*, published in 1844. Much could be written of the entextualization of Indian speech in these documents, but here I focus, in a preliminary way, on the text in which his interests in recording Indian speech and in putting an end to what he imagined to be a secret hereditary religious cult engaged in murder and thievery came together, his 1836 *Ramaseeana, Or a Vocabulary of the Peculiar Language Used by the Thugs*. The focus of my discussion will be on the ways in which the recorded speech of Thug approvers is inserted into his text, and then subsequently re-entextualized as it were, in a three-volume novel written by Captain Philip Meadows Taylor, published in London in 1839, which purports to be an authentic transcript of a lengthy conversation with a Thug murderer. Most of what Sleeman wrote about the Thugs can of course be attributed to a colonial imagining of criminality-by-birth in Indian society that is at once fantastic and also tied to specific colonial disciplinary practices (Brown 2003; Freitag 1991; Mayaram 1991, 2003; Nigam 1990a, 1990b; Raheja 1999a; Singha 1993; Suleri 1992; Woerkens 2002). In this paper I do not attempt to evaluate Sleeman's writings on Thuggee with respect to their historical accuracy or inaccuracy, but rather to point to some of the ways in which Indian speech is entextualized in the *Ramaseeana*, and thus consider it as a specimen of colonial discourse that can be analyzed along with a work of colonial fiction.

Ramaseeana was published in 1836 by G.H. Hutton, Military Orphan Press, in Calcutta. The book takes its title from the special language, Ramasee, that Sleeman reported as being used by the Thugs or Phansigars over wide swathes of Indian territory. The book is comprised of two parts. The first part opens with a preface containing notes on some of Sleeman's most frequently articulated perspectives on the nature of Thug society. He suggests for example that there are three kinds of standards governing the restraint of evil human propensities: the supposed will of a deity to which the people owe homage, 'the moral feelings of the circles of society in which they move', and the penal laws that happen to be in force. Sleeman argues that the Thugs are not constrained by the first two of these because theirs is a society wherein murder and thievery are supposedly condoned by the principal deity, the goddess Bhawani. Thus, it is in the nature of their very society and its unquestioned traditions that the logic of murder may be found, according to Sleeman. In the introduction to the volume, Sleeman is at pains to stress repeatedly that he has never met a Thug who questioned even the smallest element of Thuggee tradition and belief, which of course flies in the face of any nuanced ethnographic account.[3] The introduction also includes a brief description of the nature of the Ramasee 'dialect' and its relationship to Hindustani. The main portion of the first part of the book consists of a 'Vocabulary' of Ramasee words with English translations and a one hundred and thirty page section called 'Substance of Conversations Held by Captain Sleeman, with different Thug Approvers, while preparing the Vocabulary', which purport to be verbatim transcriptions of statements made by a number of Thug 'approvers' Sleeman questioned, usually in groups of two or three. These approvers could receive less harsh sentences if Sleeman found their testimony to be credible, but of course he does not see how this aspect of the 'ethnographic occasion' shaped the responses of the men he has assembled together.

The second part of the book is comprised mainly of letters and reports concerning Thuggee operations conducted by others in India. For the purposes of this paper I am interested in the 'Conversations' section of the book, in the ways in which the speech of the approvers is entextualized within it, and in the ways in which Taylor draws upon those dialogues in the construction of his novel *Confessions of a Thug* and recontextualizes them in ways that undermine Sleeman's assumptions about the unquestioned and fixed and invariable nature of Thug 'custom'.

Throughout the prefatory matter in the *Ramaseeana*, Sleeman asserts, in a repetitively insistent fashion, on the absence of doubt amongst the Thugs:

> There is not one among them who doubts *the divine origin of the system of Thuggee*, not one who doubts that he and all who have followed the trade of murder with the prescribed rites and observances, were acting under the immediate orders and auspices of the goddess Devee, Durga, Kalee or Bhawanee, as she is indifferently called, and consequently there is not one who feels the slightest remorse for the murders which he may, in the course of his vocation, have perpetrated or assisted in perpetrating. A Thug considers the persons murdered precisely in the light of victims offered up to the Goddes. . . . He meditates his murders without any misgivings, he perpetrates them without any emotion or pity, and he remembers them without any feelings of remorse. They trouble not his dreams, nor does their recollection ever cause him inquietude in darkness, in solitude, or in the hour of death. (Sleeman 1836: 7–8)

And he likewise insists on the inviolability of custom and the implicit belief in omens among the Thugs:

> I have never found a Thug by birth, or one who had been fully initiated in its mysteries, who doubted the inspiration of the pick-axe, when consecrated in due form,—not one who doubted that the omens described in this work were all sufficient to guide them to their prey, or to warn them from their danger; or that they were the signs ordained by the Goddess expressly for these purposes,—not one who doubted, that if these omens had been attended to, and the prescribed rules observed, the system of Thuggee must have flourished under the auspices of its divine patroness in spite of all our efforts for its suppression. (Sleeman 1836: 9)

In each of the conversations that Sleeman presents in the *Ramaseeana* there are several Thug interlocutors present. But Sleeman seems to keep a tight rein on them, either through editorial means or through his presence at those ethnographic occasions, because there are virtually no examples of disagreement among the men; if one claims that all Thugs hold a certain kind of belief, no one contradicts this or suggests another interpretation of an event or cultural practice or element of 'belief'. These are not of course idle conversations but proceedings conducted according to a penal code in which a man's life depends upon whether or not Sleeman finds the testimony to be credible and useful in his prosecution of this supposed community of criminals. The insistence on uniformity of belief in this milieu is quite different from other less fraught ethnographic reporting Sleeman did; in his *Rambles and Recollections of an Indian Official,* for example, there are many recountings of casual conversations in which he heard vigorous debate among his interlocutors about matters of ritual and belief, omens and signs. (For two particularly interesting examples, see Raheja 1999b: 40–1.) But the Thugs in the *Ramaseeana* are always made to speak in a single voice. Or perhaps they endeavored to speak in a single voice because they knew that if their testimony conflicted with Sleeman's prior assumptions about 'Thugee', their lives would be in jeopardy.

Mary Poovey's 2004 essay 'Ambiguity and Historicism: Interpreting *Confessions of a Thug*' is an intriguing meditation on some aspects of these matters. Although she focuses almost entirely on contemporary interpretations of the novel in nineteenth century England, and provides very little analysis of the *Ramaseeana* itself, she does take note of the fact that Sleeman insisted that Thugs suffered no remorse concerning murders they carried out, and this view caused him to imagine that an unbridgeable gap existed between the European and the Thug. Taylor's novel *Confessions of a Thug* was published just three years after the *Ramaseeana,* and he appears to have drawn heavily on it as he wrote the novel, although he himself had considerable experience of crime and murder in India in connection with several positions he held in the service of the Nizam of Hyderabad (Poovey 2004: 8–10; Singha 1993; Taylor 1878).

The novel is constructed as a dialogue between one unnamed English narrator and one Thug approver who tells the story of the murders and other crimes he has committed. Part of the argument of Poovey's paper is that, despite its superficial similarity to the *Ramaseeana* (which she does not analyze), the novel harbors a moral complexity and ambiguity concerning Thuggee and the East India Company that is of course completely at odds with Sleeman's text. 'It is now possible', Poovey suggests,

> to read the novel not primarily as an indictment of Thugee—and certainly not as an unequivocal justification for British rule in India—but as an oblique critique of the East India Company and everything it represented: assumptions about the racial superiority of the English, the conviction that Christianity is morally superior to any variety of Indian religion, and the belief that a Western bureaucracy is more efficient and more rational than its Eastern counterpart'. (Poovey 2004: 4)

Poovey's argument is compelling and it inspired me to read Taylor's novel and to think about it in comparison with the *Ramaseeana* and Sleeman's other writings. She does not however touch on the issue of 'doubt' and the questioning of 'tradition' that Sleeman is at such pains to insist is absent in the world of the Thugs. It is this particular aspect of the comparison between *Confessions of a Thug* and *Ramaseeana* that I want to take up here. The speech of the colonized is entextualized in very different ways in these two 1830s documents: Sleeman's text produces the speech of the colonized as an answer, in unison, to that demand that the colonized *tell us why we are here;* the speech of Ameer Ali, Taylor's approver, refuses any such demand. Although Sleeman's interlocutors and Ameer Ali, the sole Indian speaker in Taylor's novel, speak of almost identical matters of belief and worship and cultural practice, there is a quality of monoglossia to the speech of Sleeman's interlocutors (and it is the monoglossia that Sleeman notices and comments upon and he ignores the merest hint of heteroglossia in his texts) and a quality of heteroglossia that come to the fore in Ameer Ali's talk. I want to suggest here that Sleeman's prosecutorial presence in the ethnographic encounter and his authorial presence in the text have produced that monoglossic effect, whereas the critical stance Taylor assumes has produced, wittingly or unwittingly, the polyglossia in Ameer Ali's narrative.

Let us consider just one of the many topics about which both Sleeman and Taylor present Thug testimony. Sleeman is almost maniacally concerned to extract accounts of omens from his approvers, especially appearances of hares and the 'sacred pickaxe', and to show that Thugs never waver in their belief in such portents, and Taylor's Ameer Ali also speaks of them throughout his long narrative. For the purpose of comparing the two texts on these issues, I will refer to Sleeman's 1836 text and to an 1873 one-volume edition of Taylor's novel. I have consulted the original 1839 three-volume edition of Taylor's novel in the Ames Library of the University of Minnesota, but for ease of referral to this work, I provide page numbers from the more widely available one-volume 1873 edition.

Sleeman is concerned, in the *Ramaseeana,* to insist upon the unquestionability of 'custom' among the Thugs because it supports his argument that they operate in a moral universe utterly different from that of 'civilized' society, a moral universe in which they are not made to feel remorse for the criminal actions imputed to the community. Ameer Ali and Sleeman's approvers all speak of a 'sacred pick-axe' that supposedly figures prominently in Thug ritual practices. In writing of the veneration that Thugs purportedly have for the pick-axe, Sleeman remarks that 'India is emphatically the land of superstition and in this land the system of Thugee . . . has found a congenial soil and flourished with rank luxuriance . . . and spread over almost every district within the limits of our dominions' (1836: 13). Here is one of the many dialogues he adduces as evidence of this capitulation to custom, the very first of the many 'conversations' in his book. It is noteworthy that he begins the interrogation of the approvers in his book not with a question about an actual crime but with a question about a 'custom', the practice of observing the omen of the hare.

Q.—Do you ever recollect any misfortune arising from going on when a hare crossed the road before you?

Nasir, of Singnapore.—Yes; when General Doveton commanded the troops at Jhalna we were advancing towards his Camp; a hare crossed the road; we disregarded the omen . . . and went on. The very next day I, with seventeen of our gang, were seized; and it was with great difficulty and delay that we got our release. We had killed some people belonging to the troops, but fortunately none of their property was found upon us.

Q.—And do you think these signs are all mandates from the deity, and if properly attended to, no harm can befall you?

Nasir.—Certainly, no one doubts it; ask anybody. How could Thugs have otherwise prospered? Have they not every where been protected as long as they have attended religiously to their roles?. . .

Q.—And do you really believe that Bhowanee [the goddess] sends these signs to warn you of danger, and guide you to your booty?

Nasir.—Can we—can any body doubt it? Did she not in former days when our ancestors attended to rules, bury the bodies for us, and save us the trouble; and remove every sign by which we could be traced?

Q.—You have heard this from your fathers, who heard it from their fathers; but none of you have ever seen it, nor is it true?

Nasir.—It is true, quite true; and though we have not seen this, we have all of us seen the sacred pickaxe spring in the morning from the well into which it had been thrown over night, and come to the hands of the man who carried it at his call; nay we have seen the pickaxes of different gangs all come up of themselves from the same well at the same time, and go to their several bearers.

Q.—Sahib Khan, you are more sober than Nasir, have you ever seen it?

Sahib Khan.—On one expedition only.

Q.—Who were the pickaxe bearers?

Sahib Khan.—They were Imam Khan and his brother.

Q.—From what country?

Sahib.—From Arcot. I was obliged to fly from Telingana when Major Parker and Captain Sheriff made their inroad upon us . . . and I went and joined the Arcot gangs. During a whole expedition that I made with them, Imam Khan and his brother carried a pickaxe, and I heard them repeatedly in the morning call them from the well into which they had thrown them over night, and saw the pickaxes come of themselves from the well, and fall into their aprons. . . .

Q.—And you never saw any of your own gangs do this?

Sahib.—Never, I have Thugged for twenty years and never saw it.

Q.—How do you account for this?

Sahib.—Merely by supposing that they attend more to omens and regulations than we do.

In this opening conversation with the approvers, Sleeman both prods the informers to disown their supposed convictions and yet also, paradoxically, to hold fast to them. He comments on their 'soberness' and makes it clear that he regards ideas about the 'sacred pickaxe' as not worthy of belief, and yet at the same time the approvers know that if they do not provide satisfactory evidence of a Thuggee cult (and that is what Sleeman wants to get in these conversations, not mere evidence of individual guilt) they will be tried for murder. And so the presence of Sleeman himself produces the kind of speech he elicits from Nasir and so many others whose words appear in the *Ramaseeana;* and he nowhere comments on the speech of Sahib Khan, who is at pains to give evidence of 'superstitious practices' for Sleeman, even if he himself has not engaged in them. Sleeman's authorial voice has already told us that he had never found a Thug who harbored any doubts about the omens and he entextualizes the conversations in such a way as to validate this claim.

Taylor's treatment of hares and pickaxes may at first sight appear to be similar to Sleeman's but whereas Sleeman's authorial prose ignores or silences any approver whose speech betrays even the smallest hint of skepticism, Taylor's account foregrounds the ideas of a man who repeatedly comes to doubt the usefulness of omens. Here is one of Ameer Ali's tales of the hare as an omen:

'But what was that?' I eagerly asked, as something crossed our path close to my feet.

'Nothing but a hare,' said the khan; 'some prowling jackal has scared her from her form, and she seeks another hiding-place.'

'A hare!' I repeated, the current of my blood seeming to be suddenly arrested, as I thought on the fearful omen to a Thug,—one that could not be disregarded, or, if disregarded, was certain to be followed by the most dire calamities, nothing less than death or long imprisonment.

'Yes, Meer Sahib, a hare. Why should it astonish you?'

'But across my very path', I muttered involuntarily.

'Twas chance', said the man; 'what of it?'

'Nothing,' replied I; 'nothing,—we have an old superstition about it in my country, but 'tis an old woman's tale, I dare say.'

I paced on in silence. Ya Alla! what a conflict was raging in my heart! I have told you I disregarded omens; I cared not for them, only as they were the soul of Thuggee as far as my men were concerned; and to humour them I feigned to be particular in their observance. But my soul quailed when I was put to the proof. Every tale I had heard of the vengeance of Bhowauee at a conscious neglect of her commands and omens flashed in rapid succession across my mind: how one had died, eaten by worms; another been overtaken by what the world called justice; how another had lost his wife or children,—and I too had yet a child! I say I quailed in mental terror for awhile; but mine was a stout heart, a noble spirit; and it roused at my call, like that of a good steed, which worn and weary with travel, yet at the approach of strife or danger bears his master as gallantly as though he were fresh from his stall. Yes, my soul rallied. Away with such idle tales, fit only to be bugbears to children, said I mentally; Ameer Ali is 'not to be frightened by them. And to lose the charm,—the object of my anxiety, when almost within my grasp! I laughed aloud'. (Taylor 382)

Sleeman of course had insisted that he'd never found a Thug who doubted; and this almost hysterical insistence on the 'static readability' (Suleri 1992: 108) of Thuggee was necessary to his political project of constructing it as a monolithic and criminal and hereditarily organized cult. Sleeman's remarks about 'superstitions' and omens had been circulated prior to the publication of the book in 1836, so as to pave the way for the 'Thuggee Act' of 1836, with its many provisions for the prosecution of 'Thugs', provisions founded on 'the conception of communities socialized to criminality' (Singha 1993: 84). As Singha pointed out, 'At one level the 'thuggee' and 'dacoity' Acts were an effort to clothe crude devices for securing conviction with the semblance of 'due process'. But they were also defended by arguments about the peculiar characteristics of Indian society or by the 'backward' state of Indian civilization' (1993: 91). So strongly held were such ideas about the criminality of a supposed Thug community that men could be sentenced for life in connection with crimes at which they were demonstrably not present, if they had simply been proven to be 'Thugs' (Singha 1992: 126–7). The conception of 'communities socialized to criminality' was precisely what Sleeman had in mind when he wrote of 'the moral feelings of the circles of society in [the Thugs] move,' and this conception lay behind the manner in which he shaped the 'Conversations' as ethnographic occasion and as ethnographic text.

But in contrast to Sleeman's entextualizing practices, time

after time Taylor's mode of inserting Ameer Ali's speech into his text subverts that project and constructs Ameer as a man who takes matters of belief seriously, yet ponders them and comes to his own conclusions and often acts in disregard of the omens that Sleeman thought to be such central and defining mark of Indian criminality.

Subtle differences, then, in the ways that Indian speech was entextualized in *Ramaseeana* on the one hand and *The Confessions of a Thug* on the other served very different political projects. While Sleeman's entextualizations erase doubt and difference of views among Thugs and thus serve as intricately constructed justifications for the new legal procedures put into place to hunt down and prosecute 'criminals by birth' and communities rather than individuals, Taylor's text can be read, as Poovey suggests, as a critique of the East India Company and its assumptions about the racial superiority of the colonial administrators. But Taylor's novel can also be read as an implicit critique of the conception of an essentialized Thug community in which no one ever doubted what Sleeman claimed to be Thug 'superstition', and the entextualizing strategies the two authors deploy are correspondingly different.

CONCLUSION: TOWARDS A CATALOG OF COLONIAL ENTEXTUALIZING PRACTICES

Sylvia Vatuk made several acute observations in her important 1999 article on the *Qanoon-e-Islam,* substantiated by a meticulous historical and textual analysis. She pointed out that power pervaded every aspect of encounters and conversations between colonial ethnographer on the one hand and Indian informant as author or speaker on the other, and that the dialogues between them and the ethnographic accounts that were produced through these encounters always bore profound traces of changing modalities of colonial disciplinary control. And she demonstrated some of the ways in which changing historical contingencies brought about shifts not only in colonial policy but also in the ways that an ethnographic text and the words of Indians were edited and published. In the four discussions I've presented here, of the words of an imagined sati, of George Everest's reports of native speech about opposition to the Survey, of the songs of the Sansis, and of 'conversations' with Thugs, my aim has been to amplify Vatuk's observations and to consider the question of how we should think of colonial ethnographic practices more generally and of how to think with some precision about how and why the speech of the colonized is inserted into colonial texts, how competing sources of colonial knowledge are given credence or marginalized, and how particular kinds of entextualizing practices vis-à-vis native speech are tied to particular projects of discipline, control, and the production of an illusion of consent to colonial rule.

NOTES

1. Material in this section is drawn from my 1999 paper on the Survey of India, 'The Ajaib-Gher and the Gun Zam-Zammah' Colonial Ethnography and the Elusive Politics of 'Tradition' in the Literature of the Survey of India.'
2. This final section of the paper is a brief preliminary report from my broader on-going research project on Sleeman and the social life of his various books, letters and other writings.
3 Gold's brilliant analyses of doubt and disagreement among twentieth century residents of Ghatiyali concerning the efficacy of ritual performances has shaped the way I think about these issues as they surface in colonial India and the way that I think about many other issues as well (Gold 1988).

REFERENCES

Amin, Shahid. 1994. 'Introduction to William Crooke', *A Glossary of North Indian Peasant Life*, New Delhi: Oxford University Press.

Arnold, David. 1993. *Colonizing the Body: State Medicine and Epidemic Disease in Nineteenth-century India*, Berkeley: University of California Press

Arnold, David. 1994. 'The Colonial Prison: Power, Knowledge, and Penology in Nineteenth-Century India', in David Arnold and David Hardiman, eds., *Subaltern Studies VIII: Essays in*

Honour of Ranajit Guha, New Delhi: Oxford University Press, pp. 148–7.

Arnold, David. 2004. 'Race, Place and Bodily Difference in Early Nineteenth-Century India', *Historical Research* 77(196): 254–73.

Bauman, Richard. 1993. The Nationalization and Internationalization of Folklore: 'The Case of Schoolcraft's "Gitshee Gauzinee"', *Western Folklore* 52: 247–69.

Bauman, Richard, and Charles L. Briggs. 1990. 'Poetics and Performance as Critical Perspectives on Language and Social Life', *Annual Review of Anthropology* 19: 59–88.

Bhabha, Homi. 1994. *The Location of Culture,* London and New York: Routledge.

Brown, Mark. 2003. 'Ethnology and Colonial Administration in Nineteenth-century British India: The Question of Native Crime and Criminality', *British Journal for the History of Science* 36(2): 201–19.

Chatterjee, Partha. 1995. 'The Disciplines in Colonial Bengal', in Partha Chatterjee, ed., *Texts of Power: Emerging Disciplines in Colonial Bengal*, Minneapolis: University of Minnesota Press.

Cohn, Bernard S. 1985. 'The Command of Language and the Language of Command', in *Subaltern Studies IV: Writings on South Asian History and Society,* Ranajit Guha, ed., New Delhi: Oxford University Press, pp. 276–329.

Cohn, Bernard S. 1987. *An Anthropologist Among the Historians and Other Essays*, Delhi and New York: Oxford University Press.

Cohn, Bernard S. 1996. *Colonialism and Its Forms of Knowledge: The British in India*, Princeton: Princeton University Press.

Crooke, William. 1911. 'Songs About the King of Oudh', *Indian Antiquary* 40: 61–7.

Crooke, William. 1911. 'Songs from Northern India Relating to the English', *Indian Antiquary* 40: 89–92.

Crooke, William. 1911. 'Songs from Northern India', *Indian Antiquary* 40: 115–22.

Crooke, William. 1911. 'Songs of the Mutiny', *Indian Antiquary* 40: 123–4, 165–9.

Dirks, Nicholas B. 1992. 'Castes of Mind', *Representations* 37: 56–78.

Edney, Matthew H. 1997. *Mapping an Empire: The Geographical*

Construction of British India, 1765–1843, Chicago: University of Chicago Press.

Everest, George. 1830. *An Account of the Measurement of an Arc of the Meridian,* London: Parbury, Allen and Company.

Everest, George. 1830–40. 'Correspondence', Board of Control, Board's Collections F/4, India Office Library.

Fabian, Johannes. 1983. *Time and the Other: How Anthropology Makes Its Object,* New York: Columbia University Press.

Freitag, Sandria. 1991. 'Crime in the Social Order of Colonial North India', *Modern Asian Studies* 25:227–62.

Gold, Ann Grodzins. 1988. *Fruitful Journeys: The Ways of Rajasthani Pilgrims*, Berkeley: University of California Press.

Grierson, George. 1882. *An Introduction to the Maithili Language of North Bihar, Containing a Grammar, Chrestomathy and Vocabulary*, Calcutta: Asiatic Society.

Hadley, George. 1809. *A Compendious Grammar of the Current Corrupt Dialect of the Jargon of Hindostan (Commonly called Moors); with a Vocabulary, English and Moors, Moors and English*, London: J. Asperne.

Ibbetson, Denzil. 1890. 'The Study of Anthropology in India'. *Journal of the Anthropological Society of Bombay* 11.

Leitner, G.W. 1880. *A Detailed Analysis of Abdul Ghafur's Dictionary of the Terms Used by Criminal Tribes in the Panjab,* Lahore: Punjab Government Civil Secretariat Press.

Luard, Charles Eckford. N.d. *Central Indian Songs,* India Office Library: MSS. HINDI D.1.

Mani, Lata. 1984. 'The Production of an Official Discourse on Sati in Early Nineteenth-Century Bengal', in *Europe and Its Others*, Francis Barker, ed. Colchester: University of Essex, pp. 89–127.

——— 1989. 'Contentious Traditions: The Debate on *Sati* in Colonial India', in Kumkum Sangari and Sudesh Vaid, eds., *Recasting Women: Essays in Colonial History,* New Delhi: Kali for Women, pp. 88–126.

Markham, Clements. 1878. *A Memoir on the Indian Surveys*, 2nd edn., London: W.H. Allen.

Mayaram, Shail. 1991. 'Criminality or Community? Alternative Constructions of the Mev Narrative of *Darya Khan*', *Contributions to Indian Sociology* 25: 57–84.

——— 2003. *Against History, Against State: Counterperspectives from the Margins,* New York: Columbia University Press.

Narayan, Kirin. 1993. 'Banana Republics and V.I. Degrees: Rethinking Indian Folklore in a Postcolonial World', *Asian Folklore Studies* 52(1): 177–204.

Nigam, Sanjay. 1990a. 'Disciplining and Policing the Criminals by Birth, Part 1: The Making of a Colonial Stereotype—The Criminal Tribes and Castes of North India', *Indian Economic and Social History Review* 27(2): 131–64.

——— 1990b. 'Disciplining and Policing the Criminals by Birth, Part 2: The Development of a Disciplinary System, 1871–1900', *Indian Economic and Social History Review* 27(3): 257–87.

Pels, Peter. 1999. 'The Rise and Fall of the Indian Aborigines: Orientalism, Anglicism, and the Emergence of an Ethnology of India, 1833–69', in Peter Pels and Oscar Salemink, eds. *Colonial Subjects: Essays on the Practical History of Anthropology*, Ann Arbor: University of Michigan Press, pp. 82–116.

Pinney, Christopher. 1990. 'Colonial Anthropology in the 'Laboratory of Mankind', in C.A. Bayly, ed., *The Raj: India and the British 1600–1947*, London: National Portrait Gallery. pp. 222–63.

Poovey, Mary. 2004. 'Ambiguity and Historicism: Interpreting *Confessions of a Thug*', *Narrative* 12(1): 3–21.

Raheja, Gloria Goodwin. 1996. 'Caste, Colonialism, and the Speech of the Colonized: Entextualization and Disciplinary Control in India', *American Ethnologist* 23:494–513.

——— 1999a, 'The Illusion of Consent: Language, Caste, and Colonial Rule in India', in Peter Pels and Oscar Salemink, eds., *Colonial Subjects: Essays on the Practical History of Anthropology*, Ann Arbor: University of Michigan Press, pp. 117–52.

——— 1999b. 'The Ajaib-Gher and the Gun Zam-Zammah: Colonial Ethnography and the Elusive Politics of 'Tradition' in the Literature of the Survey of India', *South Asia Research* 19(1): 29–51.

Risley, H.H. 1891. *The Tribes and Castes of Bengal,* Calcutta: The Bengal Secretariat Press.

Singha, Radhika. 1993. '"Providential" Circumstances: The Thuggee Campaign of the 1830s and Legal Innovation', *Modern Asian Studies* 27: 83–146.

Sleeman, William Henry. 1836. *The Ramaseeana.* Calcutta: Military Orphan Press.

——— 1844. *Rambles and Recollections of an Indian Official,* London: J. Hatchard and Son.

——— 1850. Ms. letter to Sir H.M. Elliott, 1 March 1850, in W.H. Sleeman's Letter Book, 1849 Oct. 24–1850 Mar. 28 (bulk 1849 Oct.–Nov.). Mss B 9, Ames Library of South Asia, University of Minnesota.

——— 1858. *A Journey Through the Kingdom of Oude in 1849-1850; With Correspondence Relative to the Annexation of Oude to British India*, London: Richard Bentley.

Stoler, Ann. 1992. '"In Cold Blood": Hierarchies of Credibility and the Politics of Colonial Narratives', *Representations* 37: 151–89.

Suleri, Sara. 1992. *The Rhetoric of English India*, Chicago: University of Chicago Press.

Taylor, Meadows. 1839. *Confessions of a Thug*, 3 vols., London: Richard Bentley.

——— 1873. *Confessions of a Thug*, London: Henry S. King.

——— 1877, 2nd edn. 1878. *The Story of My Life,* Edinburgh and London: William Blackwood and Sons.

Temple, Richard. 1882. 'Folklore in the Panjab: Popular Song. Collected by Mrs. F.A. Steel, with Notes by Lieut. R.C. Temple', *Indian Antiquary* XI: 163–72.

Temple, Richard C. 1914. *Anthropology as a Practical Science: Addresses Delivered at Meetings of the British Association at Birmingham, the Antiquarian Society of Cambridge, and the Anthropological Society of Oxford*, London: G. Bell and Sons.

Vatuk, Sylvia. 1999. 'Shurreef, Herklots, Crooke, and the *Qanoon-e-Islam:* Constructing an Ethnography of 'The Moosulmans of India', *South Asia Research* 19(1): 5–28.

Walker, J.T. 1879. *Account of the Operations of the Great Trigonometrical Survey of India,* Vol. II: *History and General Description of the Principal Triangulation and of its Reduction.* Dehra Dun: Office of the Trigonometrical Branch, Survey of India.

——— 1882. *Account of the Operations of the Great Trigonometrical Survey of India,* Volume VII: *General Description of the Principal Triangulation of the North-East Quadrilateral*, Dehra Dun: Office of the Trigonometrical Branch, Survey of India.

Watson, J. Forbes and John William Kaye, eds. 1868. *The People of India: A Series of Photographic Illustrations, with Descriptive Letterpress, of the Races and Tribes of Hindustan,* London: India Museum.

Whitcombe, Elizabeth. 1972. *Agrarian Conditions in Northern*

India, Volume 1: *The United Provinces Under British Rule, 1860–1900,* Berkeley: University of California Press.

Wilson, J. 1884. *Final Report on the Revision of Settlement of the Sirsá District in the Punjáb,* Calcutta: Calcutta Central Press Company.

Van Woerkens, Martine. 2002. *The Strangled Traveler: Colonial Imaginings and the Thugs of India,* Chicago: University of Chicago Press.

11

Afterword

SYLVIA VATUK

It is a great and rare pleasure to find myself being honored for my scholarly contributions to the study of women and the Indian family. It is especially gratifying—and humbling as well—that so many of today's leading anthropologists of India have taken the trouble to prepare creative and original academic papers on topics of their own expertise that are also related in some way to my own published work. I first became interested in India through a chance encounter in Germany in 1954 with two charismatic young men who were close associates of the late Jayaprakash Narayan, working in Acharya Vinoba Bhave's Bhoodan movement. Little did I imagine what the eventual outcome of that fairly brief accidental meeting would be: an academic career of over fifty years duration, devoted almost exclusively to the study of various facets of India's society, culture and peoples! That career has brought much satisfaction and many pleasures, one of the greatest of which has been the opportunity to come to know so many wonderful scholars who have, like me, chosen to dedicate their professional lives to the study of India and of South Asia more generally.

It is especially meaningful to me that so many of these scholars are women who have focused their own research on issues related to women and the family in India, just as I have done. For when I began to seriously study Indian society, women anthropologists working on such topics were still few and far between. When I was designing my doctoral research project on the impact of urbanization in India on family and kinship relationships I, of course, relied heavily on the pioneering published work of the late Irawati Karve on Indian kinship organization. And when I eventually went to India in 1966 to do my first fieldwork I had the great good fortune of becoming acquainted with Pauline Kolenda, a woman anthropologist a few years senior to me, who had already done considerable research on family life in rural Uttar Pradesh and who ever since has been a continued intellectual mentor and a close and valued friend. Most of the other women scholars in the field of Indian studies who have become close colleagues over the past several decades came to it some years later, however, and it was several of them who last year so generously organized the two conference panels in my honor that formed the core of the set of papers that make up this volume. Others who were not able to participate in those sessions later kindly consented to make their own contributions to this publication as well.

When I reflect upon my own intellectual history and compare it with that of the junior colleagues whose papers are gathered here, I am prompted to recall that, when I was a graduate student, it was a risky strategy to propose a study of women and their concerns rather than the kinds of activities engaged in and considered important by men, if one wished—as I naturally did—to be taken seriously by one's academic advisers and peers. It was doubtless for this reason that, although my initial ethnographic fieldwork in an urban Indian neighborhood was carried out almost entirely within a female milieu and although the vast majority of those from whom I learned about the Indian family and kinship system were women, it did not occur to me at that time to explicitly frame my dissertation or the book and subsequent articles that were based on it as a study of urban Indian *women's* family and kinship relations. This was so despite the fact that by the time my book was in the press attitudes within the discipline had begun to change and a whole cohort of younger women anthropologists were building, ultimately with great success, a new sub-discipline devoted to exploring questions about women's roles and gender relations in societies around the world, including South Asia.

Each of the authors represented in this volume, including Ann Gold and Gayatri Reddy, two of those responsible for the very flattering introductory essay to this collection of papers, have during their careers made significant contributions to our scholarly understanding of women, gender and the family in India. Most have chosen to approach some aspect of this broad topic in the essays presented here. Joyce Flueckiger, Karen Leonard, Pauline Kolenda and Helen Ullrich have done so by recording and analyzing how particular individuals, as members of families whose fortunes they have followed for many years, have responded over time to changing social and economic conditions, with particular attention to the implications these have had for women, particularly for those of the present generation of young people. Werbner analyzes the sexual symbolism of a particular Muslim pre-wedding ritual as it is practiced today by Pakistani immigrants to Great Britain. Srimati Basu explores the way that the family law—and the courts through which it is administered—both transform and solidify 'traditional' understandings of the Hindu patrilocal extended family, yet somewhat contradictorily also help to promote notions of companionate marriage, with important implications for the welfare of women litigants. Bedi examines an indigenous 'feminist' discourse, by which women members of a right-wing movement that at one level valorizes the domestic roles of women, explain and justify to others and to themselves their heavy engagement in political and 'social service' activities that require spending much of their time in a very public, traditionally male arena, leaving their husbands and other family members to 'take up the slack' in terms of housekeeping, child-rearing and food preparation chores.

The two remaining papers take up other topics to which I have given attention in some of my published work: Helene Basu expands upon her extensive earlier research on the Gujarati Sidi Muslim shrine of Bawa Gor to show how the rituals performed there aid in resolving conflicts within families that others differently situated might choose to take for adjudication to the civil courts. And Gloria Raheja, whose earlier landmark work on kinship, marriage and gift exchange and on women's subversive voices as expressed in folk songs has had a major impact on our theoretical and substantive understanding of gender dynamics in India, has chosen to give us a close reading of several colonial texts from the eighteenth to twentieth centuries, showing how 'native' voices are represented there, typically in such a way as to buttress the notion that Indians are fundamentally supportive of and content to live under British rule.

Reading this stimulating collection of research papers I am especially struck with how far we have come since the mid-1960s in developing ethnographically-grounded and theoretically sophisticated understandings of Indian society and particularly of the dynamics of gender and gender relations in Indian domestic and family life. Four decades ago there was essentially one overarching theoretical question for sociologists and anthropologists studying these topics—that is, whether the 'joint family' was declining or perhaps even disappearing under the influence of the various forces of social and economic change newly affecting the subcontinent. But as the papers in this volume show, the number of issues being raised by scholars today has vastly proliferated and can no longer be encompassed under a single umbrella theme. The exceptional quantity and richness of the ethnographic data recorded by these researchers is also noteworthy. Several—including Kolenda, Ullrich, Leonard, Flueckiger and Pnina Werbner—have even kept contact with the same group of related individuals and families and returned to the same site again and again over a period of several years and even decades, which allows them to provide us with an empirically based longitudinal perspective on some of the same questions about the consequences of social, economic, educational and geographical mobility that I tried to address in my early work. But, as I realized to a certain extent even at that time, that work was seriously limited by the fact that I had no access to an actual baseline from which to measure the degree and nature of the changes that had occurred prior to my arrival on the scene with notebook and tape-recorder in hand. Only much later, in my work on a south Indian Muslim family with whom I continue to work and interact, did I begin to better appreciate the necessity of taking a long-term historical view of the family—both looking backward into the past and following its development forward into the future—rather than simply taking a snapshot at one particular point in time. Only in this way was I able to ground my ideas about social change and its effects upon solid archival and life-history data and feel confident that my conclusions about what had led up to what I observed and recorded as an ethnographer could be supported empirically.

I would like to express my heartfelt gratitude to all of the wonderful scholars who have had a part in the original conference panels and/or have contributed to this unusually rich collection of research papers on the shared theme of 'histories of intimacy and situated ethnography' in India. All of the contributors—and I in particular—owe a special debt to the editor of this volume, my good friend Karen Leonard, who has done an exceptional job of soliciting manuscripts, providing the authors with editorial suggestions and advice and making sure that every one completed and submitted her paper by the deadline. It is an honor to be in their presence on these pages.

12

Vita

SYLVIA VATUK

Education

1970	PhD	Harvard University
1958	MA	University of London, School of Oriental and African Studies
1955	BA	Cornell University

Academic Appointments—Regular

2002	Professor Emerita of Anthropology, University of Illinois at Chicago (UIC)
1983–2002	Professor of Anthropology, UIC
1972–83	Associate Professor, UIC
1970–2	Assistant Professor, UIC
1965–9	Assistant Professor of Anthropology, California State College at Hayward

Academic Appointments—Visiting and Courtesy

2001 (fall)	Visiting Scholar, Telugu University, Hyderabad, India
2000 (April)	Visiting Professor, Institute of Commonwealth Studies, London
1998–9	Visiting Scholar, Madras Institute of Development Studies, Madras, India
1998–9	Visiting Scholar, Department of Anthropology, Brown University
1994 (fall)	Directeur d'Études Associé, Centre d'Études de l'Inde et de l'Asie du Sud, École des Hautes Études en Sciences Sociales, Paris

1989-present	Associate Member, Committee on Southern Asian Studies, University of Chicago
1988 (summer)	Visiting Fellow, Center for Comparative Development Studies, Brown University.
1986–7	Fellow-by-Courtesy, Department of Anthropology, Johns-Hopkins University (Hopkins-Nanjing Center for Chinese and American Studies, Nanjing, China).
1987 (spring)	Visiting Professor, Nanjing Normal University
1986 (fall)	Visiting Professor, Nanjing University
1969 (winter)	Lecturer in Social Sciences, Cowell College, University of California, Santa Cruz.

Research Experience

2005–6	Delhi and Hyderabad, India (Muslim women and personal law)
2002–3	Chicago, IL (Marriage, family and religion among Muslim immigrants from the Indian subcontinent)
2001	Hyderabad, India (Muslim women and personal law)
1998–9	Madras, India (Muslim women and personal law)
1992 (summer)	London, England (India Office Library and Records)
1989 (summer)	London, England (India Office Library and Records)
1989 (winter)	Madras and Hyderabad, India (family records of the *khandan* of Ghulam Mahmoud)
1987 (winter)	Madras, India (family records of the *khandan* of Ghulam Mahmoud)
1983–4	Hyderabad, India (family roles of educated, employed women)
1974–6	Delhi, India and vicinity (social and cultural aspects of aging and the elderly)
1969	Delhi and U.P., India (kinship, marriage networks and gift-giving among Gaur Brahmans)
1966–7	Meerut, India (kinship, family and neighbohood among urban white-collar migrants).

Publications

Book

1972 *Kinship and Urbanization: White Collar Migrants in North India.* Berkeley and Los Angeles: University of California Press.

Edited Books

1984 *Social Structure and Social Relations*. Special Issue, *American Ethnologist* 11/4 (co-editor)

1978 *American Studies in the Anthropology of India*. New Delhi: Manohar

Journal Articles

2008 'Islamic Feminism in India: Indian Muslim Women Activists and the Reform of Muslim Personal Law', in F. Osella and C. Osella, eds., *Islam in India*, Special Double Issue, *Modern Asian Studies* 42/2–3: 489–518.

1999 'Shurreef, Herklots, Crooke, and *Qanoon-e-Islam*: Constructing an Ethnography of "the Moosulmans of India"', *South Asia Research* 19: 5–28.

1990 'The Cultural Construction of Shared Identity: A South Indian Muslim Family History', in P. Werbner, ed., *Person, Myth and Society in South Asian Islam*. Special Issue, *Social Analysis* 28: 114–31.

1975 'The Lustful Stepmother in the Folklore of North-western India', *Journal of South Asian Literature* 11: 19–43 (with V.P. Vatuk).

1975 'Gifts and Affines in North India', *Contributions to Indian Sociology* n.s. 9: 155–96.

1972 'Kinship Terminology in Northern India', *American Anthropologist* 74: 791–3.

1971 'On a System of Private Savings among North Indian Village Women', *Journal of Asian and African Studies* 6: 179–90 (with V.P. Vatuk).

1971 'Trends in North Indian Urban Kinship: The "Matrilateral Asymmetry" Hypothesis', *Southwestern Journal of Anthropology* 27: 287–307.

1969 'A Structural Analysis of the Hindi Kinship Terminology', *Contributions to Indian Sociology* n.s. 3: 94–115.

1969 'Reference, Address and Fictive Kinship in Urban North India', *Ethnology* 8: 255–72.

1967 '*Chatorpan*, a Culturally-Defined Form of Addiction in North India', *The International Journal of the Addictions* 2: 103–13 (with V.P. Vatuk).

1967 'Ethnography of *Sang*, a North Indian Folk Opera', *Asian Folklore Studies* 26: 29–51 (with V.P. Vatuk).

Chapters in Edited Books

In Press 'A Rallying Cry for Muslim Personal Law: The Shah Bano Case and its Aftermath', in *Islam in India in Practice,* ed. Barbara Metcalf, Princeton: Princeton University Press.

2009 'Islamic Learning at the College of Fort St. George in Nineteenth-century Madras', in *The Madras School of Orientalism,* ed. Thomas Trautmann, New Delhi: Oxford University Press, pp. 48–73.

2008 'Divorce at the Wife's Initiative in Muslim Personal Law: What are the Options and What are Their Implications for Women's Welfare'? in *Redefining Family Law in India: Essays in Honour of B. Sivaramayya,* ed. Archana Parashar and Amita Dhanda, London and New Delhi: Routledge, pp. 200–35.

2007 'The "Cancer of Dowry" in Indian Muslim Marriages: Themes in the Popular Rhetoric from the South Indian Muslim Press', in *Living With Secularism: The Destiny of India's Muslims,* ed. Mushirul Hasan, pp. 155–76.

2006 'Bharattee's Death: Domestic Slave-Women in Nineteenth-Century Madras', in *Slavery and South Asian History,* ed. Indrani Chatterjee & Richard Eaton, Bloomington: Indiana University Press, pp. 210–33.

2006 'Domestic Violence and Marital Breakdown in India: A View from the Family Courts', in *Culture, Power, and Agency: Gender in Indian Ethnography,* ed. Lina Fruzzetti and Sirpa Tenhunen, Calcutta: Stree, pp. 204–26.

2005 'Muslim Women and Personal Law', in *In a Minority: Essays on Muslim Women in India,* ed. Zoya Hasan and Ritu Menon, New Delhi: Oxford University Press, pp. 18–68.

2004 '*Hamara Daur-i Hayat*: An Indian Muslim Woman Writes her Life', in *Telling Lives in India: Biography, Autobiography, and the Life History,* ed. David Arnold and Stuart Blackburn, New Delhi: Permanent Black and Bloomington: Indiana University Press, pp. 144–74.

2004 '"The Family": A Contested Concept in Early-Nineteenth-Century Madras', in *Unfamiliar Relations: Family and History in South Asia,* ed. Indrani Chatterjee, New Brunswick, NJ: Rutgers University Press and New Delhi: Permanent Black, pp. 161–91.

2003 'Muslim Women in the Indian Family Courts: A Report

from Chennai', in *Divorce and Remarriage among Muslims in India*, ed. I. Ahmad, New Delhi: Manohar, pp. 137–60.

2002 'Older Women, Past and Present, in an Indian Muslim Family', in *Thinking Social Science in India: Essays in Honour of Alice Thorner,* ed. S. Patel. J. Bagchi and K. Raj, New Delhi: Sage, pp. 247–63.

2001 '"Where Will She Go? What Will She Do?" Paternalism Toward Women in the Administration of Muslim Personal Law in Contemporary India', in *Religion and Personal Law in Secular India: A Call to Judgment*, ed. G.J. Larson, Bloomington: Indiana University Press, pp. 226–38.

1999 'Family Biographies as Sources for an Historical Anthropology of Muslim Women's Lives in Nineteenth-Century South India', in *The Resources of History: Tradition, Narration and Nation in South Asia,* ed. J. Assayag, *Études Thématiques* 8: 153–72. Paris and Pondichery: École française d'Extrême Orient and Institut français de Pondichery.

1996 'The Art of Dying in Hindu India', in *Facing Death: Where Culture, Religion, and Medicine Meet,* ed. H.M. Spiro, M.G.M. Curnen, and L.P. Wandel, New Haven: Yale University Press, pp. 121–8.

1996 'Identity and Difference or Equality and Inequality in South Asian Muslim Society', in *Caste Today*, ed. C. Fuller, New Delhi: Oxford University Press, pp. 227–62.

1994 'Schooling for What? The Cultural and Social Context of Women's Education in a South Indian Muslim Family', in *Women, Education, and Family Structure in India*, ed. C.C. Mukhopadhyay and S. Seymour, Boulder: Westview Press, pp. 135–64.

1992 'Forms of Address in North India: The Family Domain', in *Concepts of Person*, 2nd edn., ed. A. Ostor, S. Barnett and L. Fruzzetti, New Delhi: Oxford University Press, pp. 56–98.

1992 'Sexuality and the Middle-Aged Woman in South Asia', in *In Her Prime: New Views of Middle-Aged Women*, 2nd rev. edn., ed. V. Kerns and J.K. Brown, Urbana and Chicago: University of Illinois Press, pp. 155–70.

1990 'To Be a Burden on Others': Dependency Anxiety among the Elderly in India', in *Divine Passions: The Social Con-*

struction of Emotion in India, ed. O.M. Lynch, Berkeley and Los Angeles: University of California Press, pp. 64–88.

1989 'Household Form and Formation: Variability and Social Change among South Indian Muslims', in *Society From the Inside Out: Anthropological Perspectives on the South Asian Household,* ed. J.N. Gray and D.J. Mearns, New Delhi and London: Sage, pp. 107–39.

1987 'Authority, Power and Autonomy in the Life Cycle of the North Indian Woman', in *Dimensions of Social Life: Essays in Honor of David G. Mandelbaum*, ed. P. Hockings, Berlin: Mouton de Gruyter, pp. 23–44.

1984 'South Asian Cultural Conceptions of Sexuality', in *In Her Prime: A New View of Middle-Aged Women*, ed. J.K. Brown and V. Kerns, South Hadley, MA: Bergin and Garvey, pp. 137–54.

1982 'Forms of Address in North India: The Family Domain', in *Concepts of Person*, ed. A. Ostor, S. Barnett, and L. Fruzzetti, Cambridge, MA: Harvard University Press, pp. 56–98.

1982 'The Family Life of Older People in a Changing Society: India', in *Aging and the Aged in the Third World*, Part II, 'Regional and Ethnographic Perspectives', ed. J. Sokolovsky and J. Sokolovsky, *Studies in Third World Societies* 23: 57–82.

1982 'Old Age in India', in *Old Age in Preindustrial Society*, ed. P. Stearns, New York: Holmes and Meier, pp. 70–103.

1982 'Purdah Revisited: A Comparison of Hindu and Muslim Interpretations of the Cultural Meaning of Purdah in South Asia', in *Separate Worlds: Studies of Purdah in South Asia,* ed. H. Papanek and G. Minault, Columbia, MO: South Asia Books, pp. 54–78.

1980 'Withdrawal and Disengagement as a Cultural Response to Aging in India', in *Aging in Culture and Society: Comparative Viewpoints and Strategies*, ed. C. Fry, New York: Praeger, pp. 126–48.

1980 'The Aging Woman in India: Self-Perceptions and Changing Roles', in *Women in Contemporary India and South Asia*, ed. A. de Souza, New Delhi: Manohar, pp. 287–309.

Contributors

HELENE BASU, Professor, Institute fuer Ethnologie, Westfaelische Wilhelms-Universitaet, Studtstrasse 21, 48149 Muenster, Germany, E-mail: hbasu 01@uni-muenster.de

SRIMATI BASU, Associate Professor, Gender & Women's Studies, Breckinridge 211, University of Kentucky, Lexington, Kentucky, 40506-0056, United States, E-mail: srimati.basu@uky.edu.

TARINI BEDI, Associate Director, South Asia Language and Area Center and the Committee on Southern Asian Studies, the University of Chicago, 5848 S. University Avenue, Kelly Hall 102, Chicago, Illinois, 60637, United States, E-mail: tbedi@uchicago.edu

JOYCE BURKHALTER FLUECKIGER, Professor, Department of Religion, Callaway Center, 537 Kilgo Drive, Emory University, Atlanta, Georgia, 30322, United States, E-mail: reljbf@emory.edu

ANN GRODZINS GOLD, Professor of Religion and Anthropology, 501 Hall of Languages, Syracuse University, Syracuse, New York, 13244, United States, E-mail: aggold@syr.edu

PAULINE KOLENDA, Visiting Scholar, Anthropology, University of California, Berkeley, E-mail: kolenda@berkeley.edu

KAREN ISAKSEN LEONARD, Professor, Department of Anthropology, University of California Irvine, Irvine, California, 92697, United States, E-mail: kbleonar@uci.edu

GLORIA GOODWIN RAHEJA, Professor of Anthropology, University of Minnesota, 395 HHH Center, 301 19th Avenue South, Minneapolis, Minnesota 55455, United States, E-mail: raheja@umn.edu

GAYATRI REDDY, Associate Professor, Gender and Women's Studies Program and Department of Anthropology, 1226 University Hall (mc 360), 601, S. Morgan St., University of Illinois at Chicago, Chicago, Illinois, 60607, United States, E-mail: gayatri@uic.edu

HELEN E. ULLRICH, M.D., Ph.D., 2434 St. Charles Ave. #303, New Orleans, Louisiana, 70130-6303, United States, E-mail: hullrich@tulane.edu

SYLVIA VATUK, 5830 S. Stony Island Avenue #11A Chicago, Illinois, 60637, United States, E-mail: vatuk@uic.edu

PNINA WERBNER, Professor of Social Anthropology, School of Sociology and Criminology, Keele University, Keele, Staffs, ST5 5BG, United Kingdom, E-mail: p.werbner@keele.ac.uk